HANDBOOK OF INTERNATIONAL DISASTER PSYCHOLOGY

Recent Titles in
Contemporary Psychology

Resilience for Today: Gaining Strength from Adversity
Edith Henderson Grotberg, editor

The Destructive Power of Religion: Violence in Judaism, Christianity,
and Islam, Volumes I–IV
J. Harold Ellens, editor

Helping Children Cope with the Death of a Parent: A Guide for
the First Year
Paddy Greenwall Lewis and Jessica G. Lippman

Martyrdom: The Psychology, Theology, and Politics of Self-Sacrifice
Rona M. Fields, with Contributions from Cóilín Owens, Valérie Rosoux,
Michael Berenbaum, and Reuven Firestone

Redressing the Emperor: Improving Our Children's Public Mental
Health System
John S. Lyons

Havens: Stories of True Community Healing
Leonard Jason and Martin Perdousx

Psychology of Terrorism, Condensed Edition: Coping with
Continuing Threat
Chris E. Strout, editor

The Psychology of Resolving Global Conflicts: From War to Peace,
Volumes 1–3
Mari Fitzduff and Chris E. Stout, Editors

HANDBOOK OF INTERNATIONAL DISASTER PSYCHOLOGY

Volume 1
Fundamentals and Overview

Edited by Gilbert Reyes and Gerard A. Jacobs

Preface by Charles D. Spielberger

Foreword by Benedetto Saraceno

Praeger Perspectives

Contemporary Psychology
Chris E. Stout, Series Editor

Westport, Connecticut
London

Library of Congress Cataloging-in-Publication Data

Handbook of international disaster psychology / edited by Gilbert Reyes and Gerard A.
Jacobs ; preface by Charles D. Spielberger ; foreword by Benedetto Saraceno.
      p. cm. — (Contemporary psychology, ISSN 1546–668X)
    Includes bibliographical references and index.
    ISBN 0-275-98315-3 ((set) : alk. paper) — ISBN 0-275-98316-1 ((vol. I) : alk.
paper) — ISBN 0-275-98317-X ((vol. II) : alk. paper) — ISBN 0-275-98318-8 ((vol. III) :
alk. paper) — ISBN 0-275-98319-6 ((vol. IV) : alk. paper) 1. Disaster victims—Mental
health. 2. Disaster victims—Mental health services. 3. Disasters—Psychological aspects.
4. Disaster relief—Psychological aspects. 5. Humanitarian assistance—Psychological
aspects. 6. Community psychology. I. Reyes, Gilbert. II. Jacobs, Gerard A. III. Contemporary
psychology (Praeger Publishers)
   RC451.4.D57H36   2006
   362.2'2—dc22   2005018786

British Library Cataloguing in Publication Data is available.

Library of Congress Catalog Card Number: 2005018786
ISBN: 0-275-98315-3 (set)
       0-275-98316-1 (vol. 1)
       0-275-98317-X (vol. 2)
       0-275-98318-8 (vol. 3)
       0-275-98319-6 (vol. 4)

ISSN: 1546–668X

First published in 2006

Praeger Publishers, 88 Post Road West, Westport, CT 06881
An imprint of the Greenwood Publishing Group, Inc.
www.praeger.com

Printed in the United States of America

The paper used in this book complies with the
Permanent Paper Standard issued by the National
Information Standards Organization (Z39.48–1984).

10 9 8 7 6 5 4 3 2 1

DEDICATION

The *Handbook of International Disaster Psychology* would not have been possible without the compassion and commitment of the international humanitarian community. In a world where millions are killed or harmed each year, either by natural hazards or because of the intentional and accidental actions of humankind, legions of caring people rise to these occasions, determined to relieve the suffering and protect the welfare of people who are in the most dire of circumstances.

The recent history of humanitarian operations has seen a surge of violence directed against these most charitable and nonpartisan individuals who have sacrificed the safety of their homes and families, and who have risked their lives to comfort distant neighbors and to promote peace in the face of force.

Those of us living in zones of relative safety, passing our days and nights in homes and workplaces equipped with modern conveniences, and having plentiful access to clean water, should feel humbled by the courage, dedication, and resilience of those who journey unarmed to enact the values and embody the virtues of our better nature.

In light of these things, it is a small thing indeed to dedicate this book to the international humanitarian personnel who are its inspiration.

Gilbert Reyes

CONTENTS

Contents

SET FOREWORD

As I write this, the media are filled with video footage and written accounts of survivors and relief workers in the aftermath of "The Tsunami." For many this is a word newly added to their vocabulary, along with words like "al Qaeda" or "anthrax" that were added a few years ago—formerly foreign and unknown, now sadly popular and common in use, as is "tsunami." But disasters—whether man-made or nature-born—share the common thread of victims in need. Historically the psychological and emotional impacts of disasters, regardless of genesis, on those impacted were largely left unconsidered. Thankfully, this has changed, and these books demonstrate another critical step in this evolving process and area of endeavor—a global consideration.

Too often, once psychological aspects of a phenomenon were considered, they were done so through a narrow lens of exclusively Western or Northern perspectives. Such work, while of definite merit, rigor, and additive benefit to knowledge, was limited in its generalizability. I very much enjoyed the turn of phrase that a reporter for the *Wall Street Journal* used in citing coeditor Gerard Jacobs: "Care for traumatic stress," he warns, "can't be delivered by Western experts parachuting into affected cultures without an appreciation of the cultures infused with strong Islamic, Hindu, and Buddhist beliefs." So true in so many additional ways, and yet so often unwittingly ignored—but thankfully changing.

At this point in time there is a growing appreciation, understanding, and grateful application of the adage that one size does not always fit all. Reyes and Jacobs have woven together a group of authors whose perspectives and work clearly demonstrate the differential aspects of dealing with the trauma of disasters from a global, diverse set of perspectives. Such is a major step forward, and I congratulate them.

For some reason still a mystery to me, it is very easy for most observers to consider post-disaster aid and relief efforts to exclusively include food, shelter,

and medical attention. But what cameras cannot capture as well as food stations, vaccination lines, and pitched tent encampments are the psychological
wounds that without intervention (when called for) can become scars at best,
or risk the infection of apathy or stigma, and result in the deadly consequences of suicide, substance abuse, and other manifest ills. Perhaps this
inability for many to "see" fosters a concomitant inability to understand.
People can see grain being trucked in and food stations preparing and dis-
tributing it, but they cannot see those who cannot eat it for lack of will.

Still More to Do

Much of my work involves medication distribution and medical interventions in areas of need. And again, and thankfully, while there is still a massive amount to be done globally in the battle for treating HIV/AIDS and
getting retrovirals distributed, it is equally important to distribute culturally
based and relevant psychosocial support for those who need such care. Both
are necessary to save their lives. Both.

It is said that there are often opportunities in crises. Perhaps we may see
some as a result of the current worldwide focus on the region impacted by
the tsunami. Many had never heard of or cared about Aceh prior to the
disaster, but there had already been a 15-year-long "disaster" when the
water hit that the world had ignored—an often brutal Indonesian military
dominion that has resulted in deaths of over 10,000 in Aceh alone, resulting
from guerrilla skirmishes with separatist rebels. Along with this loss of lives
are comorbid human-rights abuse allegations of torture and rape at the
hands of the troops. Now with Kofi Annan's pronouncement that "the UN is
the lead in the coordination of the humanitarian effort," there is renewed
hope that a side effect will have a kindling influence for the end of such
political violence. Likewise, in Sri Lanka then U.S. Secretary of State Powell
visited vis-à-vis relief efforts, and it is hoped that the tsunami will also be a
catalyst for restarting the stalled peace talks between the government and
the ethnic-based insurgency known as the Liberation Tigers of Tamil Eelam
(ETTE), or Tamil Tigers.

Psychologically trained researchers and clinicians obviously have much
to offer, as evidenced in this set of books. It is a positive evolution that such
psychological professionals are now considered along with other colleagues
when the proverbial yellow tape is strung in the aftermath of a catastrophe.
It is also important to have like involvements in preparation—be it in conflict resolution, resilience training, or other related aspects.

Irony?

Perhaps it is the psychology of indifference or just irony, but last year the
United Nations proclaimed that the world's "worst humanitarian disaster"
was . . .? The tsunami? No, in fact they were referring to the mass killings in

the Darfur region of Sudan by militias. This appears on few television screens or newspaper front pages, and thus is not on many people's minds or touching many people's hearts. Not that there is some morbid competition for compassion, response, and intervention between tsunami victims and the Sudanese, but it certainly is easier to offer relief to an area after a natural catastrophe than it is to intervene in an armed combat situation. The ghosts of Rwanda come to mind, however, and many mental health professionals are focusing efforts there a decade after the genocide, and it makes me wonder what the psychological aftermath will be in Sudan.

Most of the world has empathetically responded to those impacted by the tsunami—they have contributed, volunteered, prayed, and shed tears. And this is how it should be. But such is not so for Darfur today or Kigali a decade ago. Perhaps psychology and mental health professionals should add to their already overburdened to-do lists to work on how to move the world away from such indifference. I remain hopeful based on the work of those herein.

Chris E. Stout
Series Editor

FOREWORD

Every day millions of people in the world are affected by disasters. For many reasons, people in resource-poor countries tend to be hit especially hard by disasters. Data from Red Cross and Red Crescent societies suggest that resource-poor countries tend to be confronted with more conflict and more natural disasters compared to countries that are rich. Resource-poor countries tend to have weaker physical infrastructures that are less likely to withstand extreme conditions, such as earthquakes or cyclones. Also, resource-poor countries tend to have fewer financial resources to prepare for and respond to disaster. Most resource-poor countries often invest relative few resources in their health systems. Most resource -poor areas in the world hardly invest in mental health services and do not have well-functioning community-based mental health systems through which a post-disaster mental health response may be organized.

Disaster psychology is a complex field. Disaster psychology deals with psychological trauma (i.e., an extreme stressor that is likely to elicit a strong acute anxiety and/or dissociation reaction in most people) as a risk factor for mood and anxiety disorders and for nonpathological physical and emotional distress. Psychological trauma is an area that is generating rich research in the areas of anthropology and sociology, child protection and social work, epidemiology and health economics, history and philosophy, neuroscience and pharmacology, clinical and social psychology, psychiatry and psychotherapy, public health and health services research, political science and social policy, and alcohol and other substance abuse management. Thus, disaster psychology practitioners need to be able to think beyond their discipline. Disaster psychology deals not only with psychological trauma but also with enormous losses, which often tend to be forgotten. Affected persons may have lost family members, community support structures, employment and valued material possessions during the disaster. Like trauma, loss is a well-known risk factor for mood and anxiety disorders, for nonpathological distress as well as social problems. Thus, a disaster psychology practitioner needs to be not only an expert on psychological trauma but also an expert on loss and community change. Moreover, the practitioner needs to know how to work in and with communities in a culturally appropriate way. Also, the practitioner needs to know how to work in a collaborative and coordinated manner with others, because uncoordinated aid responses are not in the best interest of disaster survivors.

Concern for people's mental health after disasters is a relatively recent phenomenon. Disaster psychology is a young field; practitioners and researchers alike need to learn from one another. We all need to learn from one another on how to achieve meaningful objectives in a culturally appropriate and sustainable manner in order to reduce avoidable mental and social suffering without causing harm. This handbook provides a rich collection of writings by many of the world's experts on disasters. Reading these chapters will prepare both novice and experienced practitioners for a better response. This is an important book.

Benedetto Saraceno
Director
Department of Mental Health and Substance Abuse
World Health Organization

PREFACE

Catastrophic events causing great damage and destruction have been a part of human life since the beginning of world history. The earth-shaking, cataclysmic eruption of Mount Vesuvius in 79 AD, which wreaked terrible destruction and loss of life, and completely destroyed the Roman city of Pompeii, continues to be reflected in recent excavations. The devastation caused last year by four hurricanes in Florida during a period of less than six weeks and the great seawave produced by the tsunami in the Indian Ocean and Southeast Asia have received major recent attention. Hundreds of people in Florida are not yet back in their homes nearly a year after the fourth hurricane; victims who lost their lives in the tsunami disaster are still being identified and survivors are still searching for them months later.

Not so visible or readily recognized are the psychological effects of disasters for survivors, effects that can linger large and long in the minds of even those with no apparent physical injuries. Effects from the horrific and huge loss of life. Loss of home. Loss of identity. Loss of nearly all that was familiar. Sometimes, too, loss of dignity, faith, or even the will to live.

The development of theory, research, and professional practice by psychologists and other mental health specialists evaluating and helping the victims of such catastrophic events is relatively new, and much needed. This four-volume *Handbook of International Disaster Psychology* provides a solid foundation to facilitate understanding of the terrible effects of traumatic disasters. Vital information is also provided on assessment of disaster victims, and on interventions to help those who are directly affected to deal with their resulting emotional distress and physical injuries.

The general goals of these volumes are to provide information for furthering the assessment of the psychological impact of disasters, and to report procedures for developing, implementing, and evaluating the effectiveness of these programs. Many contributors to this set have been deeply involved in projects to reduce the suffering of disaster victims, and to help them adapt to life circumstances substantially and adversely altered. The editors here have remarkable experience in disaster psychology, reflected in the chapters that they have contributed. Professor Gilbert Reyes is a tireless activist and educator in the field and Professor Gerard Jacobs was recently appointed to coordinate the activities of the American Psychological Association in providing assistance for victims of the recent tsunami.

The chapters first focus on fundamental issues pertaining to international disasters. Significant political and philosophical issues are also examined, and the need for effective collaboration among culturally diverse groups providing assistance is emphasized. The critical importance of understanding the particular needs and interests of populations indigenous to a disaster site is also spotlighted, along with the necessity of assessing available resources. Several contributors show us community-based models for assessment and intervention, as opposed to Western-oriented clinical approaches. Clearly, providing effective, culturally appropriate psychosocial support requires a great deal of skill and flexibility in programs that are delivered under very difficult circumstances.

We also come to understand, with these volumes, programs and practices that have been carried out in diverse geographical and cultural settings in Europe, Latin America, and Africa. In most, the interventions have focused on small groups, along with individuals and families, as the basic targets of intervention. The critical impact of national disasters in parts of the world where poverty, disease, and civil strife have weakened the capacity for coping with adversity is especially difficult to navigate, due to a persistent sense of danger that interferes with the healing process. Yet excellent examples of interventions are described, demonstrating why organizations such as the International Red Cross and the Red Crescent are considered best suited for dealing with disasters.

Reading in these books of interventions with refugees and "special needs" populations, we see that cultural diversity compounds the difficulty of developing effective programs. A prevailing climate of hatred and violence in many refugee populations further impairs effectiveness. And special emphasis is given to interventions that address the psychosocial needs of women and children, and to crisis interventions with military and with emergency services personnel.

These four volumes on international disaster psychology will be of great interest to psychologists, mental health workers, and other professionals working with disaster victims and their families. Trauma researchers, those interested in topics such as post-traumatic stress disorder (PTSD) and related disorders, will also find a wealth of useful information here. Indeed, these books will also well serve all students, scholars, and general readers focused on understanding how the most horrific, trying, and torturous of events can tear at psychological health, and how we all might play a role in helping heal the wounds.

For the past 30 years, I have personally worked in collaborative cross-cultural research with colleagues from more than 50 countries, and in developing adaptations of our anxiety and anger measures. I have also enjoyed and greatly benefited from participation in international meetings and conferences. While international psychology has addressed a wide range of topics, including stress and emotions, which have been the major focus of my work, these volumes pioneer new directions in psychological research and professional practice. Tsunamis, earthquakes, and other worldwide disasters are frequently encountered in modern life. Effective clinical and community interventions are urgently needed to help people cope. These volumes provide both a solid foundation for the emerging field of international disaster psychology and important guidelines for future research.

Charles D. Spielberger, Ph.D., ABPP
Distinguished Research Professor
University of South Florida, Tampa
Past President, American Psychological Association

ACKNOWLEDGMENTS

It goes without saying that the writing and editing of such an extensive book as this takes a great deal of effort and patience on the part of all concerned. What is perhaps less evident is that it also takes a great deal of trust and respect. As first-time editors undertaking a project of this scope and complexity, we required the trust of our publisher that we could indeed complete what we started. In this regard, we were extremely fortunate to be working with Debbie Carvalko at Greenwood Publishing, who came at this project with such infectious enthusiasm and confidence that she inspired the same in us. She also gently but firmly guided us through the unfamiliar process of delivering an edited book in four volumes consisting of over 40 chapters by authors from around the world. Without her patience, persistence, and professionalism, it is doubtful that this project could have proceeded so successfully.

We also required a great deal of trust from our colleagues, the authors who toiled for months over these chapters, that their efforts would not be in vain and that our work as their editors would prove commensurate to their investment in us. Many of these humanitarians and scholars knew us personally, but several did not, and all had only our word that the project would be completed as promised. We thank them sincerely for their confidence in our ability to make worthy use of their contributions.

The editors also wish to acknowledge the work of Mary E. Long, Ric Monroe, Sandra Schatz, and Tina Waldron, graduate research assistants who helped us to organize and process an almost unmanageable amount of information. Particular gratitude is owed for the editorial assistance supplied by Sandra Schatz, who labored tirelessly and diligently over the final drafts to detect and correct any errors or omissions. The efforts of these assistants are greatly appreciated and are reflected in the quality of these volumes.

Overview of the International Disaster Psychology Volumes

Gilbert Reyes

The four volumes that constitute the *Handbook of International Disaster Psychology* are composed of chapters addressing most of the pressing issues being confronted in this relatively new and expanding area of research and practice. Each volume and the chapters it contains are designed to inform a diverse audience of readers about the activities that have been undertaken around the globe to improve the psychological and emotional well-being of people affected by disasters. Many of the authors are deeply involved in developing programs and projects designed to relieve the psychological suffering of people exposed to disasters. They are mostly citizens of the Western nations, though the editors have attempted to attract contributions from colleagues residing in Asia, Africa, and South America. The objectives pursued by these authors in their humanitarian roles include, among other things, the assessment of the psychosocial impacts of disasters, implementation of prevention and intervention programs, and the development of strategies for improving the effectiveness of their programs. This in turn requires a sophisticated appreciation of factors that exert influence on the success of these operations. The authors have drawn from their own experience and what they have learned from other sources to share the key ideas and practices with the greatest promise of succeeding under the least favorable conditions. Their dedication to serving the psychosocial needs of people coping with terrifying and debilitating circumstances is deserving of the highest respect and admiration. Each is a humanitarian in the truest sense.

Volume 1: Fundamentals and Overview

The first volume of the *Handbook of International Disaster Psychology* provides readers with an orientation to the field of international disaster psychology

(Reyes, 2006) and an overview of the fundamental issues that pertain across most disasters and humanitarian emergencies. Toward that aim, the contributors identify and discuss many of the political and philosophical issues and assumptions involved in the humanitarian "therapeutic" enterprise and the "psychosocial" lens that magnifies the existence and importance of trauma to suit Western expectations (Pupavac, 2006). These matters cannot be easily dismissed, disputed, or ignored and reflect a perception among some that an intentional or inadvertent cultural imperialism comparable to "White Man's Burden" is at work.

The recent blending of military operations with humanitarian relief services has further complicated these issues by blurring the boundaries between partisan use of force to coercively serve national interests and impartial initiatives compelled by empathy and compassion (Wessells, 2006). Sadly, at the same time that agents of humanitarianism are accused of having sacrificed their fundamental principles to political expediency (Rieff, 2002), the casualty rates among relief personnel have skyrocketed, leading even the most courageous of NGOs to withdraw in the face of mounting dangers (Burnett, 2004; Gall, 2004; Kelly, 2004). And while few question the benefits and necessity of providing the tradition "survival" supplies, the value of psychosocial support has been a more contentious issue than most and remains unresolved. As a matter of conscience and ethics, anyone involved in promoting services of questionable benefit under conditions of mortal danger must acknowledge and respond respectfully to these concerns (Beech, 2006).

In order for psychosocial programs to be implemented successfully, effective collaboration among culturally diverse groups of people must take place (Peddle, Hudnall Stamm, Hudnall, & Stamm, 2006). Perhaps the most distinct intercultural partnership is that which forms between the populations indigenous to the disaster-affected areas and the relief agencies that are foreign to those regions. International humanitarian agencies employ expatriate (ex-pat) staff from around the world, so there is also a great deal of cultural diversity among their personnel. However, it is an undeniable reality of the hierarchical structure of these agencies that most of the managerial staff are of European or North American origin, while middle- and lower-level personnel comprise a more diverse assembly representing the less wealthy nations. Providing culturally appropriate psychosocial support under these conditions requires considerable skill and flexibility at every level, since the people with the most useful cultural knowledge and insight are often not those who decide policies and practices. Development of approaches that could be applied in any event and context is perhaps a desirable goal, but an unlikely one given the diversity of situations, values, cultures, and customs. Nevertheless, there are similarities across events that allow for construction of flexibly structured templates based on tested principles of good psychosocial practices (Ager, 2006).

A basic necessity for any relief operation is to assess the needs and resources of the affected populations, and in this regard psychosocial programs are not substantively different. Supplies and services based entirely on typical assumptions are unlikely to accurately match the types, levels, and characteristics of what is truly required in a specific context. Moreover, this profile of needs and resources is a moving target and must be persistently assessed and modified to remain pertinent (Dodge, 2006a). Among the many options for efficiently matching needs and services and making them available and useful to those who are most likely to benefit, the preference has shifted strongly toward community-based models, both for assessments and for intervention designs. Consequently, psychosocial planners and implementing personnel are less concerned with "clinical" training and skills because of the growing importance of methods associated with community psychology (Dodge, 2006b). The roles of ex-pat personnel are also increasingly educational in nature, with direct human services often being reserved for local staff, who are more likely to have the requisite language skills and cultural knowledge to work effectively within the communities where needs are greatest.

Communities constantly gather information to inform their decisions and guide the actions of their members. Thus, the importance of public information in disaster management should never be ignored. The mass news and entertainment media, especially television and increasingly the Internet, provide a critical resource in disasters, and the effective use of these media may spell the difference between success and failure in some instances (Kuriansky, 2006). Inaccurate rumors can have destructive consequences, and urgent transmission of vital information can save lives. And given the education components of psychological support, the print and electronic media are crucial to the mission of disseminating information that can help to reduce distress and direct survivors toward resources that are most likely to meet their needs. Therefore, it is important to make effective use of these techniques and technologies, in the interest of public education and according to well-proven public health models (Cohen, 2006).

Volume 2: Practices and Programs

The second volume of the *Handbook of International Disaster Psychology* addresses various psychosocial programs and the practices they employ to provide services to a variety of populations under difficult circumstances. The contributors describe not only what they do and with whom, but also the underlying reasons for certain decisions and activities. The approaches employed in designing effective intervention programs vary according to the types of problems being targeted and the types of people being helped. Some interventions are designed to work with people one at a time, though most are conducted with small groups or across entire communities. For instance, faculty at Massey University in New Zealand have developed and refined a model for providing optimal psychosocial care to youth and families (Ronan, Finnis, & Johnston, 2006). Their approach identifies the family as the basic unit of intervention, but it also makes optimal use of community resources such as schools and the news media. Under very different conditions, however, adaptations to cultural and sociopolitical conditions such as those encountered in Southeast Asia may require very different and innovative approaches (Armstrong, Boyden, Galappatti, & Hart, 2006). As is clear in these two examples, the approaches to such interventions are also profoundly influenced by the operational assumptions made by the designers and practitioners involved.

Ongoing violent conflicts produce perhaps the most difficult situations in which to implement such services, but the psychosocial needs that became evident during the collapse of the former Yugoslavia were urgent and could not wait until more peaceful times (Kapor-Stanulovic, 2006). The fact that hostilities have not ceased creates a perpetual sense of danger and dread, making it almost impossible to promote hope and healing with any sincerity. Similar horrors have been experienced across the African continent, whether stretched out over decades in such places as Uganda (Agger, 2006), or compressed into genocidal rampages as in Rwanda (Neugebauer, 2006). Although there are many important differences between conditions of persistent violence and singular events such as the terrorist bombing of the U. S. embassy in Nairobi (Ndetei, Kasina, & Kathuku, 2006), the psychological impact on survivors and the principles of psychosocial support are mostly similar.

Natural disasters can also wreak tremendous havoc, and they often occur in parts of the world where poverty, disease, and civil strife have already weakened the local capacity for coping with adversity. Latin American countries provide an example of such conditions (Cohen, 2006), with a recent string of major earthquakes and deadly storms having killed tens of thousands and left many times that number homeless and destitute. The prime example can be found in the recent history of Venezuela. That country was overwhelmed in 1999 by flooding and mudslides that killed over 30,000 people (Blanco, Villalobos, & Carrillo, 2006) and has since experienced a military junta, rioting, a disputed election, and extreme economic hardships. Given these worsening conditions, the psychosocial interventions initially mobilized for the flood survivors taught lessons about the need for developing long-range plans to deal with a succession of crises.

Among the organizations best suited for developing such capacities are the International Federation of Red Cross and Red Crescent Societies (IFRC), which has played an important role in teaching its member societies how to develop and sustain a national program of psychological support. An exemplary application of the IFRC model took place recently in Cuba, which had invited the psychosocial training director of the Danish Red Cross to provide a "training-of-trainers" for local Red Cross staff and volunteers. Those receiving the training then became trainers of others until, in just one year's time, they had disseminated the information and skills to every corner of their country (Atherton & Sonniks, 2006). The Cuban Red Cross has sustained and implemented its psychological support activities with great success as Cuba has endured a series of hurricanes and other disasters. More recently, the IFRC has published a manual consisting of six modules that is used to train its national societies in community-based principles of psychological support (Simonsen & Reyes, 2003). Training-of-trainers workshops employing that manual were field tested in Eastern Europe, Southeast Asia, and the Middle East and have since been conducted in several other regions around the world.

Concurrently, a number of other humanitarian NGOs have developed their own training procedures and begun to proliferate them wherever such a need is identified. Additional sources of training exist across various academic and clinical institutions scattered around the globe. Some of these institutions take a general approach to disaster mental health, while others specialize in assisting with a particular problem or population. What works best in any given instance is still an open question requiring further examination and resolution. What is clear, however, is that people and institutions interested in learning about the psychosocial programs and practices employed with disaster survivors now have access to more information and training options than ever before.

Volume 3: Refugee Mental Health

The third volume of the *Handbook of International Disaster Psychology* addresses several key issues confronted by those who have been involved in mental health work with refugees. Among the most persistently troubling aspects of international affairs in the twentieth century was the sharp increase in forced international migrations, which created refugee crises on a massive scale. This was one of the earliest and most pressing issues facing the fledgling United Nations, and it led to the creation of the United Nations High Commissioner for Refugees (UNHCR) in 1951. Worldwide estimates from international relief organizations indicate that there are more than 10 million refugees and twice that number of internally displaced persons (IDPs) at this time. The psychosocial impact of the countless horrific events that characterize the refugee experience are sometimes temporary and manageable, but can also be enduring and disabling. Among survivors of war, the prevalence of psychological distress and mental disorders is often strikingly elevated, as studies of Vietnamese and Cambodian refugees demonstrated over two decades ago (Kinzie, 2006).

To accurately assess the mental health needs of displaced and transient populations is a difficult task under the best of circumstances, and to do so during the emergency phase is in some ways the most difficult option (Jacobs, Revel, Reyes, & Quevillon, 2006). However, if we are to respond with immediacy and accuracy to refugee mental health needs, such an option must be explored and developed. Furthermore, it is important to conduct research that clarifies not only the most prevalent psychopathologies seen among refugees following migration, but also the risk and protective factors that differentiate the most resilient outcomes from those requiring clinical intervention. Culturally diverse perspectives and assumptions compound the difficulty of such research, which is most often conducted in Western industrialized nations to which large populations of refugees have migrated. However, since most people displaced by forced migrations return to their regions of origin, it is important to conduct culturally sensitive research that is congruent with local customs, rather than erroneously imposing a Western psychiatric perspective (Bolton, 2006). Moreover, if we are to fully comprehend how psychosocial healing can best be supported across varying conditions and cultures, we must find ways to study the most important factors with simultaneous sensitivity and responsiveness to the needs of the survivors.

Programs serving the mental health needs of refugees are often located in the Western nations where they have settled. Europe, Australia, and North America are the most popular destinations for refugees, and nearly all of the published studies evaluating intervention programs originate from these regions. Sweden and other Scandinavian countries are among the most welcoming of refugees, and many excellent programs have been developed to help relieve postmigratory distress and improve the adjustment of forced migrants to cultural conditions that are entirely foreign to their experience (Ekblad, 2006). Australia has also experienced an influx of refugees fleeing persecution and violence, many of whom arrived from neighboring Asian nations. Innovative and culturally sensitive programs have been implemented in response to trauma and torture that can serve as models of blending individual and community intervention strategies into a more integral whole (Silove, 2006). The United States also receives large numbers of refugees and has become home to many who fled the wars and persecution across the Balkan republics following the disintegration of the former Yugoslavia. An abundance of intervention programs have been implemented in major American cities to assist refugees with psychosocial concerns, some of which have become particularly influential examples of innovation. Among those is a program in Chicago that employs family therapy and other techniques to apply a framework of intervening with groups composed of multiple families (Raina et al., 2006).

The work with refugees taking place in postmigration countries is often enhanced by experiences working with corresponding populations that remained in their country of origin. Several researchers and clinicians who work with postmigratory refugees in the West also invest great effort in working with former IDPs in the countries from which refugees have recently fled. The mental health infrastructures of such countries were often poorly developed and are typically overwhelmed and underfunded for meeting the needs of their postconflict population. International collaborations between mental health professionals from poorly resourced and highly resourced settings offer countless opportunities for improvement on both ends of such partnerships (Weine, Pavkovic, Agani, Ceric, & Jukic, 2006). Of particular merit is the movement to assign the same level of human rights, commitment to healing, and compassionate regard for mental illness as that which is felt toward those with physical ailments and injuries.

As wars and other levels of massive violence continue to erupt in repetitious cycles in many parts of the world, some patterns and principle are clear. Among those is that hatred and revenge have long memories and can reemerge after extended periods of apparent peace. One approach to breaking the cycle of violence has been to seek social justice through human rights instruments and international criminal tribunals. Another approach emphasizes rapprochement through community processes of communicative expression, such as the Truth and Reconciliation Commissions in South Africa, Peru, East Timor, Sierra Leone, and elsewhere. Unfortunately, the idealistic goals of such an undertaking often run headlong into the sheer force and brutality of the hatred they are created to alleviate. Moreover, for many who continue to endure an ever-present pain borne of atrocities that can never blend into an innocuous past, forgiveness seems like a form of betrayal that joins victims with perpetrators in a profane alliance belying all truth. Nevertheless, without forgiveness, complete psychosocial health cannot be achieved and the transmission of violence is more likely continue across generations as children enact themes of revenge in a perverse pursuit of honor and retribution (Borris, 2006).

Volume 4: Interventions with Special Needs Populations

The fourth volume of the *Handbook of International Disaster Psychology* addresses populations whose needs differ in some critical way from more general expectations. There are many reasons why this might occur, including that the "special" population is at elevated risk of harm or that key aspects of what they have endured differ from the experiences of most disaster survivors. Another reason may be that the group's needs are not well matched to the practices that are typically effective with people. Groups with "special needs" have been identified in regard to several variables, including developmental characteristics (e.g., children, the elderly), gender, types of traumatic experiences (e.g., torture, sexual assault), and occupational roles (e.g., relief workers, military personnel, journalists). Although several elements of good psychosocial practice reliably combine to form a strong core that can be applied across most populations and conditions, it is important to take special needs into account and not to expect any approach to be universally effective.

The manner in which different groups of people are treated in disasters and humanitarian crises usually reflects how they are treated under more normal circumstances. That is, if categories of people are less privileged in general, they are unlikely to receive better treatment in the worst of times. If anything, the social destabilization characteristic of most crises tends to amplify disparities in power and encourage opportunistic exploitation of the weak and vulnerable. Among the populations most often targeted for exploitation are women and children. Gender inequities are prevalent in most societies and, from a global perspective, the gains resulting from social justice movements such as feminism have been meager and fragile. Thus, while women have made remarkable progress on some issues in some nations, the worldwide economic and human rights advances for women have been shamefully slow and sporadic in their progress. Therefore, to understand the special needs of women in disasters, wars, and other crises, one must grasp the conditions and obstacles with which women are faced even in the best of times (Hudnall & Lindner, 2006).

Among the many ways in which women and girls are demeaned and exploited, one of the most humiliating and pernicious is widespread sexual violence (Reis & Vann, 2006). Sexual coercion and assault are all too commonplace in women's lives, and the protection of women and girls against such violations is pathetically inadequate. When war and social upheaval are entered into this equation, the levels of sexual depravity against women achieve sickening proportions. Tenuous social restrictions designed to at least postpone the exploitation of female children until they have reached sexual maturity are easily swept aside in times of lawlessness and war. Civilian women have historically suffered under the domination of conquering armies, who have subjected them to systematic rapes and sexual slavery. The history of these atrocities has been disputed and denied by governments unwilling to take responsibility for the heinous acts that transpire under cover of war.

Given that, there is perhaps some comfort to be taken behind international human rights protections when governments war against one another. No such restrictions exist for outlaw bands of militia and other paramilitary fighters that dominate many regions of conflict in today's world. Therefore, while the member states of the UN enact resolutions and other instruments, such as the Convention on the Rights of the Child, to protect children from harmful practices such as child labor, sexual exploitation, early marriage, and premature military service, these problems persist and worsen in the darkest corners of civilization. Wherever societies crumble into chaos and bitter conflict, children are exposed to countless hazards and may also be drawn into battle, either as fighters or as captive workers to support the troops (Boyden, de Berry, Feeny, & Hart, 2006).

While the prototypical child soldier is a young boy armed with a light machinegun, girls too are forcibly ensnared into service (McKay, 2006). In such instances, girls are used as porters, domestic servants, sexual slaves, and "wives." Whether they are boys or girls, once these children escape captivity or are otherwise returned to civilian lives, the process of reunion and reintegration is often one of stigma, rejection, and shame. Girls in particular may be viewed as damaged goods and never regain the status and opportunities that were once within reach.

The type and intensity of traumatic events can also create differential impact characteristics that translate into unique needs for certain kinds of survivors. For instance, the impact of torture on the mind can be uniquely complex and intractable, thus requiring exquisitely precise skills unlike those which suffice for other types of disaster and trauma interventions (Holtz, 1998). In response to this need, dozens of excellent facilities, such as the Rehabilitation and Research Centre for Torture Survivors in Copenhagen, have developed noteworthy expertise in helping people who have suffered terribly at the hands of others (Berliner & Mikkelsen, 2006).

A paradoxical aspect of disasters and humanitarian emergencies is that, while most people flee from these zones of mayhem and destruction, others rush into the breach to assist survivors and pursue altruistic ends. The impact of facing death and other gruesome consequences of disasters fall particularly hard upon humanitarian aid workers, emergency services personnel, members of the military, and other occupations who perform heroic services. International humanitarian organizations (Ehrenreich, 2006), civilian fire and police departments (De Soir, 2006), and other agencies have recently come to recognize the importance of responding to the psychosocial needs of their employees and volunteers. Managing occupational stress among their personnel challenges these organizations not only to add a psychosocial component to their existing employee health services, but also to modify their systems so that they are less likely to create the stress that must then be managed. It is at least ironic, if not hypocritical, that humanitarian organizations charged with the mission of relieving the suffering of any and every unfortunate soul whom they encounter often fail to treat their own staff and volunteers with comparable compassion and regard for their dignity and well-being.

As noted earlier, the role of the news media in providing reliable information about crises and relief operations has become a critically important component of marshaling resources and public opinion in helpful directions. In viewing the "media" as a mammoth multinational corporate operation involving cameras, satellites, and high technology, it is easy to overlook the fragile human elements. International correspondents and their coworkers, many of whom are poorly paid local citizens, sometimes cover these stories at great risk to their own lives. In recent events it has become clear that journalists reporting from war zones and humanitarian crises are being killed and injured at historically high rates, sometimes due to their own risky decisions, though often at the hands of military forces they had trusted to protect them. Perhaps in part because the status of war correspondents in the journalistic community is so high, they are expected to shake off the ill effects of their occupation without complaint and bask in the glory they have earned through daring deeds. But recent collaborative projects have been initiated between journalists and psychologists that examine the psychological effects of covering traumatic stories, assess the mental health needs of journalists exposed to trauma, and design proactive interventions to reduce the negative psychosocial impact on those who inform the public about these critically important events (Newman & Shapiro, 2006).

Appendix of NGO Profiles (Volume 4)

The international humanitarian relief community that developed over the past century was pioneered by a small number of organizations dedicated to serving victims of war, disease, famine, and other natural calamities. Paramount among these was the Red Cross movement, which began in Switzerland in 1863 and slowly spread throughout most of the world over the next several decades. The red cross on a white background came to be recognized as a symbol of neutrality and compassion in the face of conflict and brutality. Hospitals, ambulances, and personnel marked with the Red Cross emblem earned a status as noncombatants that allowed them to function in war zones and other dangerous places with few direct attacks upon their operations. This philosophy of mercy within a context of violence eventually led to the Geneva Conventions and other international accords designed to provide limited protection for civilians and military prisoners as an ever widening swath of war engulfed the world. As the Red Cross movement proliferated, national societies were founded in dozens of countries and a new emblem, the Red Crescent, was approved to accommodate societies in regions where Islam was the predominate faith.

The founding of the United Nations at the end of World War II fostered a period of growing humanitarian aid through both governmental ager ،es and nongovernmental organizations (NGOs). Several agencies within the UN system, such as the United Nations Children's Fund (UNICEF), the United Nations High Commissioner for Refugees (UNHCR), and the World Health Organization (WHO), developed programs and policies that saved millions of lives and improved the quality of life for untold numbers of the world's most vulnerable citizens. The scourges of war, disease, and disaster were never abolished, but a countervailing force of hope and compassion was established, and hundreds of NGOs have been founded to serve the needs of people who might otherwise perish or wither.

Perhaps the most recent of humanitarian relief activities is the formal provision of psychosocial support, though this is certainly an element of any compassionate care to the afflicted. The story of international disaster psychology cannot be fully told without repeated reference to the humanitarian NGOs that have developed and disseminated psychosocial support training and services with great dedication and determination. Moreover, volunteers who aspire to work in this field of endeavor will almost certainly work closely with several of these NGOs and will benefit from obtaining at least a cursory knowledge of their missions, philosophies, histories, and activities.

Therefore, the editors of the *Handbook of International Disaster Psychology* have included an appendix consisting of brief profiles that describe some of the prominent humanitarian organizations operating in the world today. The information contained in these profiles was gathered from public sources and may contain accidental inaccuracies. Given the rapidly evolving nature of the NGOs profiled, it is also quite likely that some of the information will soon become outdated. However, these profiles are substantially accurate, and the contact information given for each agency makes it possible for interested readers to obtain more current and detailed information.

References

Ager, A. (2006). Toward a consensus protocol for psychosocial response in complex emergencies. In G. Reyes & G. A. Jacobs (Eds.), *Handbook of international disaster psychology, Vol. 1. Fundamentals and overview*. Westport, CT: Praeger Publishers.

Agger, I. (2006). Approaches to psychosocial healing: Case examples from Lusophone Africa. In G. Reyes & G. A. Jacobs (Eds.), *Handbook of international disaster psychology, Vol. 2. Practices and programs*. Westport, CT: Praeger Publishers.

Armstrong, M., Boyden, J., Galappatti, A., & Hart, J. (2006). Participatory tools for monitoring and evaluating psychosocial work with children: Reflections on a pilot study in Eastern Sri Lanka. In G. Reyes & G. A. Jacobs (Eds.), *Handbook of international disaster psychology, Vol. 2. Practices and programs*. Westport, CT: Praeger Publishers.

Atherton, J., & Sonniks, M. (2006). Implementation of a training of trainers model for disseminating psychological support in the Cuban Red Cross. In G. Reyes & G. A. Jacobs (Eds.), *Handbook of international disaster psychology, Vol. 2. Practices and programs*. Westport, CT: Praeger Publishers.

Beech, D. R. (2006). Peace-building, culturally responsive means, and ethical practices in humanitarian psychosocial interventions. In G. Reyes & G. A. Jacobs (Eds.), *Handbook of international disaster psychology, Vol. 1. Fundamentals and overview*. Westport, CT: Praeger Publishers.

Berliner, P., & Mikkelsen, E. (2006). Serving the psychosocial needs of survivors of torture and organized violence. In G. Reyes & G. A. Jacobs (Eds.), *Handbook of international disaster psychology, Vol. 4. Interventions with special needs populations*. Westport, CT: Praeger Publishers.

Blanco, T., Villalobos, M., & Carrillo, C. (2006). The psychological support network of the Central University of Venezuela and the Venezuelan floods of 1999. In G. Reyes & G. A. Jacobs (Eds.), *Handbook of international disaster psychology, Vol. 2. Practices and programs*. Westport, CT: Praeger Publishers.

Bolton, P. (2006). Challenges in international disaster mental health research. In G. Reyes & G. A. Jacobs (Eds.), *Handbook of international disaster psychology, Vol. 3. Refugee mental health*. Westport, CT: Praeger Publishers.

Borris, E. (2006). The healing power of forgiveness and the resolution of protracted conflicts. In G. Reyes & G. A. Jacobs (Eds.), *Handbook of international disaster psychology, Vol. 3. Refugee mental health*. Westport, CT: Praeger Publishers.

Boyden, J., de Berry, J., Feeny, T., & Hart, J. (2006). Children affected by armed conflict in South Asia: A regional summary. In G. Reyes & G. A. Jacobs (Eds.), *Handbook of international disaster psychology, Vol. 4. Interventions with special needs populations*. Westport, CT: Praeger Publishers.

Burnett, J. S. (2004, August 4). In the line of fire. *The New York Times*, Late Edition–Final, p. A17, col. 1.

Cohen, R. (2006). Implementation of mental health programs for survivors of natural disasters in Latin America. In G. Reyes & G. A. Jacobs (Eds.), *Handbook of international disaster psychology, Vol. 2. Practices and programs*. Westport, CT: Praeger Publishers.

De Soir, E. (2006). Psychosocial crisis intervention with military and emergency services personnel. In G. Reyes & G. A. Jacobs (Eds.), *Handbook of international disaster psychology, Vol. 4. Interventions with special needs populations*. Westport, CT: Praeger Publishers.

Dodge, G. R. (2006a). Assessing the psychosocial needs of communities affected by disaster. In G. Reyes & G. A. Jacobs (Eds.), *Handbook of international disaster psychology, Vol. 1. Fundamentals and overview*. Westport, CT: Praeger Publishers.

———. (2006b). In defense of a community psychology model for international psychosocial intervention. In G. Reyes & G. A. Jacobs (Eds.), *Handbook of international disaster psychology, Vol. 1. Fundamentals and overview*. Westport, CT: Praeger Publishers.

Ehrenreich, J. (2006). Managing stress in humanitarian aid workers: The role of the humanitarian aid organization. In G. Reyes & G. A. Jacobs (Eds.), *Handbook of international disaster psychology, Vol. 4. Interventions with special needs populations*. Westport, CT: Praeger Publishers.

Ekblad, S. (2006). Serving the mental health needs of postmigratory adult refugees in Sweden: A transitional augmentation approach. In G. Reyes & G. A. Jacobs (Eds.), *Handbook of international disaster psychology, Vol. 3. Refugee mental health*. Westport, CT: Praeger Publishers.

Gall, C. (2004, June 3). Aid agency halts operations in Afghanistan. *The New York Times*, Late Edition–Final, p. A5, col. 3.

Holtz, T. H. (1998). Refugee trauma versus torture trauma: A retrospective controlled cohort study of Tibetan refugees. *Journal of Nervous & Mental Disease, 186*, 24–34.

Hudnall, A., & Lindner, E. (2006). Crisis and gender: Addressing the psychosocial needs of women in international disasters. In G. Reyes & G. A. Jacobs (Eds.), *Handbook of international disaster psychology, Vol. 4. Interventions with special needs populations*. Westport, CT: Praeger Publishers.

Jacobs, G. A., Revel, J. P., Reyes, G., & Quevillon, R. P. (2006). Development of the Rapid Assessment of Mental Health: An international collaboration. In G. Reyes & G. A. Jacobs (Eds.), *Handbook of international disaster psychology, Vol. 3. Refugee mental health*. Westport, CT: Praeger Publishers.

Kapor-Stanulovic, N. (2006). Implementing psychosocial programs in the Federal Republic of Yugoslavia: Was it really mission impossible? In G. Reyes & G. A. Jacobs (Eds.), *Handbook of international disaster psychology, Vol. 2. Practices and programs*. Westport, CT: Praeger Publishers.

Kelly, A. (2004, December 15). Caught in the crossfire. *The Guardian Weekly*. Retrieved March 4, 2005, from http://society.guardian.co.uk/societyguardian/story/0,,1373410,00.html

Kinzie, J. D. (2006). Personal reflections on treating traumatized refugees. In G. Reyes & G. A. Jacobs (Eds.), *Handbook of international disaster psychology, Vol. 3. Refugee mental health*. Westport, CT: Praeger Publishers.

Kuriansky, J. (2006). Working effectively with the mass media in disaster mental health. In G. Reyes & G. A. Jacobs (Eds.), *Handbook of international disaster psychology, Vol. 1. Fundamentals and overview*. Westport, CT: Praeger Publishers.

MacDonald, C. M. (2003). Evaluation of stress debriefing interventions with military populations. *Military Medicine, 168*, 961–968.

McKay, S. (2006). How do you mend broken hearts? Gender, war, and impacts on girls in fighting forces. In G. Reyes & G. A. Jacobs (Eds.), *Handbook of international disaster psychology, Vol. 4. Interventions with special needs populations*. Westport, CT: Praeger Publishers.

Ndetei, D., Kasina, R., & Kathuku, D. (2006). Psychosocial responses to the bombing of the American Embassy in Nairobi: Challenges, lessons, and opportunities. In G. Reyes & G. A. Jacobs (Eds.), *Handbook of international disaster psychology, Vol. 2. Practices and programs*. Westport, CT: Praeger Publishers.

Neugebauer, R. (2006). Psychosocial research and interventions after the Rwanda genocide. In G. Reyes & G. A. Jacobs (Eds.), *Handbook of international disaster psychology, Vol. 2. Practices and programs*. Westport, CT: Praeger Publishers.

Newman, E., & Shapiro, B. (2006). Helping journalists who cover humanitarian crises. In G. Reyes & G. A. Jacobs (Eds.), *Handbook of international disaster psychology, Vol. 4. Interventions with special needs populations*. Westport, CT: Praeger Publishers.

Peddle, N., Hudnall Stamm, B., Hudnall, A. C., & Stamm, H. E. (2006). Effective intercultural collaboration on psychosocial support programs. In G. Reyes & G. A. Jacobs (Eds.), *Handbook of international disaster psychology, Vol. 1. Fundamentals and overview*. Westport, CT: Praeger Publishers.

Pupavac, V. (2006). Humanitarian politics and the rise of international disaster psychology. In G. Reyes & G. A. Jacobs (Eds.), *Handbook of international disaster psychology, Vol. 1. Fundamentals and overview*. Westport, CT: Praeger Publishers.

Raina, D., Weine, S., Kulauzovic, Y., Feetham, S., Zhubi, M., Huseni, D., & Pavkovic, I. (2006). A framework for developing and implementing multiple-family groups for refugee families. In G. Reyes & G. A. Jacobs (Eds.), *Handbook of international disaster psychology, Vol. 3. Refugee mental health*. Westport, CT: Praeger Publishers.

Reis, C., & Vann. B. (2006). Sexual violence against women and children in the context of armed conflict. In G. Reyes & G. A. Jacobs (Eds.), *Handbook of international disaster psychology, Vol. 4. Interventions with special needs populations*. Westport, CT: Praeger Publishers.

Reyes, G. (2006). International disaster psychology: Purposes, principles, and practices. In G. Reyes & G. A. Jacobs (Eds.), *Handbook of international disaster psychology, Vol. 1. Fundamentals and overview*. Westport, CT: Praeger Publishers.

Rieff, D. (2002). *A bed for the night: Humanitarianism in crisis*. New York: Simon & Schuster.

Ronan, K. R., Finnis, K., & Johnston, D. M. (2006). Interventions with youth and families: A prevention and stepped care model. In G. Reyes & G. A. Jacobs (Eds.), *Handbook of international disaster psychology, Vol. 2. Practices and programs*. Westport, CT: Praeger Publishers.

Silove, D. (2006). The impact of mass psychological trauma on psychosocial adaptation among refugees. In G. Reyes & G. A. Jacobs (Eds.), *Handbook of international disaster psychology, Vol. 3. Refugee mental health*. Westport, CT: Praeger Publishers.

Weine, S., Pavkovic, I., Agani, F., Ceric, I., & Jukic, V. (2006). Mental health reform and assisting psychiatric leaders in postwar countries. In G. Reyes & G. A. Jacobs (Eds.), *Handbook of international disaster psychology, Vol. 3. Refugee mental health*. Westport, CT: Praeger Publishers.

Wessells, M. G. (2006). Negotiating the shrunken humanitarian space: Challenges and options. In G. Reyes & G. A. Jacobs (Eds.), *Handbook of international disaster psychology, Vol. 1. Fundamentals and overview*. Westport, CT: Praeger Publishers.

CHAPTER 1

INTERNATIONAL DISASTER PSYCHOLOGY: PURPOSES, PRINCIPLES, AND PRACTICES

Gilbert Reyes

Disasters shatter lives and societies with such force that survivors, facing futures mutilated by loss and trauma, sometimes envy the dead. Forces of nature show no respect for human designs and transgress boundaries of every kind. Much as rivers jump their banks and seawalls yield to tidal forces, so wars and natural calamities spill across borders of all kinds, be they cultural, tribal, civic, or national. Massive human migrations fleeing forces that threaten their lives create displaced populations of refugees who must struggle to survive in unfamiliar and often hostile circumstances. Resident groups and the newly arrived strive to coexist in the face of cultural and linguistic differences and the inevitable competition for status and resources. The losses endured by survivors vary in kind and magnitude ranging from more tangible costs, such as lives and property, to such intangible assets as identity, status, and dignity.

Adjusting to such profound levels of stress and loss far exceeds the normal coping resources of most people and can require more than strong personal characteristics (i.e., resilience) and the merciful passage of time. Traditionally, solace for the grief and suffering brought about by disasters and wars has been sought from spiritual or religious sources. Quite recently, however, the painful emotions, troubling memories, and other difficulties in adjusting to disasters have begun to be viewed as psychological reactions requiring professional intervention. Members of the mental health professions are now expected to comprehend the psychological and social terrain of disasters and to intervene to prevent or mitigate trauma, grief, depression, and other conditions that plague survivors. A cautiously scientific approach to psychology and psychiatric illness requires careful establishment of research evidence supporting the validity of treatments before they are widely applied. In urgent situations, however, there is little time or patience for study and deliberation, and so, somewhat hastily, the mental health field began responding to the perceived needs of disaster survivors.

Religious, governmental, and nongovernmental organizations (NGOs), including the United Nations and the International Federation of Red Cross and Red Crescent Societies (IFRC), have long provided aid to victims of wars, natural disasters, and refugee crises. The international circumstances of many high-profile disaster relief efforts compound the complexity of formulating effective response strategies that are acceptable to the recipients and congruent with the cultures and customs of the affected communities. Relief operations have traditionally supplied survival necessities (e.g., food, water, clothing, medicine, shelter, and security) at the height of a crisis while not ignoring the importance of spiritual support and morale-boosting activities. The humanitarian relief community's recognition of the need for psychosocial support came about more recently and to some extent reflects the impact of horrific events such as the genocide in Rwanda and ethnic cleansing in the Balkan wars of the 1990s. In these instances, the traumatic impact and profound grief were undeniable and began to take center stage. In response, humanitarian NGOs and the mental health professions began collaborating on ways to help reduce the psychological and emotional suffering of those who displayed the most severe reactions and impairments in functioning (Barron, 2004). This in turn evolved into a more comprehensive approach to providing psychosocial services, extending beyond the most acute and compelling instances to helping any and all who might benefit. Given the limitations of resources available for such endeavors and the many obstacles and challenges that were encountered, this has proven to be a supremely difficult enterprise requiring the harnessing of idealistic energies and the practicality to use them wisely and judiciously.

The Contexts of Disasters

People have long understood that catastrophic events result in great emotional suffering and leave their marks both on geographical landscapes and on human societies for many successive generations. Indeed, the impact of disasters on human development is writ large across thousands of years of recorded history, from great natural catastrophes like the destruction of Pompeii to the horrific world wars of the twentieth century. These events are typically sudden, unexpected, overwhelming in intensity, devastating in destructive power, and threatening to survival. The most obvious effects are gauged in the historical terms of political, social, and economic disruptions, but they have also shaped religious and cultural systems with implications for how we understand our place in the world. To the human mind and spirit, however, they are so much more than the sum of these attributes. Catastrophes of all kinds, but especially those emanating from natural forces, can lead people to deeply question their most fundamental beliefs; they have the power to transform our individual lives and our collective destiny.

In recent years, we have witnessed escalating rates of every form of hazard, including natural disasters, man-made accidental disasters, and complex humanitarian emergencies. Regardless of the source of the disaster, the impact on human societies can be devastating in almost every way imaginable. In recognition of this fact, the United Nations declared the 1990s to be the International Decade for Natural Disaster Reduction (IDNDR). The UN mandate was to instigate global cooperation across a series of programs and projects intended to increase awareness and activities that would reduce the loss of life, property damage, and social and economic disruption brought about by natural disasters. A need for such actions was perceived based on global trends toward dramatically escalating economic and human losses stemming from natural disasters. This surge was attributed to climatic changes, demographic shifts, substantial increases in population density, and a widespread failure of planning and preventive actions.

Although natural hazards cannot be eliminated, human decisions and actions play a critical role in determining whether adequate preventive measures are taken to limit the potential magnitude of the impact on societies and their most vulnerable people. However, for every society that invests heavily in preparation for earthquakes, floods, fires, and other chronic cataclysms, there are many more that lack the resources or the collective motivations and mechanisms necessary to proactively limit the impact of these natural hazards on human existence. The various nations that form the UN dedicate vastly more of their resources to issues surrounding war and other forms of human conflict, perhaps because these are perceived as more gravely threatening or more probable than natural hazards. The ambitious mission of the IDNDR—helping to create long-term, proactive disaster prevention strategies by influencing planning and decision making at every level—had limited success. The pursuit of those goals was enormously challenging, but in its 10 years, the IDNDR made strides toward a global collaboration for coordinating disaster mitigation activities and improving the resiliency of the affected communities. Nevertheless, as the decade came to an end, disasters of all kinds had become increasingly frequent and increasingly costly in terms of both money and lives.

At the time of this writing, the world received the most graphic evidence possible of just how devastating natural disasters can be, when in late December 2004, a major submarine earthquake generated tsunamis across the full expanse of the Indian Ocean. The result was widespread death and destruction across 11 countries at levels that have shocked the world and captivated the attention of the global news media. Unfortunately, this has also meant a shift of attention away from equally tragic events in other regions of the world. As with all disasters, people soon began asking how such a thing might have been prevented or its effects mitigated. Honest answers to such questions must be complex because of the numerous contributing factors involved in predicting and controlling events. In instances such as the Indian Ocean tsunami, we must bow to the unpredictability and uncontrollability of major seismic and oceanic events and look instead for strategies to limit their destructive potential. It also must be noted that although these disruptive natural phenomena (storms, earthquakes, droughts, fires, etc.) can be shockingly sudden and ferocious, they may also have highly predictable aspects that can be understood by examining historical precedents and patterns of climatic and seismic activity. And in this age of ever-advancing technology, we quickly turn to science and governments for answers as to how people could have been warned in time to spare thousands of lives. The ugly truth appears to be that the technology has long been available for early-warning systems that could substantially reduce the death toll, but nothing was done to put it to good use in affected areas (Bloomberg News, 2004). History shows that it often takes a tragedy of monumental proportions before societies and their governments are moved to take preventive actions against future occurrences of a similar nature.

The impediments to preventive planning and protection of populations are often more psychological than technological, having mainly to do with what is valued and what is feared. That is, we tend to protect what we most value from that which we most fear (e.g., vaccinating our children from infectious diseases). Preventive measures require sufficiently confident predictions to justify investing resources that might better be used for other purposes, and with a constant supply of clear and present dangers drawing on these resources, there is little remaining will to invest in the prevention of things that might not happen at all. An unfortunate aspect of the social psychology of disasters is that—much like generals planning to refight the last war—societies often prepare for the recurrence of the last worst disaster, rather than for those most likely to be coming. The most disaster-resistant societies are often those that have learned constructive lessons from prior events and dedicated sufficient resources to strengthening their capacity to withstand subsequent shocks. Nevertheless, when catastrophes of the highest magnitude occur, as in the case of Indian Ocean tsunami, most preventive measures are overwhelmed and rendered futile. In such an instance only a vast multinational humanitarian relief effort can mobilize sufficient resources to aid the millions whose lives have been shattered.

The Psychosocial Impact of Disasters

People of all ages awake each day with needs to satisfy and goals to pursue. They have learned behaviors that tend to be successful for achieving their aims and deviate from them only to the extent necessary to counterbalance variations in their environments. Thus, daily life consists mainly of predictable routines, but it is not without its challenges and upsets. Successful living becomes a matter of matching behaviors to immediate conditions in ways that will achieve expectations. This works better when environments are stable and people have time to learn adaptive lessons in relative safety. Communities can then develop collective wisdom over time and pass this wisdom along to successive generations. Such security and continuity, however, is disturbed and sometimes ruptured by disasters, which have the power to violate personal and collective expectations to a degree that terrifies people and leads them to reorganize their lives in countless ways.

A consistent goal across these events is to return as nearly as possible to what was previously normal, especially in regard to the establishment of physical safety and access to sufficient resources for survival. Once conditions become relatively stable, the rebuilding of lives and communities can proceed and accelerate. Losses will be surveyed and remaining resources salvaged. Prior values, expectations, designs, skills, and institutions are often reconsidered and reconstituted in more adaptive forms. This describes the essential nature of coping. Behaviors that meet regularly with success tend to be retained and refined and to undergo major modifications only when uncommon or unexpected obstacles arise. In other words, the wheel is not so often reinvented as it is modified to suit a changing terrain. Thus, coping, whether individually or collectively, requires responses that are well matched to the challenges or obstacles encountered and results in changes favoring the success and survival of those concerned.

Disasters suddenly (and often unexpectedly) alter the environment in ways that threaten survival and impair successful adaptation to change. People have well-worn ways of responding to losses, whether they come about gradually or rapidly. We mourn our dead and grieve the absence of things that once were or will never be, and we enact rituals that signify the meaning of our losses and unite us in a collective observance. But support is mainly lent and received among those who feel sufficient kinship, while outsiders are often left to fend for themselves or are even exploited. Memories remain that converge to form history and guide future actions. Memorials and anniversaries serve to sustain the knowledge and feelings regarding our losses that are most durably valued. Thus, that which once threatened annihilation becomes instead a source of hope and lends meaning to existence.

The transformational landscapes described above are often littered with broken hearts and injured minds that will gradually heal and adapt by various means, as people always have. But this journey is sometimes harsh and painful, and even the ancient medicines of love, faith, and compassion are poorly matched against the blights of trauma and grief. Studies of refugees and other survivors of armed conflict consistently demonstrate that some proportion of these survivors will carry emotional and psychological wounds long after they are safely removed from the violence (Fenta, Hyman, & Noh, 2004; Steel, Silove, Phan, & Bauman, 2002). This may prove particularly true when torture, human rights abuses, or other atrocities were involved (Holtz, 1998). Yet, although the meanings we attribute to intentional assaults differ profoundly from those brought about by forces of nature, survivors of natural or accidental catastrophes also suffer and may display signs of feeling traumatized and aggrieved (Goenjian, Steinberg, & Najarian, 2000). Symptoms associated with mental disorders such as post-traumatic stress disorder (PTSD), depression, anxiety disorders, and somatic complaints without clear physical sources have been found among populations of people exposed to disasters of various natures or explanations (Bowen, Carscadden, & Beighle, 1992; Friedman & Jaranson, 1994; Goenjian et al., 2000). Unhealthy behaviors, such as immoderate use of alcohol or other intoxicants, are also known to worsen in the aftermath. Hostile and aggressive interpersonal conduct may also increase as people bend others to their will as they struggle to regain control of themselves.

Thus, the impact of these events is profound, yet varied, and tends to exact some emotional toll from all concerned. The majority of persons will prove to be resilient for the most part, though they will not escape the need to adjust and integrate what has happened into what remains of their lives. And some of those who could not rebound will decline from their previous levels of functioning and well-being. For these people, memories can serve as painful reminders of their losses. Subsequent experiences may be colored by the tragic residue of their misfortune as bitterness and regret crowd out joy and optimism. Sadly, disaster psychology, with its emphasis on normalization and natural resilience, may inadvertently minimize the needs of the most severely affected survivors. The most prominent international humanitarian relief agencies tend to promote population-wide models of psychological support programming (PSP; Simonsen & Reyes, 2003), popularly known as psychological first aid (PFA; Knudsen, Hogsted, & Berliner, 1997). But what works for the resilient majority may not be adequate for those who suffer the most grievous losses or who are marginalized and ill-served within their communities. A complex and realistic understanding of the psychological, social, and political forces at work in disaster-affected communities is necessary if both majority and minority groups are to be served in proportion to their needs, and not just their numbers.

Psychosocial Interventions in Disasters

The historical development of international humanitarian psychosocial activities and the consequent emergence of disaster psychology as a discipline owe much to the field of traumatology. The major focus of concern within the refugee and disaster mental health literature has long been on trauma and PTSD and has only recently begun shifting toward a stronger emphasis on resilience and more positive adaptive outcomes. Published studies such as those describing work with refugees from World War II through the Southeast Asian Diaspora illustrate the emphasis on symptoms of pathology (especially trauma and PTSD) and clinical interventions that often include medications (Kinzie & Edeki, 1998). More recently, however, the consensus has shifted toward assessments and interventions that are community-based (Petevi, Revel, & Jacobs, 2001), and toward principles that are consistent with public health models of mental health care (van Ommeren, Saxena, & Saraceno, 2005). Nevertheless, despite the growing emphasis on normalizing intense emotional reactions and temporary decrements in functioning, PTSD and other clinical syndromes remain popular topics of interest in this field (Nicholl & Thompson, 2004).

Critics have argued that most of the psychosocial effects of disasters will abate with time, and this is true to the best of our present knowledge (e.g., Bolton, Hill, & O'Ryan, 2004). But how could one argue that these reactions, however transitory they may prove to be, do not worsen the other difficulties caused by the precipitating crisis? Yet there exists an argument that psychological support for disaster survivors is unnecessary, misguided, and imperialistic (Summerfield, 2002). Critics of post-disaster psychosocial interventions (e.g., Pupavac, 2001; Summerfield, 2005) claim that the advocates of such activities mistakenly equate disaster survivors and refugees with the mentally ill (i.e., stigmatizing) and confuse normal psychosocial reactions with symptoms of disease (i.e., "pathologizing"). To whatever extent that this is an actual danger, it should be strongly opposed, but in reviewing the literature on this subject, there is little evidence that survivors are being diagnosed as mentally ill on the basis of their exposure to disasters or other potentially traumatic events. Instead, most professionals in this field are careful to normalize short-term reactions to extremely stressful life events (Norwood, Ursano, & Fullerton, 2000). These reactions are not described as being abnormal, psychotic, or pathological, but instead are understood as normal adaptive processes occurring under conditions that strain the limits of human capacity for coping with stress (e.g., Somasundaram, 1996).

Adapting Western models of mental health, with their biomedical explanatory foundations that emphasize disorders like PTSD and approaches to healing through conversational disclosure and processing of thoughts and feelings, has presented a daunting and controversial challenge (Bracken, Giller, & Summerfield, 1995). Clinically oriented approaches employed crisis intervention techniques and psychotherapy in response to the most anticipated psychopathologies, especially trauma and PTSD. Published reports of such efforts were generally met with acceptance and even praise (e.g., Weiss & Parish, 1989), but they were also criticized by some for employing Western psychological frameworks as though they are universally valid (Summerfield, 1999) and for possibly compounding people's suffering by exacerbating negative social consequences (e.g., stigma). In response to these and related criticisms, the international humanitarian community has examined various options for enhancing mental health support following disasters that avoid the pitfall of stigmatization, "medicalization," and pathologizing.

The role of mental health professionals in such cases is not to treat a mental illness (i.e., medicalizing) but to limit the harmful psychological effects of both the acute event and the persistent and chronic stressors that often follow. Some of what is offered as psychological support can be compared to pain relief for an injury, which is simply an act of compassion. In many instances, the techniques employed amount to providing soothing or comforting support and require little professional expertise. Other types of assistance are comparable to teaching a person about helpful ways of coping until they are feeling better. All of what is done is meant to help reduce the burden of stress that people must bear so that they may experience some relief while adapting to their changing circumstances.

Good intentions, however, do not ensure that psychological support activities will actually be helpful. The histories of medicine and psychotherapy demonstrate the potential for believing that one is helping while actually having no effect—or even making things worse. This concern is supported by several facts, not the least of which is that some techniques were never systematically tested to ascertain their effectiveness with which problems, populations, or types of practitioners, and under what conditions. A prominent example of this predicament unfolded as an American technique known as Critical Incident Stress Debriefing (CISD; Mitchell, 1988) rapidly spread to almost every continent and was employed in several disasters and war-torn territories (Deahl, Earnshaw, & Jones, 1994; Dyregrov, 1997). But a recent series of research studies have cast doubt on the worth of this method (e.g., Rose, Bisson, & Wessely, 2002), leading several organizations, including the World Health Organization (e.g., World Health Organization, 2005b), to recommend against its use.

This reversal of fortune for such a prominent and respected technique may also undermine confidence in post-disaster psychosocial interventions more generally, and it is true that the approaches to intervention applied in disasters are mostly derived from methods developed in very different contexts. For a variety of reasons, the techniques preferred in clinical settings among the Western industrialized nations do not necessarily transfer well to field settings in the developing countries. As previously mentioned, cultural differences (e.g., language, customs, beliefs, and practices) are a major consideration when attempting to extend the application of psychological assessment and treatment practices beyond their cultures of origin (Stamm & Friedman, 2000). Although advocates of psychosocial assessments and interventions consistently emphasize the importance of cross-cultural translation and adaptation (e.g., Eisenbruch, de Jong, & van de Put, 2004), there are legitimate concerns regarding the quality and validity of their products (Marsella & Christopher, 2004). The problem of extending these models of practice is further complicated by the fact that most mental health techniques are designed for use in a very controlled milieu (e.g., clinics and private offices), which is far from what is typical in post-disaster settings. Thus, it is fair to complain that these assessments and interventions have not been rigorously tested for use across culturally diverse populations of refugees or disaster survivors in the uncontrolled and often chaotic environments in which they are likely to be encountered.

Nevertheless, there are dedicated humanitarians whose experience with traumatized and dejected populations of refugees and disaster survivors have convinced them that palpable psychosocial needs exist among these people that cannot be ignored in good conscience. Research literature demonstrates the presence of psychological symptoms consistent with Western mental health frameworks of trauma among substantial proportions of refugees and disaster survivors (Mollica et al., 1999; Norris, Friedman, & Watson, 2002). Other studies have provided evidence that culturally adapted approaches to intervention are also promising in their effectiveness and acceptance in the communities where they have been applied (Cardozo, Talley, Burton, & Crawford, 2004; Peltzer, 1989). Moreover, the core elements of psychological support (e.g., protection from further harm, concerned interest for emotional distress, compassionate care, encouragement toward recovery, and respect for human dignity) are not fundamentally Western in their values and provide a generally useful foundation from which a more specific approach can be developed to fit a given set of circumstances.

Establishing Standards and Practices

Various relief and humanitarian agencies have published papers and guidebooks describing what they consider to be the best practices known at this time for providing psychosocial care for disaster survivors (Cohen, 2000; Knudsen et al., 1997; Lakshminarayana, Murthy, & Prewitt Diaz, 2004; Loughry & Ager, 2001; Psychosocial Working Group [PWG], 2004; Simonsen & Reyes, 2003; United Nations High Commissioner for Refugees [UNHCR], 2001; Weine et al., 2002; WHO, 2003 2005a). The cumulative knowledge and expertise within these volumes form an excellent base from which to create psychosocial programs and projects that are well suited to serve the needs of disaster survivors. Among the key activities that tend to be emphasized are the identification of highly exposed or otherwise at-risk populations, assessment of psychosocial needs, identification of existing psychosocial resources, incorporation of important cultural information for improving the service model, stress management and counseling techniques, and community participation. A great deal of space is also dedicated to cautionary statements designed to discourage certain goals, activities, and perspectives that are likely to prove ineffective or harmful. Other important issues include services for groups who have either special needs (e.g., children) or particular risks and mitigating factors (e.g., people with HIV/AIDS), and the needs of relief personnel working in difficult situations (IFRC, 2001).

The goals of psychosocial services for disaster-affected populations are to avert further harm while relieving immediate distress and supporting effective coping. These require activities that are preventive, responsive, and progressive. Conventional talking therapies are less advantageous than crisis intervention methods that focus on identifying immediate problems and needs and developing practical and effective coping strategies. Although discussions focusing on detailed accounts of traumatic events and the processing of emotional reactions are not uncommon, they are discouraged by many of the most prominent voices in the field. Rather than focusing on pathology, the emphasis is placed on empowering the affected population and fostering resilient adaptations that are solution-focused, locally controlled, and sustainable. The term *capacity building* is used to convey the principle aim of strengthening local resources beyond their pre-disaster limits. For several reasons, community-level interventions are often preferred over individualistic services. This may allow more efficient and effective use of resources, improve the match between services and local characteristics, and help reduce the stigma associated with receiving psychosocial assistance. Moreover, if local leaders and their constituents buy in to the benefits and values of psychosocial programming, they are more likely to develop a sense of community ownership of those services and seek to sustain them. This last aspect is an issue that is often neglected, and it is all too common for externally initiated and funded projects to evaporate once the news media and humanitarian relief agencies shift their attention to a more compelling hotspot.

Conclusion

The field of international disaster psychology has recently emerged as a distinct discipline focusing on the mental health and psychosocial needs of people affected by catastrophic events. Human societies have endured the effects of disasters throughout the ages and developed remarkable resiliency in the face of horrible tragedies and massive trauma. Nevertheless, both natural and man-made disasters have been found to have profound short-term psychological and social effects and may cast a long shadow over the well-being of survivors. Immediate compassionate attention appears to be prudent and warranted by the risk of further harm if psychological services are withheld. The empirical foundations of this field, however, are not yet sufficient to provide convincing evidence of what is needed, by whom, from whom, and at what time. Clearly, it is imperative that a progressive and systematic program of research continues to be pursued. Thus, psychosocial support must never be imposed or mandated and should be well integrated with other types of practical services for which the necessity is clear and unquestioned. Moreover, psychosocial support is not intended to be a panacea for human suffering and is no substitute for physical security, social justice, and human dignity. The altruistic motives of Western practitioners, their methods, and their culture-bound assumptions have also been questioned and scrutinized (e.g., Summerfield, 1999), and the burden of proof that this humanitarian endeavor is justified rests with those individuals and institutions who promote and perform these services.

References

Barron, R. A. (2004). International disaster mental health. *Psychiatric Clinics of North America, 27*, 505–519.

Bloomberg News. (2004, December 30). Indian Ocean tsunami warning plan ignored for 15 years, UN Says. Retrieved December 30, 2004, from www.bloomberg.com/

Bolton, D., Hill, J., & O'Ryan, D. (2004). Long-term effects of psychological trauma on psychosocial functioning. *Journal of Child Psychology & Psychiatry, 45*, 1007–1014.

Bowen, D. J., Carscadden, L., & Beighle, K. (1992). Post-traumatic stress disorder among Salvadoran women: Empirical evidence and description of treatment. *Women & Therapy, 13*, 267–280.

Bracken, P. J., Giller, J. E., & Summerfield, D. (1995). Psychological responses to war and atrocity: The limitations of current concepts. *Social Science & Medicine, 40*, 1073–1082.

Cardozo, B. L., Talley, L., Burton, A., & Crawford, C. (2004). Karenni refugees living in Thai-Burmese border camps: Traumatic experiences, mental health outcomes, and social functioning. *Social Science & Medicine, 58*, 2637–2644.

Cohen, R. (2000). *Mental health services in disasters: Manual for humanitarian workers.* Washington, DC: Pan American Health Organization.

Deahl, M. P., Earnshaw, N. M., & Jones, N. (1994). Psychiatry and war: Learning lessons from the former Yugoslavia. *British Journal of Psychiatry, 164*, 441–442.

Dyregrov, A. (1997). The process in psychological debriefings. *Journal of Traumatic Stress, 10*, 589–605.

Eisenbruch, M., de Jong, J. T. V. M., & van de Put, W. (2004). Bringing order out of chaos: A culturally competent approach to managing the problems of refugees and victims of organized violence. *Journal of Traumatic Stress, 17*, 123–131.

Fenta, H., Hyman, I., & Noh, S., (2004). Determinants of depression among Ethiopian immigrants and refugees in Toronto. *Journal of Nervous & Mental Disease, 192*, 363–372.

Friedman, M., & Jaranson, J. (1994). The applicability of the posttraumatic stress disorder concept to refugees. In A. J. Marsella & T. Bornemann (Eds.), *Amidst peril and pain: The mental health and well-being of the world's refugees* (pp. 207–227). Washington, DC: American Psychological Association.

Goenjian, A. K., Steinberg, A. M., & Najarian, L. M. (2000). Prospective study of posttraumatic stress, anxiety, and depressive reactions after earthquake and political violence. *American Journal of Psychiatry, 157*, 911–916.

Holtz, T. H. (1998). Refugee trauma versus torture trauma: A retrospective controlled cohort study of Tibetan refugees. *Journal of Nervous & Mental Disease, 186*, 24–34.

International Federation of Red Cross and Red Crescent Societies (IFRC). (2001). *Managing stress in the field.* Geneva: Author.

Kinzie, J. D., & Edeki, T. (1998). Ethnicity and psychopharmacology: The experience of Southeast Asians. In S. O. Okpaku (Ed.), *Clinical methods in transcultural psychiatry* (pp. 171–190). Washington, DC: American Psychiatric Association.

Knudsen, L., Hogsted, R., & Berliner, P. (1997). *Psychological first aid and human support.* Copenhagen, Denmark: Danish Red Cross.

Lakshminarayana, R., Murthy, R. S., & Prewitt Diaz, J. O. (2004). *Disaster mental health in India.* New Delhi: Indian Red Cross.

Loughry, M., & Ager, A. (Eds.). (2001). *The refugee experience: Psychosocial training module* (Rev. ed.). Oxford, England: Refugee Studies Centre. Retrieved January 27, 2005, from http://earlybird.qeh.ox.ac.uk/rfgexp/start.htm

Marsella, A. J., & Christopher, M. A. (2004). Ethnocultural considerations in disasters: An overview of research, issues and directions. *Psychiatric Clinics of North America, 27,* 521–539.

Mitchell, J. T. (1988). The history, status and future of critical incident stress debriefings. *Journal of Emergency Medical Services, 13,* 47–52.

Mollica, R. F., McInnes, K., Sarajlic, N., Lavelle, J., Sarajlic, I., & Massagli, M. P. (1999). Disability associated with psychiatric comorbidity and health status in Bosnian refugees living in Croatia. *Journal of the American Medical Association, 282,* 433–439.

Nicholl, C., & Thompson, A. (2004). The psychological treatment of post traumatic stress disorder (PTSD) in adult refugees: A review of the current state of psychological therapies. *Journal of Mental Health, 13,* 351–362.

Norris, F. H., Friedman, M. J., & Watson, P. J. (2002). 60,000 disaster victims speak: Part I. An empirical review of the empirical literature, 1981–2001. *Psychiatry: Interpersonal & Biological Processes, 65,* 207–239.

Norwood, A. E., Ursano, R. J., & Fullerton, C. S. (2000). Disaster psychiatry: Principles and practice. *Psychiatric Quarterly, 71,* 207–226.

Peltzer, K. ((1989). Assessment and treatment of psychosocial problems in refugees in Zambia. *International Journal of Mental Health, 18,* 113–121.

Petevi, M., Revel, J. P., & Jacobs, G. A. (2001). *Tool for the rapid assessment of mental health needs of refugees, displaced and other populations affected by conflict and post-conflict situations: A community-oriented assessm*ent. Geneva, Switzerland: World Health Organization.

Psychosocial Working Group (PWG). (2004). *Considerations in Planning Psychosocial Programs.* Retrieved February 15, 2005, from http://www.forcedmigration.org/psychosocial/papers/PWGpapers.htm

Pupavac, V. (2001). Therapeutic governance: Psycho-social intervention and trauma risk management. *Disasters, 25,* 358–372.

Rose, S., Bisson, J., & Wessely, S. (2002). Psychological debriefing for preventing post traumatic stress disorder (PTSD) (Cochrane Review). In *The Cochrane Library* (issue 2). Oxford, UK: Update Software.

Simonsen, L. F. & Reyes, G. (2003). *Community-based psychological support: A training manual.* Geneva: International Federation of Red Cross and Red Crescent Societies.

Somasundaram, D. J. (1996). *Post-traumatic responses to aerial bombing. Social Science & Medicine, 42,* 1465–1471.

Stamm, B. H., & Friedman, M. J. (2000). Cultural diversity in the appraisal and expression of traumatic exposure. In A. Shalev, R. Yehuda, & A. McFarlane (Eds.), *International handbook of human response to trauma* (pp. 69–85). New York: Plenum.

Steel, Z., Silove, D., Phan, T., & Bauman, A. (2002). Long-term effect of psychological trauma on the mental health of Vietnamese refugees resettled in Australia: A population-based study. *Lancet, 360,* 1056–1062.

Summerfield, D. (1999). A critique of seven assumptions behind psychological trauma programmes in war-affected areas. *Social Science & Medicine, 48,* 1449–1462.

———. (2002). Effects of war: Moral knowledge, revenge, reconciliation, and medicalised concepts of "recovery." *British Medical Journal, 325,* 1105–1107.

————. (2005). What exactly is emergency or disaster "mental health"? *Bulletin of the World Health Organization, 83*, 76.

United Nations High Commissioner for Refugees (UNHCR). (2001). *Managing the stress of humanitarian emergencies.* Retrieved January 31, 2005, from http://www.the-ecentre.net/resources/e_library/doc/managingStress.PDF

van Ommeren, M., Saxena, S., & Saraceno, B. (2005). Mental and social health during and after acute emergencies: Emerging consensus? *Bulletin of the World Health Organization, 83*, 71–76.

Weine, S.M., Danieli, Y., Silove, D., van Ommeren, M., Fairbank J., & Saul, J. (2002). Guidelines for international training in mental health and psychosocial interventions for trauma exposed populations in clinical and community settings. *Psychiatry, 65*, 156–164.

Weiss, B. S., & Parish, B. (1989). Culturally appropriate crisis counseling: Adapting an American method for use with Indochinese refugees. *Social Work, 34*, 252–254.

World Health Organization (2003). *Mental health in emergencies: Mental and social aspects of health of populations exposed to extreme stressors.* Retrieved September 30, 2005, from http://www.who.int/hac/techguidance/pht/8656.pdf

————. (2005a). *Manual for community level workers to provide psychosocial care to communities affected by the tsunami disaster* (World Health Organization Project ICP EHA 011 XD 04). World Health Organization Regional Office for SouthEast Asia, New Delhi, India. Retrieved January 31, 2005, from http://www.rcpsych.ac.uk/members/tsunami/ManualForCommunityIndiaJan05.pdf

————. (2005b). *Single-session psychological debriefing: Not recommended.* Retrieved February 12, 2005, from http://www.who.int/hac/techguidance/pht/13643.pdf

CHAPTER 2

HUMANITARIAN POLITICS AND THE RISE OF INTERNATIONAL DISASTER PSYCHOLOGY

Vanessa Pupavac

Introduction

International disaster psychology work has expanded rapidly in the last decade. In the 1980s international emergency responses were often synonymous with famine relief. Yet in the 1990s, the image of the traumatized victim displaced the famine victim as the iconic figure of suffering in the disaster literature. Before the end of the Cold War, psychosocial intervention did not feature in international humanitarian work, but within just a few years, psychosocial programs became standard in disaster relief. The chapter analyzes the rise of international disaster psychology in relation to humanitarian politics. International disaster relief is not apolitical (de Waal, 1997; Macrae, 2001; Vaux, 2001), nor is disaster psychology an apolitical aspect of the international disaster relief agenda. The nature of humanitarian aid provided to disaster-affected populations is entwined with the relationship of international humanitarian organizations, overwhelmingly Western, to their own societies and governments. This chapter explores how developments within donor countries and their humanitarian sectors at the end of the Cold War shaped the growth and character of international disaster psychology. The aim of the chapter is threefold. First, the chapter discusses the contemporary Western ethnopsychology and the psychologizing of life experiences in donor countries. Second, the chapter examines the crisis of belief in the aid sector and how this has facilitated the psychologizing of disaster relief. Third, the chapter outlines problems with the international psychosocial approach and argues for the importance of social meaning for recovery after disaster.

Western Ethnopyschology

The rapid growth of international disaster psychology has essentially been spurred by developments within Western donor countries. These developments have encouraged the application of psychological models to social problems, alongside changed cultural expectations about how people cope with adversity. Psychology has come to dominate how Western societies conceptualize experiences, and its influence is not confined to professionals. Psychology's dominance arises from how personal emotions are the standpoint from which people today in Western societies understand their lives as a consequence of atomization and the erosion of tradition and shared political or communal beliefs.

As personal feelings have come to the fore, Western emotional norms have shifted from emotional reserve to openness. Yet the Western individual of today is not a robust creature, for all its cult of the self (Furedi, 2003; Lasch, 1984). Instead, individuals appear insecure and disorientated by the loss of communal bonds and beliefs. Individuals' psychological security is related to the security of their relationships and communal purpose. Selfhood is bound up with what the philosopher Charles Taylor calls "an orientation towards the good," or a moral, philosophical, or political framework (1989). The psychoanalyst Erik Erikson's identification theory sets out the importance of how individuals identify with other people and conceive of what is good for their own development, while suggesting reasons for the contemporary crisis of selfhood (1968, 1980). Strong beliefs and relationships foster strength of character. However, post-traditional, post-political, and postmodern Western societies lack both strong beliefs and relationships that foster strength of character (Furedi, 2003; Lasch, 1984; Sennett, 1998). Relativism rather than conviction, suspicion rather than belief, and mistrust rather than trust typify the Western outlook today, along with a growing skepticism over the possibility of human progress and its gains. The weakened sense of personal or communal purpose has fostered a more passive, plaintive personality type that is prone to demoralization. These characteristics influence the social and personal effect of disasters.

People's lives have a tenuous coherence, and they feel psychologically vulnerable in the face of any obstacles or setbacks. Victor Frankl, whose logotherapy is expressly concerned with "the will to meaning," identifies an existential vacuum underlying many contemporary psychological disorders (Frankl, 1992). Psychological insecurity is illustrated by the widespread diagnosis of post-traumatic stress disorder (PTSD) in the West. PTSD has been insightfully analyzed as a disorder of meaning, which represents an acute manifestation of the general cultural insecurity over identity and meaning (Bracken, 2002; Young, 1995). The psychologically fragile personality seems to find meaning in the diagnosis of post-traumatic stress disorder (PTSD) as a disorder that captures contemporary existential fears (Furedi, 2003; Nolan, 1998). Cultural critics have diagnosed Western society today as a post-traumatic culture (Farrell, 1998). However, if PTSD is understood as a disorder of meaning (Bracken, 2002), this suggests both the culturally specific appeal of PTSD counseling and its limitations in addressing both individual and the wider social crisis of meaning.

The psychologization of human experience today is not simply led by professionals but is also facilitated by individuals seeking social recognition through diagnosis (Shaw & Woodward, 2003). Diagnosis as social recognition accords with the standpoint of the demoralized and atomized individual. Diagnosis also epitomizes how social action has mutated into professional intervention at the level of the individual as political activism has receded. At the same time, social improvement is increasingly tackled by policy-makers through self-improvement strategies for enhancing self-esteem and perfecting interpersonal communication skills, rather than the New Deal–type mass employment and construction initiatives of previous eras (Giddens, 1994; Samuels, 2001). Public policy interest in emotional communication further accords with new business methods requiring flexible soft skills to facilitate communication and adaptability in fast-moving markets (Sennett, 1998). From school pupils becoming playground peacemakers to self-esteem coaching for the unemployed to staff development training for self-awareness, there is a converging demand for individuals to be trained in "emotional literacy." Individuals commonly come across these schemes in their day-to-day lives. My daughter's primary school has set up a playground peacemakers initiative, as have other schools in Nottingham and across Britain. In addition, I have been offered courses in self-esteem and self-analysis; for example, by the University of Nottingham staff-development program. Emotional literacy has become central to strategies seeking to enhance personal performance or improve the social environment. Organizations increasingly provide preventive therapeutic programs even when individuals do not ask for psychological support. Culturally, individuals are increasingly expected to need professional emotional assistance to cope with any changes in their lives.

Proponents argue that these trends should be welcomed as creating a more caring environment and as enhancing emotional sensitivity and expression (Giddens, 1994; Kraemer & Roberts, 1996; Samuels, 2001). Yet critics have drawn attention to the coercive potential of emotional management and the risks of estranging people from their emotions under the instrumentalization or "McDonaldization" of the emotions (Mestrovic, 1997; see also Furedi, 2003; Hochschild, 1983; Stearns & Stearns, 1986). The stress on the importance of psychological well-being for social well-being is leading to our emotions—not simply our behavior—becoming more regulated in public policy and business practice. Emotional management involves the validation of specific emotional norms and the invalidation of others toward the development of a specific model of the self. This model of the self not only embodies the notion of the self as psychologically vulnerable but also tends to pathologize the previous ideal type of the self as the robust self-disciplined character. Notably, passion and anger tend to be viewed with suspicion and have been singled out for treatment in Western emotional management approaches, which seem fearful of spontaneous expression (Furedi, 2003; Nolan, 1998; Stearns & Stearns, 1986). Under contemporary Western "emotionology," unregulated expression appears to be associated with emotional dysfunctionality.

A fear of emotional dysfunctionality arising from untreated trauma is one imperative that drives mass trauma counseling programs. Another imperative for mass trauma counseling programs is how therapy has now become an integral part of public ritual in Western societies, conferring social recognition of suffering. The next section explores the social role of counseling in contemporary Western emotionology.

Social Role of Counseling

Our changed cultural expectations and political climate have meant both greater receptivity to therapy and therapy acquiring a new public significance. Our psychologically disposed culture has encouraged the proliferation of counseling and mediation services and professionals. Significantly, therapeutic rather than religious rituals now dominate the contemporary culture. If diagnosis confers social recognition, therapy authenticates claims. Strikingly, today any media report of a crime or tragic incident states how the victims are being offered counseling to underscore the seriousness of their suffering. Thus, a BBC radio news report on the recent tragic drowning of Chinese cockle pickers in Britain stated that the survivors were receiving counseling, "which indicates . . . how difficult things have been for them" (BBC, 2004). Here we see how Western cultural expectations of emotional vulnerability and the need for therapeutic intervention are being projected onto people from other societies. Significantly, legal advocates have found that asylum seekers to Britain or other European states are expected to exhibit trauma, or doubt is cast on the authenticity of their claims to refugee status. Well-prepared asylum claims now almost invariably highlight how the applicant is suffering from PTSD and has required counseling.

Therapists have been characterized as the new priesthood, supplanting religious figures as guardians of social norms (Nolan, 1998). Religious observance too has become more therapeutic in style, with prayer and religious services adopting therapeutic forms and justifications. The therapeutic approach as a form of religion indicates how social expectations of psychological fragility have become normative. On the one hand, by demonstrating psychological vulnerability and seeking therapy, people show that they are responsible caring citizens in today's ethos. On the other hand, individuals who do not display psychological vulnerability or who dismiss counseling risk being branded as uncaring and socially reckless. In Britain, the traditional stiff upper lip is vilified, and conspicuous compassion is endorsed (West, 2004). Even the British royalty is not excused from the precepts of contemporary emotionology. Members of the royal family were attacked in the British media for being undemonstrative in public at Diana's death. In turn, unemotional reporting in the face of tragic events is increasingly unacceptable (Mayes, 2000). In the contemporary therapeutic culture, emotional reserve risks being equated with being unfeeling and denying the suffering of victims. Likewise, the buzz and excitement experienced in disaster relief work is becoming socially unacceptable to express, because it transgresses therapeutic precepts. The cultural validation of psychological vulnerability as an empathetic reaction helps account for the apparent growth of secondary trauma among the emergency services today. In today's therapeutic culture, relief workers may find themselves under cultural pressure to express psychological vulnerability as an expression of empathy toward victims in a disaster. Tellingly, secondary traumatic stress has been outlined by psychologists as a condition that sometimes overwhelms therapists, journalists, and other professionals who respond empathically to sharing the traumatic experiences of others (Ochberg, 2003). However, the professional or wider cultural validation of vicarious psychological vulnerability as an empathetic response does not necessarily represent a more compassionate professional outlook. Arguably, the phenomenon represents a more self-centered response in which professionals' attention has become subtly reoriented toward their own feelings toward the victims' suffering, rather than toward the suffering itself. Amid this validation of psychological vulnerability, it should perhaps be restated that professionals becoming overwhelmed by what they see is not very useful for victims, who need practical actions to be undertaken to alleviate their situation.

Because counseling routinely accompanies ordinary life events, it is not surprising that counseling should become a standard response in disasters both domestically and internationally. Therapeutic responses are devised on the assumption of vulnerability, with debriefing teams being sent to an area and proactively giving counseling—not waiting for individuals to request support. Salutogenic studies, which explore people's resilience, are relatively rare in the trauma literature and have been overlooked in disaster planning in recent decades (Almedom, 2004; Waysman, Schwarzwald, & Solomon, 2001). This neglect is unsurprising culturally because salutogenic approaches go against the grain of contemporary Western emotionology. Western emotional norms validate even virtual experiences as inducing trauma that requires psychological intervention (Coward, 2001). That individuals at risk of psychological emotional trauma now encompass those who see disaster scenes on the television demonstrates the normalization of psychological vulnerability in Western societies. Various Western universities, for example, discussed offering counseling over the Iraq War to students at their institution, whose only encounter with the war was liable to be through their television sets. Trauma counseling has become culturally expected, so that even close communities with effective informal networks invite professional support. In this vein, a mass trauma debriefing program for all pupils and their parents was immediately proposed at an English Lincolnshire village school following the shooting dead of a pupil by a fellow pupil (my thanks to Roger Bretherton, Lincolnshire National Health Service). Yet by all accounts the rural village enjoyed good social networks that belied the need for mass professional support. Indeed, the local Lincolnshire NHS trauma center considered the proposal for a mass debriefing program inappropriate for the community and declined to undertake one. The efficacy of mass psychological debriefing programs is increasingly questioned not just in cross-cultural psychology but also more broadly (Ørner & Schnyder, 2003; Rose, Bisson, & Wessely, 2003a, 2003b; Sensky, 2003). The continuing advice of the Cochrane Review has been that, "There is no current evidence that psychological debriefing is a useful treatment for the prevention of post traumatic stress disorder after traumatic incidents" (Rose et al., 2003b). However such is the cultural expectation of the need for professional intervention that this advice may be ignored. The BBC, for example, decided to press ahead with debriefing counseling for its journalists reporting on the Iraq War.

Irrespective of whether people appear resilient, they are presumed in the prevailing therapeutic model to require preventive therapeutic support. Proponents are self-consciously eschewing reference to "traumatized community" and "victims," using "affected community" and "survivors," respectively, instead, so as not to pathologize and demean populations (Smith, 2004). Nevertheless, these semantic changes do not signal a rolling back of psychosocial programs and their pathologization of populations, but, rather, a pathologizing of the meaning of survival and resilience. In the model, resilience too is understood as a condition that requires professional assistance to process emotions and is thus effectively pathologized. The model tends to conflate the experience of distress with emotional dysfunction requiring therapeutic management (de Jong, Ford, & Kleber, 1999). As such, trauma counseling programs may be experienced as an education on vulnerability. That professional interventions should have become the norm even for tight-knit communities illustrates how the therapeutic ethos lacks confidence in ordinary people's capacity to support each other. The prevailing therapeutic model ignores or at best pays lip service to the fact that the way people respond to tragic events is influenced by communal, political, or religious beliefs and networks and cannot be reduced to the scale of casualties (Shephard, 2000). Crucially, the model ignores how the very experience of tragedy may actually bring people together, counter social atomism, and reinvigorate fragmented communal ties (Joseph, Williams, & Yule, 1993). Disaster may actually foster social integration, rather than social disintegration, which helps support people in their adversity. Again, the model conceptualizes the effect of war solely in terms of causing social disruption (Strang, 2004), ignoring how mobilizing for war, including civil war, requires mobilizing a constituency, and that communal identities have historically commonly been forged through the very experience of war (Duffield, 2001; Wrong, 1994). In other words, although war may break particular social ties, it equally depends on mobilizing social ties and may therefore strengthen those ties and support networks.

We do not have to go back many decades to see very different emotional norms operating. The present expectation of vulnerability may be compared to past validation of resilience. Popular magazines such as the *Picture Post* in Britain saw featuring stories of dignity and heroism among ordinary people as part of their mission. The Welsh Aberfan landslide disaster of 1966, which killed over a hundred children and adults, exemplifies past stoicism. Therapy was not provided to the bereaved families, and the surviving children were returned to classes as soon as practically possible to avoid them dwelling on the tragedy (Furedi, 2003). The villagers were commended in the media coverage at the time for how well they were supporting themselves. Such responses would be unthinkable and condemned today. Indeed, Aberfan and other past disasters are being reinterpreted in line with present emotionology, resulting in retrospective demands for trauma counseling to deal with the tragedy. But would trauma counseling have eased the bereaved community's suffering? Would teams of counselors coming to the village have been experienced positively? Or negatively, as "disaster tourists"? Accounts of the tragedy have referred to the villagers' wariness and distrust of the many outside visitors.

The cultural change is often regarded as a sign of a more sensitive culture, yet the presumption of the need for mass counseling is insensitive to the disruptive consequences of professionals descending on an area and managing people's grief—as if people do not grieve properly unless supervised by professionals. The normalization of mass counseling programs implicitly disparages how family, friends, and neighbors respond to each other in the wake of a tragedy. An unspoken mistrust of the community's moral and emotional capacity to comfort the bereaved underlies the imperative to bring in professional support. Even a community that appears fragmented may be pulled together by the very experience of disaster (Rogers, 2003), but this phenomenon is overlooked in current disaster psychology. The parachuting in of professionals to manage people's feelings according to the prevailing professional emotional script unwittingly distances people from each other. The dominance of professional intervention represents a technical quick fix that individualizes the experience of disaster and interrupts how communal bonds are remade in shared experiences and reciprocal relationships.

The psychiatrist Sally Satel has explored the lessons of 9/11 for professional trauma responses (2002; Satel & Sommers, 2001). Satel has described the responses to 9/11 as a "missed opportunity"—missed in the sense that although mass psychiatric damage among New Yorkers did not materialize, the professional therapeutic responses ran the risk of suggesting to individuals a pathological interpretation of normal reactions (sleeplessness, crying) and encouraging them to think of themselves as defeated or sick (Satel, 2003). The responses were also a missed opportunity in another sense: Although the mass trauma predicted did not materialize, the professional therapeutic responses disrupted the potential renewal of a shared communal outlook and purpose, which could have been galvanized by the horrific act. Instead, the professional responses reinforced the culture's atomized nature rather than challenging it. Hence, the efficacy of mass trauma counseling is questionable not just at the level of the individual but also at the communal and national level. The dominant therapeutic model, even in its newly declared affirmation of resilience, invites people both to see themselves as unable to move on without professional support and to focus inward on their personal feelings. Whether through individual or group therapy, the therapeutic model tends to affirm personal passivity and disengage people from social action through which society could transcend disaster.

In summary, what I am questioning here is not simply the dangers of imposing Western disaster psychology on non-Western societies but, equally, problems with contemporary Western disaster psychology for Western societies. Nevertheless, controversial therapeutic programs continue to be promoted for disaster-affected populations globally and to influence international humanitarian responses. Furthermore, today's politicization of disasters in the international sphere tends to attribute the disaster to some fault of the community. We will see below how the concept of complex (political) emergency in international aid work questions the capacity of the affected community to rehabilitate itself without outside intervention.

Crisis of Humanitarianism

The rise of international disaster psychology programs was further propelled by developments within the humanitarian sector. Humanitarian organizations have become increasingly important voices in public discourse since the end of the Cold War with the erosion of previous political affiliations. The U.S. writer David Rieff has described humanitarianism as "the last coherent saving ideal" of the West (Rieff, 2002). Humanitarianism's appeal to empathy for people suffering corresponds with the prevailing ethos of Western societies. Personal emotions are the standpoint from which people today in Western societies understand their own lives, and empathy has become a key principle of ethical behavior in Western countries, which lack strong beliefs following the erosion of traditional values and ideologically based politics.

Yet the focus on humanitarianism over the last decade has involved fundamental questioning of its mission, even as humanitarian programs have massively expanded. Modern humanitarianism was born out of an aspiration to recognize a common humanity transcending political, national, or social differences. But, as I will return to below, a tension lurks in charitable or welfare provision between the affirmation of a common humanity versus a judgment as to the worthiness of the recipient—that is, a tension between the provision of aid to the needy and their moral reform. Notably, Western individualism has been disposed to understand social problems in terms of personal character. To be dependent on charity has frequently been associated with a failing of character, but traditional humanitarianism did not make the character of the recipients an issue, as their plight in war or disaster was regarded as exceptional and temporary, existing through no fault of their own. However, the humanitarian debates of the last decade have led to new attention being paid to the character of recipient communities.

The broader loss of confidence in donor societies has eroded confidence in humanitarianism and cast doubt on the validity of humanitarian work and the humanitarian recipient alike. Humanitarianism as a symbolic gesture of empathy from donor to recipient informs humanitarian ideals, but as former Oxfam official Tony Vaux acutely observes, altruistic motives and actions not underpinned by convictions become subject to endless doubt (Vaux, 2001). The humanitarian sector was riddled with doubt over its mission in the 1990s, notwithstanding its public standing and impressive growth. Indeed the very high profile of humanitarianism and the support aid organizations received from official donors created unease among humanitarian workers. Humanitarians found it hard to cling to a belief that their work was altruistic and improved the lives of recipients. A raft of publications were written highly critical of humanitarianism, notably Mary Anderson's *Do No Harm* (1999), Alex de Waal's *Famine Crimes* (1997), Michael Maren's *Road to Hell* (1997), Timothy Morris's *The Despairing Developer* (1991), John Prendergast's *Crisis Response* (1997), David Rieff's *A Bed for the Night* (2002), Ian Smillie's *The Alms Bazaar* (1995), David Sogge's *Compassion and Calculation* (1996), Fiona Terry's *Condemned to Repeat?* (2002), and Tony Vaux's *The Selfish Altruist* (2001), to name some of the more prominent critiques. Damning reports on aid work also seeped into newspapers and magazines, which compared humanitarians to imperial missionaries of the nineteenth century (*The Economist*, 2000; Hilsum, 1995; Jenkins, 1999). Even popular culture, which has previously treated humanitarian work as sacrosanct, has voiced criticisms. The cartoon *South Park* conspicuously ridiculed humanitarian activities in its "Starvin' Marvin" episode (Parker, 1997), which portrays humanitarianism as an overblown industry leeching off others' suffering and harming its purported beneficiaries.

Some of the most trenchant attacks on humanitarianism have strikingly come from within the humanitarian sector: Michael Maren, for example, has worked for USAID and Tony Vaux for Oxfam, and Fiona Terry is a director of research for Médecins Sans Frontières. These accounts testify to a profound internal crisis of legitimacy, the particular character of which facilitated the adoption of psychosocial work. The humanitarian crisis of legitimacy revolved around three themes: humanitarian principles, the bureaucratization of aid, and the efficacy of material aid. Many aid workers were dismayed at the technologies of humanitarian relief as the sector grew and feared that humanitarianism was becoming driven by the expediencies of organizational growth rather than altruism (Maren, 1997). The perception that the technologies of aid were becoming dehumanizing was exacerbated by questions over the usefulness of humanitarian aid work. Was relief work doing any good, or was it even doing harm? The altruism of aid organizations could no longer be taken for granted, and the motives of individual aid workers were challenged as well. Vaux writes of the "selfish altruist" (2001), and Rieff of the "moral alibi" (Rieff, 2002). Racked by self-doubt, for these writers, empathy for the suffering of others had become an insufficient guide to action.

New codes of conduct were developed in the 1990s, but definitive principles to inform work proved elusive. The very preoccupation with codes spoke of disorientation within humanitarianism, as well as uncertainties with its mission and mistrust of aid workers. Humanitarianism was charged with being "short-termist" and with jeopardizing people's long-term security. Accounts such as Mary Anderson's *Do No Harm* (1999), Alex de Waal's *Famine Crimes* (1997), and Fiona Terry's *Condemned to Repeat?* (2002) have drawn attention to how humanitarian aid could aggravate crises, destabilize precarious local economies, and fuel conflicts. The cry that "we are part of the problem" is a sentiment that runs through humanitarian accounts of the last decade. As Vaux explores, "providing a few sacks of food was virtually the same as providing a Kalashnikov rifle" in conflict situations in which humanitarian aid would be exchanged for weapons (Vaux, 2001, p. 82). It has long been argued that there are "no humanitarian solutions to humanitarian problems"; however, the earlier aspirations for international development have not come to fruition and have been abandoned. The prospect of significant material advancement of the world's population is off the international policy agenda. Populations in the South remain far more vulnerable to natural disasters than postindustrial populations, as the devastating Bam earthquake of 2004 testifies. Instead of development eradicating humanitarian disasters, a state of humanitarian crisis has become normalized, and humanitarian aid has become a key form through which Northern countries relate to those in the South. At the same time, humanitarian relief has become burdened with developmental responsibilities as international development has retreated.

Arising from this developmental burden, the greatest attacks on the aid sector of the last decade have been on their traditional emergency relief work, condemned as short-termist and irresponsible. Furthermore, having normalized a state of humanitarian crisis as characteristic of particular societies, moral concerns over the character of recipient societies and their rehabilitation now pervade humanitarian work, with its additional developmental responsibilities. Critics have typically argued that humanitarian organizations need to reflect on their role, on how aid may create dependency and reinforce inequitable structures, and to address how humanitarian relief might address the root cause of disasters and promote developmental and human rights goals (Anderson, 1999). Yet the developmental burden being placed on humanitarianism arose out of despair with the development project itself. Unsurprisingly, the experience of repeated disasters and long-standing conflicts with little prospect of material transformation, together with the questioning of humanitarian principles and efficacy of aid, have demoralized humanitarianism and humanitarians. As one UN official is quoted as saying, "This will be the third time I've rebuilt this place. . . . I can't see doing it a fourth time" (Rieff, 2002, p. 22).

The crisis of humanitarianism, the normalization of humanitarian crises and humanitarianism's developmental burden all have implications for how aid recipients are treated and have influenced how the emotional well-being of these recipients has been used in international aid policy. The normalization and politicization of disasters has meant that humanitarian victims are no longer exempt from moral and political judgments. As humanitarianism is burdened with developmental responsibilities, so too is psychosocial aid as part of the contemporary humanitarian program. Before I examine this aspect of disaster psychology work further, however, I want to explore the attractions of psychosocial programs for humanitarian workers. An important appeal of psychosocial work has been as a reaction against the bureaucratization of aid and the treatment of people as abstractions and undifferentiated victims. International trauma counseling seeks to address how people and communities personally experience disaster or conflict. Western relief workers are also imputing their feelings of vulnerability and demoralization onto disaster or conflict-affected populations. However, populations do not simply experience disasters passively, but do so within political, spiritual, or moral frameworks. Groups or individuals having a sense of purpose, whether from political or religious convictions, communal duties, professional commitment, or personal pride, may interpret distressful experiences as challenges to be surmounted and tests of courage, rather than in just negative terms (Bracken, 2002; Cherniss, 1995; Waysman et al., 2001).

Relief workers in earlier decades have seemed extraordinarily resilient despite the enormities of their mission. In the so-called golden age of humanitarianism in the 1970s and 1980s, relief workers enjoyed considerable personal independence in their role and had tremendous confidence in the efficacy of their work. In contrast, today relief workers' dedication and sense of pride in the humanitarian mission, which helped make previous generations of relief workers remarkably resilient, have been severely strained by humanitarianism's crisis of legitimacy. Relief workers have found themselves subject not just to new physical hazards but also to new ethical and political attacks over their mission. The endless chasing of grants and donor funding requirements, as well as institutional responses to humanitarianism's crisis, involving more auditing mechanisms and paperwork, have tended to constrain the autonomy previously enjoyed by relief workers and to compound general feelings of frustration and demoralization in their work. More fundamentally, the meaning of humanitarianism has been thrown into doubt by attempts to create a robust humanitarianism. The concept of humanitarian enforcement, whereby the use of coercive force is justified when human rights are being violated, seems intended to invigorate humanitarianism, but also risks imploding the very identity of humanitarian organizations as humanitarians. If humanitarians can no longer be defined by their nonviolence because of their advocacy of military intervention, and Western military forces also define themselves as humanitarians, then what is left of the humanitarian identity today? What makes humanitarian organizations different from any other organization? The accumulation of these developments makes it harder to feel humanitarian work to be redeeming.

The growing prominence of PTSD as an explanatory framework among relief workers (Bracken, 2002) may be considered an extreme expression of the broader crisis of legitimacy in humanitarianism. The importance of humanitarianism's crisis of legitimacy has been neglected in the existing literature on PTSD in humanitarian staff. Analysis does highlight the bureaucratization of aid work, but it primarily draws attention to external dangers and stressors and to the need to develop support systems and training for staff (Eriksson, Kemp, Gorsuch, Hoke, & Foy, 2001; McCall & Salama, 1999; Smith, Agger, Danieli, & Weisaeth, 1996). It has been contended that aid workers experience more stressful emergencies today than in earlier "straightforward natural disasters" (Salama, 1999, p. 12)—as if past emergencies were ever straightforward; the humanitarian emergencies of the past were potentially as complex as today's so-called complex political emergencies. However, the Cold War solidarist framework and humanitarianism's more tightly defined mission of relief simplified both the humanitarian goals and the ethical issues that humanitarian workers were confronted with in their work. In essence, the solidarist framework assumed the legitimacy of host governments and humanitarian organizations and did not override official representations of humanitarian disasters or investigate any political culpability in creating or exacerbating the disaster. The Ethiopian famine of 1984, for example, was not a straightforward natural disaster, but humanitarian responses treated the famine as if it were, rather than as a disaster arising from a regional conflict involving the government (Vaux, 2001). Today's concept of "complex political emergencies" would treat the Ethiopian famine differently and would complicate how humanitarian staff approached their mission. The new responsibilities placed on humanitarian aid, the charge that aid may exacerbate crises, and the concept of humanitarian (military) intervention have all created new ethical dilemmas and anxieties for humanitarian staff.

Humanitarianism's crisis of legitimacy, rather than simply the severity of exposure to danger or suffering in the field, needs to be taken into account in explaining the increasing instances of PTSD among humanitarian staff.

Mental health problems among humanitarian staff have been a conspicuous feature of troubled missions in which staff have been most demoralized in their work. The Somalia mission of 1992 pointedly revealed humanitarianism's disorientation and despair, even before the outrage over responses two years later in Rwanda. Oxfam, for example, documented after its Somalia operation significant mental health problems among its staff, arising from a muddled and ill-fated mission in which staff experienced feelings ranging from "personal inadequacy to anger and disillusion with aid work" (Vaux, 2001, p. 154). Rapid growth in trauma counseling for international aid workers, peacekeepers, journalists, and human rights workers has followed humanitarianism's troubles in the 1990s. Yet counseling, irrespective of its cultural resonance, cannot overcome a broader crisis of morale within humanitarianism, or within society more generally.

Pathologizing Affected Populations

Moreover, international psychosocial programs may be expanding alienating technologies by instrumentalizing the emotions. This aspect touches on the allure of psychosocial intervention for international aid thinking. Psychosocial approaches were enthusiastically embraced as revitalizing the international aid project in the wake of the international development policy debacle. Psychosocial intervention is seductive in aspiring to address the dual aspects of charitable and welfare provision—both the suffering of recipients and their improvement—and in seemingly overcoming the perils of material aid, which has been attacked for feeding killers and creating dependency. I have already alluded to how Western societies are disposed to understand society as the sum of its individuals and equate reforming society with reforming individuals. The Anglo-American therapeutic ethos essentially conceptualizes social problems as being rooted in a defective ethnopsychology: Improve the psychological well-being of people and how they interact with each other, and the social environment will be improved. Conversely, when the psychological well-being of people is threatened, their behavior and their relationships deteriorate, according to the model, creating a vicious cycle in which the social environment is damaged. International reports typically link psychological suffering with social instability (World Health Organization [WHO], 2002). Both preventive and curative psychosocial interventions are therefore regarded as vital to rehabilitating populations whose culture and personality are seen as being complicit in the crisis, and especially war-affected populations (Volkan, 2001). Thus, the agenda of international psychosocial work is not simply concerned with relieving suffering, but rather with prescribing a particular emotional script to reform the recipient society. As a consequence, the emotions of disaster or war-affected populations have become a legitimate area of external intervention under the prevailing therapeutic model, which assumes universal vulnerability rather than general resilience and has even redefined resilience and self-help as a condition requiring professional management. International psychosocial thinking has become very critical about medicalized treatment models and has shifted to more community based activities. Thus, reports may speak of how "Psychosocial support is not so much about treatment but about helping people to find their own strengths" (Rodenburg, 2004).

Unacknowledged by advocates are the disciplining aspects of international psychosocial work, perhaps revealed in the reluctance to accept that a community might not want or need therapeutic interventions. Again, unacknowledged by proponents is the tension between the psychosocial programs' goal to alleviate the psychological suffering of a community and rehabilitate a community. The recipient community has an ambiguous place in the international therapeutic model because the ultimate causes of humanitarian crisis are traced in international psychosocial thinking to the character of the community. Indeed, the very strength of communal relations in the face of crisis can be treated as an obstacle to the community's rehabilitation when the community's problems are seen as bound up with the character of its communal relations. Hence, irrespective of whether a community appears to be holding up, it is deemed to be in need of psychosocial aid, for in not admitting its psychosocial needs, as manifested in the crisis, the community is determined to be in denial and storing up problems for the future.

The prevailing international therapeutic model is not only inappropriate to address the needs of disaster-affected populations but also demoralizes them as moral agents. More significant, perhaps, than questions about the efficacy of the numerous international psychosocial programs is their insidious redefining of the problems facing preindustrial or semiindustrial societies globally in terms of their psychological state. Psychological distress, for example, has been cited in a WHO report as the greatest health problem facing people in Afghanistan (WHO, 2001). The diagnosis of mental health as the worst health problem confronting Afghanistan, a country suffering one of the lowest rates of life expectancy and highest rates of infant mortality in the world, seems perverse. However, the idea has gained currency in international policy through Western psychosocial models' influence, which would conceptualize the crisis in Afghanistan in terms of intergenerational cycles of psychosocial dysfunction. But are the humiliation and hazards of Afghani women begging, for example, psychological problems or material ones? How do psychosocial programs address the women's poverty, which drives their begging? Of questionable efficacy, international psychosocial programs may be experienced negatively as stigmatizing and compounding recipients' humiliation. Disaster- or war-affected populations, aid officials acknowledge, may view trauma counseling programs as stigmatizing and irrelevant to their needs (Wiles et al., 2000). In the high-profile Kosovo humanitarian operation in 1999, relief workers admitted seeing few people who would regard themselves as suffering from any psychological disorder (Wiles et al.). Yet international psychosocial programs have had little to offer

these cases. Indeed, the basic needs of the long-term mentally ill were surprisingly overlooked even in the relatively resource-rich emergencies in
Southeast Europe, despite all the hype over "traumatised populations" in the
aid literature. This neglect belies the hopes of some international aid officials
that the new interest in trauma would help foster the interests of the mentally
ill. Yet all the vast sums and concern poured into post-9/11 trauma counseling has not discernibly furthered the interests of the long-term mentally ill on
the streets of New York. So there is little ground for believing that the preoccupation with trauma furthers the interests of the mentally ill elsewhere.

The call for therapeutic interventions as "preventive medicine" (Volkan,
2001), following the precautionary principle of psychosocial risk management, even where populations appear resilient, may perpetuate psychological ill-being by denying populations' own coping strategies and creating
unaccountable relations of dependency. As salutogenic studies suggest
(Waysman et al., 2001), those who view themselves as being in charge of
their fates are more likely to have positive outcomes. Ironically, however,
the rise of the international psychosocial model has been bound up with the
erosion of sovereign equality in the international system and has helped
legitimize the suspension of local political control and the establishment of
de facto international protectorates under the international community,
notably in Bosnia (Pupavac, 2004). International dependency has been high-
lighted as negative for a population's psychological well-being (de Jong et
al., 1999). Longitudinal studies of mental health in these informal protectorates must take into account loss of political control in their analysis. Psychosocial interventions are correctly viewed with suspicion by many societies,
for their premise is a mistrust of the populations' psychological and moral
capacity, with implications for their rights and freedoms.

The predominant international disaster psychology model only compli-
cates recovery by endorsing vulnerability and making resilience conditional
on professional interventions. The renunciation—even denunciation—of
resilience in contemporary Western emotionology has been validated until
recently. The dangers of validating vulnerability became apparent to policy
makers in the wake of the terrorist attack on the World Trade Center. A nervous, post-traumatic ethnopsychology is particularly susceptible to terrorist
strategies designed to promote fear. Policy has to address how people may
be discouraged from being resilient in present Western cultural sensibilities.
Researchers at the International Policy Institute of the War Studies Group at
King's College London have recommended "an approach that clarifies people's values rather than emphasising their vulnerabilities" (Durodie & Wessely, 2002). Their approach is useful in recognizing how a society's weak
sense of social purpose makes people more psychologically vulnerable. A
relativistic age does not encourage the development of strong characters fostered by the strong belief systems of the past. A loss of belief in humanity
and human progress informs the contemporary humanitarian agenda and
the malaise in Western societies more broadly and has made it difficult to

project an inspiring vision globally. Psychological recovery can only be real-ized from the overall circumstances and meaning of people's lives and can-not be treated as a technical problem deliverable through emotional literacy programs (Summerfield, 2002). However, the psychosocial aid package, as the new hope of humanitarianism, with humanitarianism itself being the last hope of the West (Rieff, 2002), embodies a misanthropic vision that casts doubt on the moral capacity of affected populations to recover.

Nevertheless, the breakdown of meaning and its expression in psycholog-ical vulnerability is not universal. Western-inspired psychosocial programs represent a global lesson on vulnerability. The practical, problem focused coping style common to non-Western societies is far more useful than the emotion focused coping style of contemporary Western therapeutic cultures in recovering from catastrophes (Summerfield, 2001). Therapeutic approaches, focused on feelings rather than activities, can legitimize the assumption of sick roles, furthering social disengagement and atomization. A first step in national and international policy should be the revalidation of resilience. Individuals or groups should not be deemed in need of psychoso-cial preventive interventions simply because they have been through dis-tressing experiences. Against the prevailing emotionology, it should be reiterated that distressing experiences may foster strength of character and stimulate latent communal support networks (Joseph et al., 1993). There is new interest in findings of resilience (Kendra & Wachtendorf, 2003; Rogers, 2003), but one should be wary of how resilience itself is being pathologized in international psychosocial thinking as a condition that needs professional management. Even where a shared belief system remains elusive, strength of character may be encouraged by affirming people's professional abilities and courage displayed in emergency situations. Voluntarism to encourage latent communal responsiveness and social action, rather than fostering social disengagement in a sick role, could also be useful, but again volunta-rism has been affected by the declining belief in social progress, as indicated in humanitarianism's crisis of mission.

The lessons of resilience and social purpose are crucial for devising poli-cies for disaster- and war-affected populations internationally and for devel-oping national responses to the new security threats confronting Western societies. Psychosocial interventions are inadequate and inappropriate for the task. A sense of meaning and social purpose is crucial to psychological well-being. The disorientation of the humanitarian mission underlies both the rise of PTSD among humanitarian workers and the impulse to manage the psychology of war- and disaster-affected populations. At the heart of the humanitarian mission and modern ethics was the belief in the moral capac-ity of fellow human beings, but the international psychosocial model's equa-tion of traumatization with dysfunction is dehumanizing and offensive. Affirmation of this core principle of humanism is fundamental to the future of humanitarianism and the resolution of the contemporary crisis of social purpose and meaning.

References

Almedom, A. (2004). Factors that mitigate war-induced anxiety and mental distress. *Journal of Biosocial Science, 36*, 445–461.

Anderson, M. (1999). *Do no harm: How aid can support peace—or war.* Boulder, CO: Lynne Rienner.

BBC. (2004, February 7). *Radio 4 Today* [Radio broadcast].

Bracken, P. (2002). *Trauma: Cultural meaning and philosophy.* London: Whurr.

Cherniss, C. (1995). *Beyond burnout: Helping teachers, nurses, therapists, and lawyers recover from stress and disillusionment.* New York: Routledge.

Coward, R. (2001, March 4). Seeing is reliving. *The Observer.* Retrieved March 1, 2005, from http://www.guardian.co.uk/selby/story/0,7369,446174,00.html

de Jong, K., Ford, N., & Kleber, R. (1999, May 8). Mental health care for refugees from Kosovo: The experience of Médecins sans Frontières. *The Lancet, 353*, 1616–1617.

de Waal, A. (1997). *Famine crimes: Politics and the disaster relief industry in Africa.* Oxford, UK: James Currey.

Duffield, M. (2001). *Global governance and the new wars: The merging of development and security.* London: Zed Books.

Durodie, B., & Wessely, S. (2002). Resilience or panic? The public and terrorist attack. *The Lancet, 360*, 1901–1902.

The Economist. (2000, January 29). *Sins of the secular missionaries,* 25–28.

Erikson, E. (1968). *Identity: Youth and crisis.* London: Faber.

———. (1980). *Identity and the life cycle.* New York: W.W. Norton.

Eriksson, C., Kemp, H., Gorsuch, R., Hoke, S., & Foy, D. (2001). Trauma exposure and PTSD symptoms in international relief and development personnel. *Journal of Traumatic Stress, 14*, 205–212.

Farrell, K. (1998). *Post-traumatic culture: Injury and interpretation in the nineties.* Baltimore: Johns Hopkins University Press.

Frankl, V. E. (1992). *Man's search for meaning: An introduction to logotherapy* (4th ed.). Boston: Beacon Press.

Furedi, F. (2003). *Therapy culture: Cultivating vulnerability in an age of uncertainty.* London: Routledge.

Giddens, A. (1994). *Beyond left and right: The future of radical politics.* Cambridge, MA: Polity Press.

Hilsum, L. (1995, December 31). Save us from our saviours: Good intentions are not enough. *The Observer.* Retrieved March 2, 2005, from http://www.netnomad.com/hilsum.html

Hochschild, A. (1983). *The managed heart: Commercialization of human feeling.* Berkeley, CA: University of California Press.

Jenkins, S. (1999, November 26). Weep for poor Orissa. *The Times.* London.

Joseph, S., Williams, R., & Yule, W. (1993). Changes in outlook following disaster: The preliminary development of a measure to assess positive and negative responses. *Journal of Traumatic Stress, 6*, 271–279.

Kendra, J., & Wachtendorf, T. (2003). Elements of resilience: After the World Trade Center disaster: Reconstituting New York City's Emergency Operations Center. *Disasters, 27*(1), 37–53.

Kraemer, S., & Roberts, J. (Eds.). (1996). *The politics of attachment: Towards a secure society.* London: Free Association Books.

Lasch, C. (1984). *The minimal self: Psychic survival in troubled times.* New York: W.W. Norton.

Macrae, J. (2001). *Aiding recovery? The crisis of aid in chronic political emergencies.* London: Zed Books.

Maren, M. (1997). *Road to hell: The ravaging effects of foreign aid and international charity.* New York: Free Press.

Mayes, T. (2000). Submerging in therapy news. *British Journalism Review, 11*(4), 30–36.

McCall, M. & Salama, P. (1999, January 9). Selection, training, and support of relief workers: An occupational health issue. *British Medical Journal,* 318, 113–116.

Mestrovic, S. (1997). *Postemotional society.* London: Sage.

Morris, T. (1991). *The despairing developer: Diary of an aid worker.* London: I.B. Taurus.

Nolan, J. (1998). *The therapeutic state: New York: Justifying government at century's end.* New York University Press.

Ochberg, F. (Ed.). (2003). Secondary traumatic stress disorder. In *PTSD 101.* [online text]. Dart Center for Journalism and Trauma. Retrieved March 24, 2003, from http://www.dartcenter.org/articles/special_features/ptsd101_6.html

Ørner, R. & Schnyder, U. (Eds.). (2003). *Reconstructing early intervention after trauma.* Oxford University Press.

Parker, T. (Writer). (1997). Starvin' Marvin [Television series episode]. In A. Garefino & D. N. White (Producers), *South Park.* Burbank, CA: Comedy Central.

Prendergast, J. (1997). *Crisis response: Humanitarian band-aids in Sudan and Somalia.* London: PlutoPress.

Pupavac, V. (2004). The emotionology of the new international security paradigm. *European Journal of Social Theory, 7,* 149–170.

Rieff, D. (2002). *A bed for the night: Humanitarianism in crisis.* London: Vintage.

Rodenburg, J. (2004). The emotional aftershocks of the earthquake in Bam. *Coping with Crisis* [newsletter], *9.* Reference Centre for Psychological Support, International Federation of Red Cross and Red Crescent Societies. Retrieved March 2, 2005, from http://www.ifrc.org/cgi/pdf_pubs.pl?health/psycholog/newsletter0104.pdf

Rogers, L. (2003, March 16). How tragedy changed lives for the better. *The Sunday Times,* p. 14.

Rose, S., Bisson J., & Wessely, S. (2003a). A systematic review of single-session psychological interventions (debriefing) following trauma. *Psychotherapy and Psychosomatics, 72*(4), 176–184.

Rose, S., Bisson, J., & Wessely, S. (2003b). Psychological debriefing for preventing post traumatic stress disorder (PTSD) (Cochrane Review). In *The Cochrane Library* (issue 2). Oxford, UK: Update Software.

Salama, P. (1999). The psychological health of relief workers: Some practical suggestions. *Relief and Rehabilitation Network, 15,* 12–14.

Samuels, A. (2001). *Politics on the couch: Citizenship and the internal life.* London: Profile Books.

Satel, S. (2002, July 26). New Yorkers don't need therapy. *The Wall Street Journal,* p. A-10.

Satel, S. L. (2003). The Mental Health Crisis That Wasn't. *Psychiatric Services, 54,* 1571.

Satel, S., & Sommers, C. H. (2001, October 15). Good grief: Don't get taken by the trauma industry. *The Wall Street Journal,* p. 24.

Sennett, R. (1998). *The corrosion of character: The personal consequences of work in the new capitalism.* New York: W.W. Norton.

Sensky, T. (2003). The utility of systematic reviews: The case of psychological debriefing after trauma. *Psychotherapy and Psychosomatics, 72*(4), 171–175.

Shaw, I., & Woodward L. (2003). The medicalisation of unhappiness? The management of mental distress in primary care. In I. Shaw & K. Kaupinnen (Eds.), *Constructions of health and illness: European perspectives* (pp. 125–138). Aldershot, UK: Ashgate Press.

Shephard, B. (2000). *War of nerves: Soldiers and psychiatrists 1914–1994.* London: Jonathan Cape.

Smillie, I. (1995). *The alms bazaar: Altruism under fire.* London: IT Publications.

Smith, B., Agger, I., Danieli, Y., & Weisaeth, L. (1996). Health activities across traumatized populations: Emotional responses of international humanitarian aid workers. In Y. Danieli, N. Rodley, & L. Weisaeth (Eds.), *International responses to traumatic stress* (pp. 397–423). Amityville, NY: Baywood.

Smith, M. (2004, March 31). *Asylum—An end or a beginning?* Presentation at Psychosocial support for children & families affected by armed conflict workshop. Centre for Trauma Studies, Nottinghamshire Healthcare Trust, Nottingham, UK.

Sogge, D. (Ed.). (1996). *Compassion and calculation: The business of private foreign aid.* London: Pluto.

Stearns, C. Z., & Stearns, P. N. (1986). *Anger: The struggle for emotional control in America's history.* University of Chicago Press.

Strang, A. (2004, March 31). *Exploring a conceptual framework for psychosocial programming in regions affected by conflict.* Presentation at Psychosocial support for children & families affected by armed conflict workshop. Centre for Trauma Studies, Nottinghamshire Healthcare Trust, Nottingham, UK.

Summerfield, D. (2001). The invention of post-traumatic stress disorder and the social usefulness of a psychiatric category. *British Medical Journal, 322,* 95–98.

———. (2002). The effects of war: Moral knowledge, revenge, reconciliation and "recovery." *British Medical Journal, 325,* 1105–1107.

Taylor, C. (1989). *Sources of the self: The making of the modern identity.* Cambridge, MA: University Press.

Terry, F. (2002). *Condemned to repeat? The paradox of humanitarian action.* Cornell, NY: University Press.

Vaux, T. (2001). *The selfish altruist: Relief work in famine and war.* London: Earthscan.

Volkan, V. (2001). Traumatized societies and psychological care: Expanding the concept of preventive medicine. *Mind and Human Interaction, 11*(3), 177–194. Retrieved March 3, 2005, from http://www.healthsystem.virginia.edu/internet/csmhi/volkan.cfm

Waysman, M., Schwarzwald, J., & Solomon, Z. (2001). Hardiness: An examination of its relationship with positive and negative long term changes following trauma. *Journal of Traumatic Stress, 14*(3), 531–548.

West, P. (2004). *Conspicuous compassion: Why sometimes it really is cruel to be kind.* London: Civitas.

Wiles, P., Bradbury, M., Buchanan-Smith, M., Collins, S., Cosgrave, J., Hallam, A., et al. (2000). *Independent evaluation of expenditure of DEC Kosovo appeal funds. Phases I and II, April 1999–January 2000:* Vol. 2. London: Overseas Development Institute (ODI) with Valid International.

———. (2001, November 6). *The invisible wounds: The mental health crisis in Afghanistan* [Special report]. WHO Central Asia Crisis Unit. Retrieved March 3, 2005, from http://www.who.int/disasters/repo/7399.pdf

World Health Organization (WHO). (2002, March). Breaking the vicious circle. *Health in Emergencies, 12,* 6.

Wrong, D. (1994). *The problem of order: What unites and divides societies.* Cambridge, MA: Harvard University Press.

Young, A. (1995). *The harmony of illusions: Inventing post-traumatic stress disorder.* Princeton, NJ: Princeton University Press.

CHAPTER 3

Toward a Consensus Protocol for Psychosocial Response in Complex Emergencies

Alistair Ager

Despite the increasing profile of psychosocial programming in the context of complex emergencies over the last 10 years, work in this area remains deeply contested. Four consistent themes are found at the core of these debates, concerning the cultural appropriateness of models and interventions, ways in which "psychopathology" or "suffering" are conceptualized, the relative priority of mental health within complex emergencies, and approaches to delivering psychosocial interventions to large populations. This chapter addresses these key sources of contention in an attempt to clarify how a consensus might be reached regarding a protocol for psychosocial responses in complex emergencies.

Cultural Appropriateness of Models and Interventions

Much of our contemporary understanding of the human consequences of disaster draws very heavily on the disciplines of psychology and psychiatry (Ager & Loughry, 2004). To the extent that such disciplines reflect Western epistemologies, models and interventions can be seen to bring tacit "Western" assumptions that may undermine local understandings (Pupavac, 2001; Summerfield, 1999). The humanitarian world has long been exhorted to support local agendas and resources (Harrell-Bond, 1986), and humanitarian policy now increasingly reflects such an emphasis. Accordingly, any perceived dependence on culturally alien interventions is a major obstacle to incorporation of such work by humanitarian organizations. Much current development in the field thus involves exploration of means of using generalized (or "etic") understandings of psychosocial processes that relate to indigenous (or "emic") perspectives and resources (e.g., Mercer, Ager, & Rawanapuri, 2004).

Conceptualization of "Psychopathology" or "Suffering"

Discourses of intervention are often structured around concepts of psychopathology and the consequent need for treatment interventions of a "clinical" nature. There is indeed a growing body of evidence indicating that exposure to conflict and displacement is reliably associated with increased frequency of symptom report on mental health screening measures (de Jong, 2003). However, critics have argued that such conceptualization may be inappropriate for both technical and humanitarian reasons (Summerfield, 1999). Technically, identification of psychopathology with respect to the diagnostic criteria of a measure such as the *Diagnostic and Statistical Manual of Mental Disorders* generally requires a judgment regarding the functional impairment associated with the reported symptoms. Baseline assessments of population groups affected by complex emergencies have often, for practical reasons, not pursued such appraisal of function, risking significant overreporting of disorder (Ager, 2002). In addition, from a humanitarian perspective, such clinical frameworks risk neglect of important social, cultural, and moral dimensions of the experience of affected communities (Bracken, Giller, & Summerfield, 1995; Muecke, 1992).

Such concerns have encouraged, alternatively, conceptualizing the human consequences of war and conflict as suffering that may, but not must, be alleviated. The implications of such a differing conceptualization can be considerable (Kelley, McDonald, & Mollica, 2002). The potential for structured measurement of need may be far less with such an approach, but it can usefully prompt different forms of intervention response that are more closely related to local understandings of the effect of conflict and of the resources locally valued in addressing such an effect (Eyber & Ager, 2002).

Prioritization of Mental Health within Complex Emergencies

Even when the psychological needs of populations affected by conflict and displacement are acknowledged, it can be argued that such needs are less pressing than physical health needs, such as the need for food and provision of adequate shelter (Médicins sans Frontières, 1997; Simmonds, Vaughan, & Gunn, 1983). Harrell-Bond (1986) has argued that such views reflect an "oversocialised model of man" that assumes social and psychological aspects of experience to be of lesser import to populations, or that mechanisms for addressing needs in these areas will survive complex emergencies more effectively than will mechanisms of food production and economic livelihood. Over the last decade, humanitarian agencies appear to have been decreasingly inclined to make such assumptions. In our work with such agencies, it is not uncommon to now hear such views as the following:

> Saving lives is not just to feed or treat people. That makes them breathe but they might not feel alive.
>
> —Humanitarian Agency Fieldworker

However, there are nonetheless clear operational constraints on humanitarian actions, which generally require prioritization of actions. As a consequence, in contemporary discussions of the place of psychosocial work in humanitarian response, it is becoming increasingly common for psychosocial intervention not to be proposed as a discrete component of intervention that must "compete" against other programming priorities. Rather, attention is focusing on the manner in which interventions can simultaneously address both "basic" and psychological needs.

Structures for Delivery of Interventions to Large Populations

The scale of complex emergencies demands approaches that are effective and appropriate at a population level. A major emphasis is thus commonly given to interventions that can be delivered by relatively unskilled personnel at a "grassroots" level. However, mechanisms for effective supervision of such personnel are rarely in place, and the integrity of intervention effectiveness is thus potentially compromised (Loughry & Kostelny, 2002). Psychosocial programming thus has to grapple with the potential to "go to scale" in humanitarian crises, all the while ensuring the effectiveness and appropriateness of the intervention that is delivered.

The Need for a Draft Protocol

Given such debates, the field of psychosocial intervention can often appear very abstract and inaccessible to humanitarian workers (Fyvie & Ager, 1999). In circumstances that need purposeful and decisive action, the lack of consensus on so many issues can be disturbing. However, recent moves to incorporate psychosocial guidelines within the Sphere Standards for humanitarian work (Sphere Project, 2000) mark an acknowledgment that there is some emerging consensus on key issues that can guide humanitarian practice (van Ommeren, Saxena, & Saraceno, 2005).

This chapter builds on such an emerging consensus to propose a draft protocol for addressing psychosocial needs in the specific context of complex emergencies. This protocol draws on a conceptual framework developed by the Psychosocial Working Group (PWG), a consortium of research institutes and humanitarian agencies engaged in the psychosocial field. The protocol illustrates how the ideas in the framework may be worked out in practice to guide field practice.

Such a protocol may be seen to have a number of purposes. First, it may be seen as a presumptive guide to generic workers, who may not have specific training in the field of psychosocial work. In such circumstances, the protocol is serving as a broad guide, or "map," to help nonspecialists take appropriate actions to incorporate psychosocial needs and response within their overall strategy.

Second, such a protocol provides a reflective tool for appraisal of past programs. Although it is widely acknowledged that agencies can benefit immensely from reflection on the strengths and weaknesses of their programming, such reflection can be difficult to facilitate within agencies (Fyvie, 2001). Having a protocol with respect to which fieldworkers can consider specific actions taken in a given setting—and the bases for the judgments that led to these actions—may usefully enable such reflection.

Third, such a protocol may serve as a focus for debate, disagreement, and development. Notwithstanding the first point above, consensus in the field may be emerging, but it is far from robust. Having a concrete protocol can valuably serve as a "rallying point" for both agreement and disagreement. The debate, and the research activity prompted by it, can only serve to strengthen the evidence base underpinning the psychosocial field.

Suggested Principles

To move toward the definition of such a protocol, the conceptual framework of the PWG needs to be outlined and explained. Even before this step, however, it may be best to assert certain key principles underlying the following analysis. The four major foundational principles for this approach follow:

- Psychosocial issues are of potential relevance in all complex emergencies.
- The *psycho* and *social* orientations are potentially complementary.
- All impacted communities have some relevant coping resources.
- Psychosocial support needs to be integrated within emergency response.

The bases of such principles may be seen as the emerging consensus regarding the themes addressed above and the conceptual insights offered by the PWG framework.

The PWG Conceptual Framework

The framework (PWG, 2003) begins with the assumption that in the context of most initiatives, the needs of individuals are generally appropriately conceptualized within the context of a family or household, which, in turn, is located within an "affected community" (Hobfoll, 1998). The community is considered to be "affected" by some particular series of events, related to war and displacement, that has disrupted or diminished the resources available to that community. In terms of the "psychosocial well-being" of the community, three particular domains are recognized as being of significance: human capacity, social ecology, and culture and values.

Human Capacity

Conflict and displacement can lead to a loss of "human capacity" within the community. This domain is taken to constitute such resources as the physical and mental health of community members and the skills and knowledge of people (which can be referred to as the "human capital" of the community). Events can clearly reduce such human capacity by many means. Physical disability, loss of skilled labor, social withdrawal, and depression all serve to degrade human capacity, as do less tangible effects such as a reduced sense of control over events and circumstances.

Social Ecology

The circumstances of war and refuge also frequently lead to a disruption of the "social ecology" of a community, involving social relations within families, peer groups, religious and cultural institutions, links with civic and political authorities, and so forth (which can be referred to as the "social capital" of the community). Targeted disruption of such structures and networks is often the central focus of contemporary political and military conflict (Summerfield, 1999), as effects on the social ecology of an affected community frequently include changes in power relations between ethnic groups and shifts in gender relations (Lorentzen & Turpin, 1998).

Culture and Values

Events may also disrupt the "culture and values" of a community, challenging human rights, cultural values and mores, and so on (which can be referred to as the "cultural capital" of the community). Conflict can threaten cultural traditions of meaning that have served to unite and give identity to a community (Wessells, 1999). Conflict can also serve to reinforce hardened images of other political or ethnic groups, encouraging escalation of violence and hatred (Kostorova-Unkovska & Pankovska, 1992).

Although psychosocial well-being is appropriately defined with respect to these three core domains, loss of resources (physical, economic, environmental, etc.) clearly has a major effect in many refugee settings, defining the broader context within which individuals, families, and communities seek to protect their well-being. Although resource availability or loss in these broader domains clearly has an effect on psychosocial well-being, it is assumed that such an effect is felt through the core domains of human capacity, social ecology, and culture and values. To do otherwise is to define psychosocial well-being and its determinants so broadly that is becomes a concept of little conceptual or humanitarian programming value.

Engagement

The framework serves not simply as a means of mapping the disruption and depletion of community resources in the context of war and displacement but also, most crucially, as a means of mapping emerging engagement by communities in protecting and promoting well-being. This notion of local engagement is crucial to the use of the framework. The resources that an intervention brings to the community need to be matched to the existing, emergent processes of engagement, rather than used to promote coping or development processes that are "alien" to that community.

Negotiation

The process by which the community assents to the receipt of external resources (which again can be mapped as involving human, social, or cultural capital; see Figure 3.1) is one of negotiation. This interaction between powerful external agencies and relatively weaker local communities clearly relates to the conceptual tensions of the field identified earlier and must be seen as the key to effective, sustained intervention.

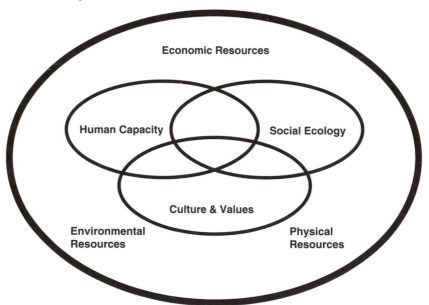

Figure 3.1   The PWG Conceptual Framework

Transformation

Finally, it is tempting in working with war-affected communities to think of the process of community engagement as one with the goal of "restoration" of the situation existing before the events—a perspective emphasized by a number of authors. The goal of intervention would thus be to restore human, social, and cultural capital, and the interaction between them, to a situation similar to that before the conflict. Settings such as Rwanda and East Timor, in which elements of a preconflict situation have contributed directly to the onset of violence, indicate that it may be more helpful to think of this process as one of transformation, involving new relationships between the capacities, linkages, values, and resources of that community.

Using the Framework to Develop an Intervention Protocol for a Complex Emergency

The PWG framework links together three major sources of resource (human capacity, social ecology, and culture and values) with three interactive processes (engagement, negotiation, and transformation), all of which are key to supporting the psychosocial well-being of a community. Taking these ideas into practice requires that they be sufficiently clearly operationalized in a specific setting to be identifiable within a draft intervention protocol.

In the specific context of a complex emergency, however, what actions do such concepts encourage? A protocol is a means of translating concepts and principles into concrete actions relevant to a particular situation. With the draft protocol suggested here, distinctions are made among the following:

- Presumptive actions: actions that may be appropriately deployed in most settings without prior assessment
- Assessment and appraisal: guidance on the collection of data that will shape subsequent deployment
- Potential strategic actions: the broader set of interventions from which selection is made reflecting identified strengths and needs

Putting these elements together suggests a draft protocol of the form presented in Table 3.1.

Table 3.1
Draft Protocol for Psychosocial Response in Complex Emergencies

Acute phase	Presumptive actions
	• Briefing of camp workers (registration officers, health and sanitation workers, etc.) in basic psychosocial principles (e.g., normalization, solidarity, grief and loss, participation)
	• Participation by community sought in basic health, water and sanitation, and shelter provision

(continued)

Table 3.1
Draft Protocol for Psychosocial Response in Complex Emergencies (*Continued*)

Acute phase	**Initial psychosocial assessment**
	
	Rapid assessment techniques deployed to identify
	
	• Human capacity
	   ○ Levels of disability and severe and enduring mental ill health
	   ○ Households vulnerable to poor access to assistance resources
	• Social ecology
	   ○ Level of household fragmentation
	   ○ Potential for intergroup conflict and gender-based violence
	   ○ Level of human rights abuse
	• Culture and values
	   ○ Disruption of preexisting civic or religious institutions
	
	Strategic actions
	
	Initial assessment informs general emergency response strategy regarding
	
	• Linkage with preexisting mental health provision
	• Protection and support to vulnerable households
	• Fostering contact/reunification by households
	• Promotion of good intergroup relations
	• Engagement with key preexisting civic and religious institutions
	• Protection regarding human rights abuses enhanced

Postacute phase	**Presumptive actions** • Reestablishment of schooling • Reinstitution of core cultural, social, and religious activities (e.g., dance, singing, worship)

(continued)

Postacute phase	**Comprehensive psychosocial assessment**

Comprising the following elements:

- Stakeholder analysis
- Epidemiological assessment
- Participative rapid appraisal
- Appraisal of local human resource and institutional capacity

Strategic actions

Assessment to inform general strategy regarding

- Facilitation of group activities (targeting key groups, e.g., youth, women, sports)
- Strengthening local capacity (e.g., teachers, community leaders) for psychosocial and related support
- Establishment of appropriate primary health screening and referral facilities for severe mental health problems
- Establishment of dialogue with community with regard to obstacles to recovery (e.g., social justice issues, ethnic divides, spiritual sequelae of conflict)

Key Elements of the Draft Protocol

Acute Phase

Complex emergencies are generally characterized as having an "acute" and a "postacute" phase. The precise definitions of such phases differ, and although specific criteria (e.g., excess mortality rates) can be used, the intention here is effectively to distinguish an acute phase in which urgent actions need to be put in place and there are constrained opportunities for assessment of—and engagement with—affected populations. Transition to the postacute phase would be marked by deeper negotiation with local populations and the development of less reactive and more proactive forms of humanitarian response. This does not mean that response in the acute phase is marked by a lack of commitment to understanding processes of local engagement. It is simply to acknowledge that opportunities for negotiation with the local community are more constrained in this period.

Presumptive actions in this period are few, but significant. Those interacting with members of the affected community—be they camp officials, health workers, or food aid distributors—can serve to foster effective engagement by beneficiaries, or to undermine it. Harrell-Bond's (1986) powerful description of one method used to enumerate refugees in a camp setting—herding refugees like cattle in the middle of the night—testifies to the potential for such interactions to foster withdrawal and humiliation rather than positive engagement. The principles of "psychological first aid" (Knudsen, Hogsted, & Berliner, 1997) indicate that a basic training of workers can equip them to perform functions that promote well-being during their interactions with beneficiaries. The principle of normalization, for instance, involves reassurance that emotional responses are generally a normal part of response to violence and loss and do not represent pathology. Such sentiments are core to many traditional support systems within communities (Eyber & Ager, 2002), although support from such mechanisms is often compromised during conflict and displacement. Promoting participation follows as a key principle, noting the PWG analysis of the centrality of effective engagement to psychosocial well-being (PWG, 2003).

Although the opportunity for detailed assessment is likely to be limited during the acute phase of an emergency, rapid assessments of resource availability in the domains of human capacity, social ecology, and culture and values are key to shaping strategic actions in this phase. Those listed are suggestions of appropriate and feasible assessment. Disability and severe and enduring mental ill health are significant risk factors for descending a rapid spiral of resource loss in the context of a complex emergency (Hobfoll, 1998) but are frequently ignored in psychosocial assessments (van Ommeren et al., 2005). Households where ill health, care responsibilities, and other factors constrain human capacity such that they are unable to effectively engage with assistance efforts similarly warrant identification.

Household fragmentation gives insight into the number of single-headed households and unaccompanied minors for which particular provision may need to be made. Female-headed households were the most vulnerable educationally, socially, and economically in an analysis of Mozambican refugee well-being during the civil war (Ager, Ager, & Long, 1995). Unaccompanied minors are appropriately considered a major programming priority in the context of complex emergencies, with significant protection needs. Social linkage may generally be an asset, but intergroup conflicts (whether based on tribal, religious, ethnic, or other differences) have clear potential for disrupting effective engagement in postconflict recovery (Colletta and Cullen, 2000).

Summerfield (1999) has documented how the disruption of civic or religious institutions is a common goal of military actors, given its effect on the broader well-being, morale, and identity of the community. It makes clear sense, therefore, to assess the extent of such disruption as a precursor to potential rehabilitative actions. Human rights abuses, including violence against women (who are especially vulnerable during periods of instability and conflict; Callemard, 1999), will further erode community capacity for engagement and need to be effectively monitored such that they can be systematically addressed.

The strategic actions that then follow should clearly be shaped by the outcomes of the rapid assessments outlined above. These actions will be informed not only by the needs noted through such assessments but also by the resources and capacities thereby identified. Importantly, the PWG framework assumes that resource availability in one domain can be used to support resource development in another. Thus, for example, strong community linkages can be exploited to bolster the human capacity available to otherwise vulnerable households, or strong religious institutions can be used to foster peace-building between conflicting social groupings.

Postacute Phase

The postacute phase, as discussed above, is marked by the opportunity for deeper negotiation with affected communities. Nonetheless, there is arguably a case for identifying a small set of actions that can be made presumptively, given their widespread appropriateness in complex emergency settings. Such actions should clearly be shaped by negotiation with the affected community where possible, but the protocol indicates that certain actions are both so crucial to recovery and so widespread in their applicability that it may be appropriate to advance them presumptively. Reviews of community recovery indicate that just two actions fulfill such criteria. The reestablishment of schooling not only minimizes disruption to children's educational progress, which is of potential relevance to their future social and economic advancement, but it provides a structure that is generally significantly protective of children's social, emotional, and cultural development (Ahearn Loughry, & Ager, 1999). Schools, for instance, have provided a vital structure for supporting the psychosocial well-being of Palestinian children and youth through the second *intifada* (Arafat & Boothby, 2003). The importance of the reinstitution of preexisting cultural, social, and religious activities flows from the value of such structures in mobilizing resources of community engagement and the negotiation of shared accounts of resilience and recovery (Ager, 1999; Summerfield, 1999). Facilitating burial feasts, cleansing rituals, and other symbolically rich activities can have significant utility in fostering community recovery (Ager et al., 1995; Wessells & Monteiro, 2000).

The next action that is proposed is a more detailed psychosocial assessment, building on earlier, rapid analyses and involving deeper processes of negotiation with the affected community, regarding both needs and capacities. The precise nature of this assessment will vary on circumstance, and there is a range of assessment tools and practice guides now available to help structure such processes (e.g., Arnston & Knudson, 2004).

There are four components of such analysis that should be seen as being core to comprehensive psychosocial analysis. Stakeholder analysis identifies the constituent groups and interests within a community. Early rapid appraisal will generally have had to involve negotiating access to communities through key position holders. To the extent that such positions reflect power relations within affected communities, they may not serve to give comprehensive access to community perspectives. It is common, for instance, for refugee representational structures to be dominated by men (Ager et al., 1995; Callemard, 1999), and at this stage of assessment, it will likely be important to identify appropriate structures for consultation with women. Similarly, initial access will often involve adults representing the interests of children and youth, and assessment methodologies need to be used that access such perspectives directly. Epidemiological assessment is a structured approach to assessing the prevalence of ill health and should appropriately include some measure of mental ill health. Participatory rapid appraisal involves a range of exercises and activities seeking to identify local constructions of the challenges facing a community or group and, typically, the distribution of resources available to address them. Eyber and Ager (2004), for example, describe participatory approaches used to access the views of adolescent refugees in postconflict Angola. The final, often neglected, component of comprehensive psychosocial assessment involves the appraisal of local human resource and institutional capacity. There is a great danger that planned interventions ignore or, worse still, undermine locally available people and institutions (Adjukovic & Adjukovic, 1998). Alternatively, planned interventions can assume support from preexisting services that are, in fact, incapable of reliable delivery (either because of existing capacity constraints or as a result of the effects of the emergency). Thorough appraisal of available resources in this area is thus a vital foundation for coherent determination of subsequent strategic actions.

The protocol lists a number of potential strategic actions that may be put in place following such assessment, although the list provided is in no way meant to be seen as exhaustive of such options. Essentially, actions will be supported when they address an identifiable need, using identifiable resources, in a manner that strengthens processes of community engagement. Group activities can bolster social linkage, promote cultural values and rights, and strengthen—through training components—human capacity (Agger, 2001). Strengthened human capacity regarding psychosocial support can prompt community development and foster approaches to peace and reconciliation (Wessells & Monteiro, 2000). Primary care screening provides linkage and referral to services, where available, for those with severe and enduring mental health needs. Most broadly, extension of dialogue with stakeholders across the community mobilizes existing human capacity, social linkage, and cultural capital to identify major obstacles to recovery. Such actions should not being taken forward in a vacuum. The proposed protocol prompts such actions to be based on a foundation not only of rapid and more comprehensive assessment but also of experiences from implementing presumptive and strategic actions earlier in the emergency.

Conclusion: The Problems and Promises of Protocols

This protocol is offered as a tool for debate and development. It is not intended as a last word in the determining psychosocial response in complex emergencies but, rather, an "early word" in shaping the development of an evidence base and consensus. For instance, any notion of "presumptive actions" will be anathema for some and represents a threat to the centrality of local voices in shaping intervention strategy. Seeking to articulate such actions, however, forces us to identify what generalized lessons or principles we may have learned that provide any sort of basis for external agencies to assume qualification to intervene in supporting community response to emergencies.

More generally, protocols have a number of weaknesses: they can appear to be too rigid in shaping response or, alternatively, too vague in specifying appropriate actions. They can be seen to go beyond available evidence in asserting a recommended response. They can suggest an overly rational model of planning, when circumstances require a flexible response that properly accounts for various complicating factors. They may also emphasize the agenda of an intervening agency over local needs and priorities that ought to carry greater influence.

All these weaknesses are risks in the use of the proposed draft protocol. However, if it is used as a reflective guide rather than an inflexible programmatic script, it is hoped that the effect of the protocol will be positive in shaping humanitarian response. Above all, it must be a framework for debate, leading to the development of an increasingly effective response on the part of agencies seeking to support the engagement of populations affected by complex emergencies.

References

Adjucovic, M. & Adjucovic, D. (1998). Impact of displacement on the psychological well-being of the children, *International Review of Psychiatry, 10,* 189–195.

Ager, A. (1999). Perspectives on the refugee experience. In A. Ager (Ed.), *Refugees: Perspectives on the experience of forced migration* (pp. 1–23). London: Pinter.

———. (2002). Psychosocial needs in complex emergencies. *The Lancet, 360,* 43–44.

———, Ager, W., & Long, L. (1995). The differential experience of refugee women and men. *Journal of Refugee Studies, 8,* 1–23.

———, & Loughry, M. (2004). Psychology and humanitarian assistance. *Journal of Humanitarian Assistance.* [Online]. Retrieved January 27, 2005, from http://www.jha.ac/articles/a131.htm

Agger, I. (2001). The problem of the wool. In M. Loughry & A. Ager (Eds.), *The refugee experience: Psychosocial training module* (Rev. ed.). Oxford: Refugee Studies Centre. Retrieved January 27, 2005, from http://earlybird.qeh.ox.ac.uk/rfgexp/start.htm

Ahearn, F., Loughry, M., & Ager, A. (1999). The experience of refugee children. In A. Ager (Ed.), *Refugees: Perspectives on the experience of forced migration.* London: Continuum.

Arafat, C., & Boothby, N. (2003). *Psychosocial assessment of Palestinian children.* Washington, DC: Save the Children. Retrieved January 27, 2005, from http://www.caresaveupdate.org/FinalCPSPAssessmentEnglish.pdf

Arnston, L., & Knudson, C. (2004). *Psychosocial care and protection of children in emergencies: A field guide.* Westport, CT: Save the Children.

Bracken, P., Giller, J. E., & Summerfield, D. (1995). Psychological responses to war and atrocity: The limitations of current concepts. *Social Science & Medicine, 40* (8), 1073–1082.

Callemard, A. (1999). In A. Ager (Ed.), *Refugees: Perspectives on the experience of forced migration.* London: Continuum.

Colletta, N. J., & Cullen, M. (2000). *Violent conflict and the transformation of social capital.* New York: World Bank.

de Jong, K. (2003). Mental health programmes in war stricken areas. *Intervention, the International Journal of Mental Health, Psychosocial Work and Counselling in Areas of Armed Conflict, 1*(1), 14–33.

Eyber, C., & Ager, A. (2002). Conselho: Trauma and healing in Angola. *The Lancet, 360,* 871.

———. (2004). Researching young people's experiences of war: Participatory methods and the trauma discourse in Angola. In J. Boyden & J. de Berry (Eds.), *Children and youth on the front line: Ethnography, armed conflict and displacement.* Oxford: Berghahn Books.

Fyvie, C. (2001). Innovation in development assistance non-governmental organizations: Characteristics, constraints and constructions. Unpublished doctoral dissertation. Edinburgh: Queen Margaret University College.

———, & Ager, A. (1999). NGOs and innovation: Organizational characteristics and constraints in development assistance work in the Gambia. *World Development, 27* (8), 1383–1395.

Harrell-Bond, B. (1986). *Imposing aid: Emergency assistance for refugees.* Oxford: Oxford University Press.

Hobfoll, S. (1998). *Stress, culture and community: The psychology and philosophy of stress.* New York: Plenum.

Kelley, S. D., McDonald, L., & Mollica, R. (2002). *Worldview approach to understanding the nature of human suffering and psychosocial interventions in post-conflict situations.* Final Report to the Mellon Foundation, Harvard Program in Refugee Trauma, Harvard University, Cambridge, MA.

Knudsen, L., Hogsted, R., & Berliner, P. (1997). *Psychological first aid and human support.* Danish Red Cross. Copenhagen, Denmark. Retrieved January 27, 2005, from http://www.ifrc.org/docs/pubs/health/bestpractices_07.pdf

Kostorova-Unkovska, L., & Pankovska, V. (1992). *Children hurt by war.* Skopje: General Children's Consulate of the Republic of Macedonia.

Lorentzen, L., & Turpin, J. (1998). *The women and war reader.* New York: New York University Press.

Loughry, M., & Kostelny, K. (2002). *Mapping psychosocial interventions in East Timor.* Retrieved January 27, 2005, from http://www.forcedmigration.org/psychosocial/papers/PWGpapers.htm

Médicins sans Frontières. (1997). *Refugee health care: An approach to emergency situations.* London: Macmillan.

Mercer, S., Ager, A., &, Rawanapuri, E. (2004). Psychosocial distress of Tibetans in exile: Integrating western interventions with traditional beliefs and practice. *Social Science & Medicine, 60* (1), 179–189.

Muecke, M. A. (1992). New paradigms for refugee mental health problems. *Social Science & Medicine, 35,* 515–523.

Psychosocial Working Group. (2003). A conceptual framework for psychosocial intervention in complex emergencies. [Working paper]. Edinburgh: Queen Margaret University College. Retrieved February 3, 2005, from http://www.forcedmigration .org/psychosocial/papers/PWGpapers.htm

Pupavac, V. (2001). Therapeutic governance: Psycho-social intervention and trauma risk management. *Disasters, 25* (4), 358–372.

Simmonds, S., Vaughan, P., & Gunn, S. W. (1983). *Refugee community health care.* Oxford: Oxford University Press.

Sphere Project. (2000). *Humanitarian charter and minimum standards in disaster response.* Retrieved January 22, 2005, from http://www.sphereproject.org/handbook/hdbkpdf /hdbk_full.pdf

Summerfield, D. (1999). Socio-cultural perspectives on the experience of war. In A. Ager (Ed.), *Refugees: Perspectives on the experience of forced migration.* London: Continuum.

van Ommeren, M., Saxena, S., & Saraceno, B. (2005). Mental and social health during and after acute emergencies: Emerging consensus? *Bulletin of the World Health Organization, 83* (1), 71–77.

Wessells, M. (1999). Culture, power and community: Intercultural approaches to psychosocial assistance and healing. In K. Nader, N. Dubrow, & B. Stamm (Eds.), *Honoring differences: Cultural issues in the treatment of trauma and loss.* New York: Taylor & Francis.

———, & Monteiro, C. (2000). Healing wounds of war in Angola: A community-based approach. In D. Donald, A. Dawes, & J. Louw (Eds.), *Addressing childhood adversity* (pp. 176–201). Cape Town, South Africa: David Philip.

CHAPTER 4

IN DEFENSE OF A COMMUNITY PSYCHOLOGY MODEL FOR INTERNATIONAL PSYCHOSOCIAL INTERVENTION

Gordon R. Dodge

Defining a "Community Psychology" Model

The field of disaster psychology, especially when applied internationally, raises many concerns about how to properly serve the needs of people of differing cultures and experiences. Assessments must accurately reflect the psychosocial reactions present and reveal the most important needs of the affected populations. Interventions must not only match the assessed needs but also prove themselves accessible, acceptable, and convincing if they are to be at all effective. The potential obstacles are too numerous to list, but of major concern are the following:

1. Gaining access to those who might benefit from psychosocial services: The affected population is often spread across geographic territories with many distinct communities, rather than one homogeneous group in a concentrated location. The ability of "outsiders" to detect psychosocial needs is limited by barriers of geography, language, culture, and permeability of the affected community. There are also issues of physical safety to be considered when venturing into unfamiliar territory.

2. Overcoming the stigma surrounding mental health concerns and the potential to inadvertently stigmatize survivors: It would be unrealistic to think that most people around the world welcome attention to their psychosocial needs. Most cultures still view anyone with a "mental problem" as inferior and potentially dangerous. People who are

having difficulty adjusting to the terrible consequences of a disaster might justifiably fear being stigmatized by the attention of mental health professionals. Because most of these people can expect to regain their prior level of well-being over time, a potential exists for psychosocial response teams to complicate recovery by adding stigma to the mix of challenges facing survivors.

3. Making optimal use of existing resources: The resources that psychosocial response personnel can provide are typically quite limited and are therefore inadequate for serving each and every survivor individually. Although disasters destroy many of the assets of an affected community, there are usually some human and institutional resources and capacity that remain useful. These "community" resources often have inherent benefits of being culturally familiar, accessible, and acceptable. Resourceful local people are typically knowledgeable about their communities in ways that outsiders simply cannot match. Moreover, making use of these resources begins the rebuilding of community capacities and sends a much more empowering message than relying entirely on external resources (Paton & Bishop, 1996).

These goals and obstacles will sound familiar to those who are acquainted with the principles of community psychology (e.g., Levine & Perkins, 1997). In contrast to a "clinical" perspective, emphasizing pathological symptoms and behaviors among individuals, community psychology identifies ecological factors that predict greater or lesser resilience in the face of adversity. As a consequence, the sources of both functional and malfunctioning adaptations are located in the community ecology, rather than in stigmatized or "scapegoated" individuals or groups. From this perspective, collective goals and needs require collective (i.e., collaborative and cooperative) action. Ideas like dependency and deficiency are to be discouraged in favor of empowering communities to use their competencies and capacities for resilient adaptation (Iscoe, 1974). Great emphasis is placed on inclusiveness and participation across all levels and sectors of society, resulting in more diversity of views and values being represented. Perhaps most important, as unfavorable adaptations are not "medicalized," interventions need not require specialized clinical expertise. This allows for a more multidisciplinary approach that takes proper advantage of the skills and abilities of community members with healing talents.

Given the collective social effect of disasters and armed conflicts, the principles of community psychology provide a particularly well-suited framework for meeting the psychosocial needs of diverse groups of people with efficient use of available resources (Trickett, 1995). Coupling this approach with adequate safety measures for detecting and responding to acute psychosocial disturbances requiring clinical expertise may provide the most effective model for serving disaster-affected populations. Additional benefits of mobilizing and empowering community resources include the building of durable local capacity for responding to subsequent adversities and the flexibility to adjust interventions as needs evolve.

The Need for Improving Our Present Models and Methods

To maintain and improve the effectiveness of our professional efforts, it has been important for us to stay abreast of relevant theory and research, as well as best practices from the field. We have, for the most part, trusted that others interested in identifying effective methods and improving on them will at least do the same. Unfortunately, in the international psychosocial arena, we too often find bureaucratic and political interests surpassing common sense and compassion, arrogance guiding programmatic decisions, and authoritatively asserted opinions lacking any factual basis. Given the relative immaturity of this field, such characteristics are understandable but are nonetheless disappointing and ultimately unacceptable. We have ethical and moral responsibilities to the recipients of our efforts to overcome these impediments to providing better services.

Fortunately, the time appears ripe for improving our international services. There is a growing interest and understanding among our researchers and academicians, an increasing awareness within nongovernmental humanitarian organizations (NGOs) of the relevance of psychosocial services to their missions, and an expanding capacity and desire across disciplines and cultures to learn from each other. In recent years, humanitarian organizations like the International Federation of Red Cross and Red Crescent Societies (IFRC) have begun developing formal guidelines for psychosocial intervention that stress the importance of community-based approaches (e.g., Simonsen & Reyes, 2003). If we proceed with humility, flexibility, creativity, objectivity, and open minds, we can make good use of this historic opportunity to reduce the psychological damage following conflict and disasters while employing the principles and strategies of community psychology.

Obviously, there is much that is not well understood regarding which approaches are useful, and correspondingly, the confidence we can have in the available models of service varies extensively. For the purposes of this chapter, I have constructed an argument for change based more on professional experience than on research literatures. Therefore, I have limited the citing of relevant research and program evaluation references, this being more a matter of personal conclusions and not a scientific thesis. What follows is therefore based mostly on my familiarity with work performed by others, as well as the work in which I have been personally involved, and I have carefully qualified my statements as to what degree of confidence might be placed in any of these approaches, given the available evidence.

Applying Community Psychology Internationally

Perhaps the most fundamental question we must ask is, "Can those of us from Western cultures and training effectively help people in other parts of the world to cope with trauma and other mental health issues?" This is a complex question, but with the right balance of modifications, sensitivities, and humility we can safely answer "yes." There is an increasing body of knowledge suggesting that, in much of the world, the core aspects of trauma and loss are considerably similar, although the social meanings and modes of expression may vary in important ways (Stamm & Friedman, 2000). By better understanding cultural variations in the expression of trauma, we can also learn principles for specifying acceptable modes of intervention for a given context. Already, as many of the chapters in this handbook attest, much of what we have learned is beginning to demonstrate helpfulness in various international settings. Our awareness of which approaches might be most useful with differing groups has benefited from international assignments. This, in turn, informs our work with the increasing numbers and varieties of immigrant populations whom we seek to serve in our own countries.

How do we continue to improve our international work? The answer seems obvious, but typically it is ignored. Many of our clinical, sociological, and educational research models are sufficiently well developed to be adapted to international settings, and there are established international research and evaluation precedents in other fields such as public health and agriculture. Cooperative research and evaluation agreements between countries and their respective academic and humanitarian organizations need to be a priority. Similarly, program evaluation, if it is to be at all useful in improving the effectiveness of services, must be designed and implemented from the beginning of an intervention program, rather than as an afterthought. Exchange programs, scholarships, and international internships will also add to our interest and knowledge base. Conferences and other forums for exchange of both research and applied findings have been increasing over the last several years, but sponsorships for participants from less-affluent countries to attend these are few.

When is it best to intervene? This is as much a policy question as an analytical one. Some NGOs limit their overall involvement to short-term interventions (e.g., medical care, food, and shelter) in the emergency phase following a disaster. Many organizations have policy limits on types of services, such as educational or health, and others by type of recipient, be it children, elderly, and so forth. This means that if psychosocial interventions are to be offered, they need to fit within that overall parameter and the priorities of the relief operation. This may be seen as a limitation, but in many ways, it is a developmental strength and advantage for our work. With this in mind, let us go back to the question of timing the psychosocial intervention.

Several reasons can be offered to support providing psychosocial services in the earliest possible time frame following a disaster (often referred to as the emergency phase). There are typically immediate psychosocial needs that can be partially served in conjunction with the provision of other emergency services. Early intervention is meant to both relieve immediate distress and decrease the long-term effects of traumatic events, thus serving a preventive role. Survivors and staff are educated about what to be aware of and how they might later address psychosocial needs should the occasion arise. An increasingly useful body of knowledge is available to guide us in identifying who is at risk for long-term complications and which actions are most helpful in early stages of recovery. Early intervention allows for assessment, planning, and training for evolving psychosocial program needs. Early involvement also provides for building an awareness of the importance of psychosocial services and for establishing necessary trust and working relationships with the survivor population, as well as with the many other organizations participating in response services. Staff themselves often have psychosocial needs from the beginning that can be addressed constructively to reduce vicarious traumatization, burn-out, organizational fatigue, and other stress-related complications.

Arguments, however, can also be presented against early involvement. For instance, in the emergency phase, we typically have little information available on the individuals, communities, and cultures involved. Also, in situations in which rapid decisions need to be made, there is greater risk of making errors in judgment that would do more harm than good. Concerns have been raised regarding the risk of inadvertently undermining natural and spontaneous recovery, creating dependency, or stigmatizing instead of truly reducing suffering and distress. Furthermore, during emergency phases, NGOs are usually involved in providing basic life-preserving services (e.g., food, water, and sanitation), and the scarcity of financial resources fuels arguments about these "necessities" taking precedence over mental health care. Such strong and legitimate concerns as these need to be addressed thoroughly and objectively. Even within the mental health field itself, there is a tenable position that we are best at working with established clinical conditions, so why not wait and use our limited resources with those who do not recover through other existing resources. In general, however, with careful assessment criteria and processes, there are often emergency phase disaster situations that can significantly benefit from psychosocial interventions.

Conducting a Psychosocial Needs Assessment

How and when to conduct a psychosocial needs assessment is a complex matter and is difficult to summarize. I have addressed the topic of psychosocial assessment in depth elsewhere in this volume (see Dodge, 2006). Suffice it to say that most NGOs now have at least some awareness of the importance of psychosocial needs assessment, and several are incorporating assessments into their overall models of service delivery. What is lacking is a

forum for exchange of assessment experiences and interorganizational training in psychosocial needs assessment. The reader is also advised to remember that assessment methodology must be consistent with program
methodology. More specifically, if one anticipates the possibility of using a
community psychology intervention model, then critical organizational, system, and community variables require identification in assessment activities.
Given accurate needs assessments, awareness of resources available to meet
those needs, and knowledge of what interventions likely will be most effective in meeting the identified needs, an organization can implement services
accordingly.

Current Intervention Models

A preventive model of intervention with considerable acceptance internationally is often referred to as psychological first aid (PFA) or psychological support (PSP). This includes the training of organizational staff in the
basics of stress management, communication skills, supportive counseling,
crisis intervention, initial individual assessments, and referral for clinical
care when that is needed. In practice, this is carried out on a "training of
trainers" basis so that it can be rapidly and widely disseminated and implemented at a relatively low cost. The most extensive development of this
model has been through the efforts of the Reference Centre for Psychosocial
Support in Copenhagen. This jointly managed collaboration between the
Danish Red Cross and the IFRC has been influential in helping to establish
PSP in many Red Cross and Red Crescent national societies around the
world. Attempts are usually made to modify the basic curriculum to make it
more culturally acceptable to the locale where it is to be employed. This
approach has been applied in postdisaster settings and also in disaster preparedness training in various countries (Taylor, 2003). Information about
post-trauma effects is usually included, with general suggestions of what may
be useful in response. In spite of its extensive use and popularity, however,
the psychological first aid model has yet to be evaluated to any significant
degree, especially with regard to the question of whether its application pre-
vents the development of psychological consequences following conflict or a
disaster.

Psychological debriefing, especially the Mitchell model of Critical Incident Stress Debriefing (CISD; Mitchell, 1983), has been taught quite extensively internationally. This approach is much more specific and limited in its
scope and intent than the PSP or PFA models, but it is consistent with the
same preventive concept. Recent controversial arguments over the merits of
psychological debriefing (see Litz, 2004, for a thorough discussion) have
clouded the issue and led some organizations to disavow its use (e.g., World
Health Organization, 2003, 2005). Nevertheless, countless examples of psychological debriefing interventions have and will continue to be found in
many conflict and disaster situations throughout the world.

At least two basic premises are involved in psychological first aid and psychological debriefing. The first is that the survivors of a disaster are understandably distraught or distressed, and that temporary but formalized supportive interventions help them get through the period until their lives can get back to normal or until local resources can be accessed if they need such. Although I know of no empirical support for this conclusion, there is popular recipient, professional, and organizational support for this contention. The second premise is that such interventions reduce the severity and frequency of long-term complications such as post-traumatic stress disorder (PTSD), depression, and traumatic grief. Obviously this conclusion is more difficult to reach, and there are mixed research findings. Postdisaster social support in general, however, has been identified as a significant mitigating variable. The opposing argument is that money may be better spent by more precisely identifying those who are at highest risk for long-term complications and working more intensively with them, assuming that the majority of the population does not really need support services other than what spontaneously occurs without designed psychological intervention. That argument is weakened by the fact that this often does not have to be an either/or question, in that general psychological support interventions can be incorporated as part of other services already being provided. For example, pairing psychological care with basic services like health care may facilitate both mental health education for the majority of recipients and prompt identification of those who are at elevated risk for long-term complications.

Psychological triage and crisis intervention services are often provided, either in conjunction with general support services or as a component of medical services. This is more common and acceptable in Western cultures and usually presupposes the availability of pharmaceutical agents and psychiatric facilities for those needing such. Yet even in Western settings, people in acute psychological crisis may avoid crisis intervention resources when they are offered in accordance with a clinical model. Moreover, this approach is unfamiliar in many cultures and consequently not likely to be sought out in conflict and disaster situations. In settings in which medical services are readily used by recipients, the incorporation of crisis intervention strategies can be partially effective psychologically but requires specialized training, cooperation, and flexible temperaments among the staff involved. The work done by Médecins Sans Frontières (Doctors Without Borders) has used this model in some of its international missions with apparent success.

Clinical model services also can be provided on a long-term basis, either in a typical Western format or modified for more cultural effectiveness. The more we modify our methods, however, the less sure we can be of their potential usefulness because of our inability to generalize from the original effectiveness studies. This is costly and complex work that takes literally years of commitment and a willingness to spend extended periods of time working in hardship and sometimes dangerous conditions. However, when such services can be provided for those with long-lasting psychological trauma difficulties, some highly useful progress can be made for those clients. Such programs can also demonstrate the potential beneficial incorporation of Western knowledge in other settings.

The Center for Victims of Torture in Minneapolis has a project in western Africa that is an example of this approach. The incorporation of cognitive-behavioral therapeutic behavioral methods for PTSD into culturally acceptable models has had more attention than work with other clinical areas of concern following disasters such as depression, traumatic grief, psychosomatic disorders, and spiritual conflict. A complication that often occurs with long-term clinical programs as they gain acceptance in international settings that have limited mental health resources is pressure to provide those services to the chronically mentally ill, who are also usually indigent. Obviously this population is in need of assistance, but attending to the extensive needs of this group can quickly deplete program resources so that adequate services cannot continue to be provided to others seriously affected psychologically by the disaster.

Another long-term model that is gaining considerable appeal in the international humanitarian community focuses on building or restoring personal resiliency. This is attractive because it does not emphasize pathology and is therefore less stigmatizing. There are difficulties with this approach, however, in that we have such limited knowledge of how to identify and foster resilient characteristics in cultural settings that rely less on individualism and autonomy. It is probably best to view the resiliency model as having sufficient potential worth to warrant further evaluation along with better exploration of what constitutes resiliency in various cultures. The work being done on developing mediation and conflict resolution skills, especially in postconflict settings, is also likely to have relevance to resiliency efforts.

Mass education is an approach that can be applied on a preventive, early intervention, or long-term basis. It can be initiated quickly and with low cost as long as there are written or oral modes of communication available to reach the populations of concern. Care, of course, needs to be taken to have respectful and meaningful translation of materials used. In this regard, and to help maintain supportive local social structures, where possible it is best to provide mass education through existing indigenous community and leadership resources (Edwards, 2002). Basic information on typical effects of trauma and on what can be helpful psychologically for ourselves, our children, and our communities are examples of this approach as commonly used and typically appreciated. Pamphlets, newspaper articles, radio and television presentations, and public meeting forums can all be used.

It is important to know that general information that provides access to resources, connection with family and friends, knowledge of the status of conditions "back home," flood levels, information regarding ongoing peace negotiations, and so on can have a profoundly calming effect on people following conflict or a disaster. For example, the International Committee of the Red Cross distributed inexpensive radios among Kosovar refugees in Albania and provided a variety of practical information to these groups. The savvy person developing mental health services in a disaster situation will be aware of such dynamics and will encourage these and similar informal interventions. This is also a good working example of a community-based psychosocial intervention.

A number of international psychosocial programs employ a social rehabilitation model. These include promoting efforts such as "healing" activities in public schools, craft and garden clubs, drama groups, and classes on sewing or computers. The therapeutic principles underlying these approaches emphasize group support, confidence building, relaxation, and ventilation through safe and acceptable activities. Many non-Western cultures prefer access to troubling thoughts and feelings through indirect rather than straight discussion approaches and respond more readily on a group and community basis than one on one; hence the appeal of these methods. In a few initiatives, for similar reasons, mental health programs are blended with social welfare programs. What is lacking in most social rehabilitation approaches is documentation of their psychological therapeutic effectiveness, or measurement of functional improvement. Perhaps one of the best developed programs that fits under the social rehabilitation umbrella and has evolved documentation of clinical and functional improvement is the Danish Red Cross' Children Affected by Armed Conflict (CABAC) initiative and its offspring. These are school-based interventions with conflict-affected children and involve the training of teachers and other school staff in therapeutic group activities, with most of these program efforts occurring in the Balkans over the last 10 years.

There is also a psychosocial community organizational model. This has variations in organizational and institutional development but typically incorporates a primary goal of capacity building so that the target institutions can continue services or be capable of handling the next disaster after external resources are withdrawn. Many humanitarian organizations and governmental entities support, if not require, this approach. This usually requires a long-term availability from a project, program flexibility, and staff competence in community development. Most mental health personnel do not have these skills, and to be effective in this model, they either need additional training or need to work in partnership with personnel who have that capacity and role. In recent years, there have been some attempts at least in some organizations to combine psychosocial efforts with other capacity-building resources, but good models of this combination are lacking. Ironically, the inclusion of an evaluation of even two or three psychosocial capacity-building efforts on an international basis likely would do more for the consideration and awareness of psychosocial programs among NGOs and governmental entities than any other similar level of effort. There has been a slow but growing community organizational psychosocial awareness and evolvement internationally, primarily associated with organizational capacity-building efforts. The terms "community resiliency," "community empowerment," and "community mobilization" are being introduced (and to some degree reintroduced, but with better articulation) as effective methods for postconflict and postdisaster psychological care. Many of the principles and methods associated with these concepts will be seen in the community psychology model encouraged later in the chapter.

The extent to which staff care may influence beneficiary mental health also warrants discussion as an intervention model. Most people agree that providing any postdisaster service with respect, empathy, calmness, and dependability usually has reassuring effects on the recipients of those services, compared with not displaying those characteristics. Creating a calm and supportive environment may be a worthwhile short-term mental health programmatic goal. A corollary premise is that maintaining physically and emotionally healthy staff is also to the advantage of the service recipients. This is the basis, in general, for employee assistance programs and occupational stress management programs. Disaster and humanitarian workers, no matter how well selected and trained, because of the nature of their work, are considered to be at higher risk for critical incident and cumulative stress—thus the added rationale for a comprehensive occupational stress management program, including on-site services if the disaster is of significant stress. There has been an increase in interorganizational discussion on this topic, and a few publications. Similarly, over the last couple of years, at least two professional service organizations have been established to provide employee assistance services to international staff for several NGOs as their clients. I am acquainted with two organizations that have attempted to provide professional stress management support directly to field staff on an international basis, these being World Vision International and the International Committee of the Red Cross. However, what is lacking is an evaluation of actual benefits of an occupational stress management program not only for the organization and its staff but even for the disaster service beneficiaries themselves. An evaluation design for this question is certainly feasible. Greater barriers are encountered in convincing organizational decision makers of its potential usefulness and in the requirement of obtaining support across organizational functions such as human resources, security, desk officers, and the donor community. It is imperative that these obstacles be overcome in the interest of humane treatment for humanitarian personnel. The potential benefits of more effective staff mental health care may well be the most cost-efficient of all international psychosocial interventions.

This examination of intervention models reveals that, although several approaches have been tried in various contexts and configurations, there is still much we do not know about the usefulness of our international psychosocial initiatives. Progressing beyond this point will require openness to many possibilities, along with professional and theoretical humility. With these cautions in mind, the things that we have learned thus far may be sufficient to guide our focus and emphases with several theoretical and professional principles of intervention.

An initial needs assessment is uniformly needed to provide for accurate decision making on whether or not psychosocial assistance is warranted and what are likely the best approaches, given a review of all critical variables. In most major conflict and disaster circumstances, some level of intervention will be indicated—increasingly so, of course, depending on the severity of human loss. For staff care, needs assessment, general psychological support, triage and crisis care, and the development of interorganizational agreements and community trust, the identification of high-risk individuals and high-risk communities and possible early prevention efforts and capacity-building needs, psychosocial participation in the emergency phase will most often be indicated over delaying involvement for several months.

Suggested Future Directions

Working through established disaster relief services, activities, and personnel, both indigenous and those provided by external organizations, will in general be more acceptable, efficient, and effective compared with using independent clinical services. This approach, however, requires us to identify which activities and opportunities exist within a given community, as well as which will also have beneficial psychosocial effects. Several of my international disaster response assignments over the last few years provide specific examples relevant to a community psychology approach in psychosocial work.

Yugoslavia

During the 1990s, both expatriate and indigenous humanitarian staff consistently informed me that expressions of supervisory support, friendships, and contact with family were the most important needs they had for maintaining their emotional well-being. Assisting the organizations involved in improving the likelihood of these opportunities certainly was not a clinical service, but it was beneficial nonetheless.

Albania

While working during the Kosovo Crisis with an assessment team for the IFRC, we found that basic information, reunion with family, and safety and security were the most critical factors affecting emotional stability in the emergency phase for the refugees. Working with existing "non–mental health" organizations and systems to maintain and improve response to those needs was a very appropriate psychosocial intervention.

Kenya

When providing organizational consultation following the American embassy bombing, one affected group that was difficult to help were those who directly experienced and witnessed the bombing and then went back to their villages ("up-country"). Working with and through the tribal leaders and in conjunction with home-based health workers was determined to be the best approach. We found it much more acceptable to develop a functional assessment instrument to assist staff and clients in determining needs and measuring improvement, especially, again, in the nonurban settings.

India

In 2001, I conducted a psychosocial needs assessment following the Gujarat earthquake on behalf of the American Red Cross and the Indian Red Cross Society. The disaster killed more than 20,000 people and injured or left homeless many thousands more. It was decided that a strategy of incorporating emotionally healing approaches into services such as child care, educational, religious, and public health programs and institutions offered the best opportunities for psychosocial intervention. A training of trainers and consultation services model was developed. This program struggled getting started but eventually evolved into a nationwide community-based, supportive, preventive, and educationally focused program. Perhaps its best long-lasting benefit was the establishment of a local problem-solving model that subsequently was applied to other disaster and conflict situations.

Kosovo

In 2001, I led a team sent by the IFRC to evaluate a Red Cross program that had been functioning there for 2 years. This program contained several elements that are consistent with a community psychology orientation. These included decentralization, village outreach, use of paraprofessionals, and an emphasis on occupational training. The client participation, the sense of local ownership, and the occupational and educational functional emphasis all contributed to improvements in self-reliance, mobilization, and recovery orientation.

Thailand

More recently, in the spring of 2004, I conducted a psychosocial needs assessment for refugees from Burma living in camps along the Thai–Burmese border. Most of these refugees have been in camps for many years, resulting in a remarkable range of psychosocial needs and resources to address those needs. Perhaps most important was the excellent opportunity to utilize to a high degree refugee participation in the assessment process and plan development. These activities in themselves were "therapeutic" in several respects, allowing for ventilation, support, self-control, problem-solving, mobilization, recognition, pride, increased knowledge, and consensus building. Mild but pervasive depression, perhaps better termed malaise; domestic and gender-based violence; and psychosomatic disorders were the most prevalent conditions of concern.

The camps had notable strengths in family support, a sense of concern for one's neighbor, and strong self-help groups and political, educational, health, and religious institutions. A range of services was recommended on the basis of the assessment process, but the predominant service by far was to improve the number and variety of employment opportunities for the camp residents, both within and outside of the camps. There was consistent agreement among the camp residents, study participants, and external providers that employment improvement would have a dramatic effect on the primary areas of emotional concern. This was consequently recommended to become the main psychosocial intervention focus. Most other psychosocial interventions were deemed to best be provided through existing community systems, with community organization, education, and case and program consultation being provided to leadership, professional, paraprofessional, and voluntary persons in those systems.

A very reassuring thing to me was that the refugees interviewed not only were able to articulate and agree with the wisdom of helping people do well emotionally through normal, spontaneous, and socially desirable activities and institutions but also understood how many of those activities could have significant "therapeutic" benefit to those more seriously impaired—persons whom we would otherwise label with a *Diagnostic and Statistical Manual of Mental Disorders, Fourth Edition* diagnosis.

Conclusion

Writings on the definitional characteristics of community psychology have been around for several decades, but applying the principles involved has come along very slowly. Terms and concepts such as societal improvement, the good community, furthering normal development, natural and spontaneous healing systems, primary prevention, professional–community collaboration, multidisciplinary approaches, innovative research methodology, and applied psychology keep popping up. Newer concepts and terms of mobilization and community resiliency fit in well with these. Understanding not only the conceptual link between individual and society but also how to constructively intervene to improve human functioning and emotional well-being differentiates community psychology from social psychology. In addition, with a community psychology orientation, the self-defeating argument of whether or not conflict and disasters cause psychiatric disorders becomes less important because we find it more useful to identify postconflict and postdisaster psychosocial difficulties in functional and social terms and to intervene with them accordingly.

By incorporating influences from related disciplines, both within psychology (e.g., social, organizational, and developmental psychology) and from other relevant fields (e.g., social work, sociology, economics, education, and anthropology), community psychology offers the most comprehensive model for postdisaster psychosocial programming. This is not to say that international psychosocial work cannot be conducted successfully by some other approach. However, following careful consideration of the collective effect of disasters and the overwhelming needs facing psychosocial workers, the principle and practices of community psychology are undeniably well matched to the tasks.

References

Dodge, G. R. (2006). Assessing the psychosocial needs of communities affected by disaster. In G. Reyes & G. A. Jacobs (Eds.), *Handbook of international disaster psychology, Vol. 1. Fundamentals and overview*. Westport, CT: Praeger Publishers.

Edwards, S. (2002). Evaluating models of community psychology: Social transformation in South Africa. *International Journal of Behavioral Medicine, 9*, 301–308.

Iscoe, I. (1974). Community psychology and the competent community. *American Psychologist, 29*, 607–613.

Levine, M., & Perkins, D. V. (1997). *Principles of community psychology: Perspectives and applications* (2nd ed.). New York: Oxford University Press.

Litz, B. (Ed.). (2004). *Early intervention for trauma and traumatic loss*. New York: Guilford.

Mitchell, J. T. (1983). When disaster strikes . . . the critical incident stress debriefing process. *Journal of Emergency Medical Services, 8*, 36–39.

Paton, D., & Bishop, B. (1996). Disasters and communities: Promoting psychosocial wellbeing. In D. Paton & N. Long (Eds.), *Psychological aspects of disasters: Impact, coping and intervention* (pp. 255–268). Palmerston North: Dunmore.

Simonsen, L. F., & Reyes, G. (2003). *Community-based psychological support: A training manual*. Geneva: International Federation of Red Cross and Red Crescent Societies.

Stamm, B. H., & Friedman, M. J. (2000). Cultural diversity in the appraisal and expression of trauma (pp. 69-85). In A. Y. Shalev, R. Yehuda, & A. C. McFarlane (Eds.), *International handbook of human response to trauma*. Netherlands: Kluwer Academic.

Taylor, A. J. W. (2003).Cross-cultural interaction in the appraisal of disaster trauma in three Pacific Island countries. *Asia Pacific Viewpoint, 44*, 177–193.

Trickett, E. J. (1995). The community context of disaster and traumatic stress: An ecological perspective from community psychology. In S. E. Hobfoll and M. deVries (Eds.), *Extreme community stress: Impact and intervention*. The Hague: Martinus Nijhof.

———. (2003). *Mental health in emergencies: Mental and social aspects of populations exposed to extreme stressors*. Retrieved January 29, 2004, from http://www.who.int/ mental_health/media/en/640.pdf

World Health Organization (2005). *Single-session psychological debriefing: Not recommended*. Retrieved July 21, 2005, from http://www.who.int/hac/techguidance/pht/ 13643.pdf

CHAPTER 5

ASSESSING THE PSYCHOSOCIAL NEEDS OF COMMUNITIES AFFECTED BY DISASTER

Gordon R. Dodge

Rationale for Conducting Psychosocial Needs Assessments

Why bother with assessing psychosocial needs? Why not just get in there and do whatever you think is best to do? How can you stand back and just gather information when it is obvious that people need your services? Sorry to say, but that kind of thinking is simply wrong. Although there may be a few very specific and circumscribed incidents that warrant an immediate international disaster mental health response without a formal needs assessment (e.g., a mass-casualty plane crash with a multinational passenger manifold), in virtually all disasters involving potential international intervention, an assessment is essential. Before stating the most important reasons for needs assessment I want to clarify that quality assessment is ongoing in principle, and in a major disaster, there typically is a need for several formally written needs assessment reports over the course of the disaster.

Perhaps the most important reason to conduct a needs assessment is that our understanding of what likely are useful interventions to use following disasters is at a rudimentary level, especially in non-Western cultural settings. Without identifying the needs as precisely as possible, we run the risk of providing relatively ineffective or possibly counterproductive services. Correspondingly, without precise definition of needs and subsequent interventions, we are not able to determine what has been helpful, and thus are not able to continue to increase our knowledge and professional skills. Even if research is not to be part of a program, an evaluation should always be included, and good evaluation is dependent on, an accurate objective needs assessment.

Applying the most appropriate and sufficient services, as identified through needs assessment procedures, is dependent on financial, personnel, and other resources. Donors and others who make expenditure decisions have a right and responsibility to assign limited funds in as effective a manner as possible. Similarly, both within organizations as well as with cooperative interorganizational planning and response, recruiting and assigning the best staff available are key to effectiveness. There is the potential need for a wide range of skills in psychosocial services, and choosing the most appropriate personnel is dependent on adequate needs assessment procedures. No one professional or single organization is most competent across all potential helpful psychosocial interventions following a disaster.

There still is considerable misunderstanding and skepticism among humanitarian organization administrators and policy-makers regarding psychosocial services. Given the infancy and complexity of the field this is understandable, and even helpful to methodological improvement. This uncertainty, however, often results in disagreements on what to do and in delays and decisions based more on personal bias and politics than effectiveness. Well-conducted needs assessments help reduce these unfortunate influences and, in turn, can improve organizational professionalism and administrative effectiveness.

A caution and reminder is in order at this point because the reader may tend to think that considerable time and expense are necessary to conduct an adequate and useful needs assessment, thus possibly defeating the same effective interventions one may have identified as most appropriate to the needs. We now have methods of rapid, time-sensitive, and cost-efficient psychosocial needs assessment available, with sufficient accuracy in most disaster situations to make well-founded program planning decisions. These methods will be addressed in depth later in this chapter.

Qualifications

Several factors will influence which qualifications are necessary for a person or persons to conduct a psychosocial needs assessment. Typically, within a few days following a disaster, an organization will gather basic information that, in turn, may prompt an in-depth psychosocial needs assessment. That initial data gathering does not require a specialized person as long as the organization has people on its fact-finding team who are cross-trained, and there are specific indicators that will prompt the request for a psychosocial needs assessment. Second, as will be discussed later, there often is a need for more than one assessment over the course of responding to a disaster, and each assessment may require at least a differing emphasis of qualifications. Certainly, if an organization has a policy on what types of services it will be willing to offer in response to a disaster, this will influence who will be most qualified to conduct an assessment. For example, if an organization will only consider offering short-term crisis interventions, then a person with skills in identifying longer-term organizational development needs may not be necessary. I will now provide a summary of qualifications needed across psychosocial needs assessment assignments, with advisement to the reader that not all personnel will always need all of these qualifications, depending on some of the above and related factors. Also, it is important to keep in mind that two or three people may be assigned to conduct an assessment to save time as well as increase comprehensiveness, and a balance on the team may be possible to more broadly cover the qualifications desired.

A person must be able to handle at least three or four weeks of hardship conditions. These may include lengthy travel by plane and vehicle, limited housing and food accommodations, long work hours, adverse weather, safety and security concerns, and witnessing and responding to physical and psychological trauma. Although when one is assigned to conduct a needs assessment there is little time to provide any direct services, exceptions will typically occur, and one will need to provide some psychological service to beneficiaries as well as staff. Keep in mind that doing so also provides some useful needs assessment information and serves as an educational as well as trust-building step in the early stages of disaster response.

Good overall communication skills are essential, both written and oral, as well as being able to work in group and cooperative efforts. Especially in early phases of disaster response, staff need to share resources and pitch in to take care of basic facilities, accommodation, and equipment needs. Also, being in effective close cooperation with our local counterparts and other organizations' staff is essential.

Some grounding in cultural awareness, respect, and understanding is essential, especially on international assignments. Education in anthropology, sociology, geography, economics, and comparative religions all are helpful in this regard. Obviously we cannot be fully versed in all of these disciplines, but basic subject knowledge is important because of its relevance to understanding local mental health needs and subsequent effective interventions. Hopefully, one's organization provides background information on the locale where one is assigned, but that does not always occur, and sufficient knowledge of relevant cultural factors and the ability to correctly gather that information while on assignment are critical. It is important to take the initiative in gathering information to improve your understanding of the principles, policies, structure, and services of the organization that you are representing. This is especially true if the organization offers a variety of services and if the potential to provide psychosocial services may be in cooperation with or even through one or more of the other organizational services, such as health or social welfare.

Basic skills in needs assessment, planning, research and evaluation, and program development are needed. There may be particular assessment and planning formats that the organization for which one is working requires to be used as a matter of administrative uniformity and decision making. Sometimes prior training in these formats is necessary. Evaluation design skills are important because it is best for the person conducting the needs assessment to present baseline information in ways that can be measured to determine program effectiveness. If certain program services are antici- pated, the person conducting the assessment is expected to draft the plans for those services. This is usually done in cooperation with administrative staff in one's own organization, local counterparts, and other agencies. Thus, planning skills are crucial. In some situations the person conducting the assessment and planning may also be asked to initiate the program and to provide leadership at least until other staff can be hired. This both helps to ensure continuity of effort and facilitates prompt implementation of services.

Awareness of research and program literature on disaster mental health methodology with an emphasis on international and cross-cultural applica- tions is of course essential to psychosocial assessment and planning. Without knowledge of what has been effective and what has not across a variety of circumstances and settings, the plan that is most likely to succeed cannot be developed, and there is no one correct response to all psychosocial need sit- uations. Similarly, one needs to know the literature on psychosocial needs assessment itself, as well as having associated knowledge of predictors of short- and long-term postdisaster mental health outcomes.

Yet someone might be told what information to gather without needing to know why because our field is not so precise as to be able to decide if, what, how, and how much should be done by some predetermined formula. In addition to adequate background knowledge, hands-on experience in disas- ter mental health work on a large-scale basis is important, to know what may work from a practical point of view. Clinical skills are also helpful because we are looked to for those and at times may have to apply them in crisis sit- uations, even if that is not the primary intent of our assignment. Readers may note that training in a major mental health discipline (e.g., psychology, psychiatry, and social work) has not been mentioned as being necessary. That is because, although any one of these backgrounds could be important, without the above-mentioned skills, none of them are sufficient. Indeed, rigid adherence to disciplines and their doctrines is typically an impediment to conducting a useful needs assessment.

Often an expectation of involvement by an external organization is that assistance will be provided to local agencies for capacity building. This is another aspect of needs assessment that typically requires some attention in initial assessments, but more so in later months. If capacity building is possi- bly going to be part of the services provided, then the person conducting the needs assessment will benefit from having organizational development skills. Often that is not a background available in mental health professions, so a team or collaborative approach typically is required to address this assessment need. It is very important, however, to note that the assessment process itself is part of capacity development as well as a useful method of mobilization. As a consequence, conducting the assessment with an empha- sis on participation to the greatest extent possible by the beneficiaries is highly recommended and constructive. This has to be balanced out with the realization that the beneficiaries, as well as responding organizations, are already very busy, especially in the emergency phase, and time involved in assessments can add to burdensome and already hectic demands.

Foreign language skills are obviously helpful, but many of the most widely known languages are not always the primary or even secondary local language in a disaster context. If we are able to identify local interpreters in those countries who are also capable in human relations skills we can often be even more effective in our needs assessment work than when trying to struggle along by ourselves with a less-than-fluent grasp of the language. Sometimes we are lucky enough to be working with a local professional counterpart who also knows English, or another language in which we are also fluent, and this may be the most ideal arrangement. This is not to minimize the importance of knowing sociological, meaning, and cultural variation aspects of languages, especially if we intend to do any questionnaire work or to develop educational materials for local use. The upshot is that there are constructive ways of working around language limitations, and fluency in the local language is not an essential qualification for conducting an effective needs assessment.

When to Conduct a Psychosocial Needs Assessment

Several conditions need to be considered before a decision to conduct a psychosocial needs assessment can be made at all, much less when and where to begin. The organization considering the possibility of conducting the assessment must be in a position to provide interventions based on the assessment results. Similarly, knowing what types of interventions are within the organization's mandate, budget capabilities, and interest will directly influence when and how a needs assessment is conducted. For example, one organization may only be available to provide short-term emergency phase services, whereas another organization may have a mission of providing community restoration or reconciliation services; obviously these two sets of circumstances will dictate not only when to conduct an assessment but also how to go about doing it. Safety and security considerations as well as the availability of external and local personnel and other resources will also influence when an assessment is conducted. With due consideration of these issues, a sequential decision-making process can determine the proper timing for conducting a needs assessment.

When a major disaster prompts an international response, most organizations that typically provide one or more emergency-phase services will quickly send an initial assessment team to gather basic information and arrange for the provision of services, as indicated. Often these teams are cross-trained so that, regardless of individual discipline, information is gathered for decision making in several functions such as health, housing, food, and water and sanitation. Other organizations may have a narrower focus but will follow a similar initial procedure. With regard to decisions on emergency phase psychosocial intervention, some basic information can be gathered in this assessment phase, even if the personnel involved are not of a mental health background. Details of this basic, first-phase, psychosocial assessment will be described in greater depth later in this chapter, but such information as the number of deaths, cause of the disaster, local and other international resources available, and whether or not there is a local request for services will provide the basis for deciding whether or not a more in-depth psychosocial needs assessment should be conducted.

To my knowledge, no organization that provides international services in response to a disaster uniformly includes either an in-depth psychosocial assessment or psychosocial services in all or even most disasters to which it responds. It is worth noting, however, that when the American Red Cross activates its national team for domestic disasters, a mental health component is always included. This approach results in the planning and implementation of psychosocial services within hours of the team's activation. The assessment and intervention functions of such a team are designed to be closely intertwined. Many other national Red Cross or Red Crescent societies, as well as other humanitarian organizations, are increasingly offering psychosocial services to their own affected citizens. Correspondingly, they will be able to conduct their own needs assessments with timing and methods that are appropriate to those organizations' roles and structures. Although this chapter is written primarily from an international response perspective, many of the same principles and recommendations for organizational and professional development likely can be applied to local and national responses.

If psychosocial services might be provided in the emergency phase, then a needs assessment should be conducted as soon as possible. Ideally, an assessment person or team would arrive no later than one week after the decision to begin has been made. If a team is to be involved, it is best to have all members start at the same time and travel to the site together, thus establishing roles and working relationships from the beginning. However, if assembling the team before departure results in counterproductive delays, one member of the team certainly can be dispatched early and can get started. In addition to this arrangement allowing an earlier completion of the assessment, having a member of the team arriving later often allows that person to stay on longer, providing an opportunity for continuity of services into the program development phase. An example of how this has worked out to program development advantage is given later.

A psychosocial needs assessment in the early weeks of an emergency phase allows for timely decision making, hopefully coordination with other organizations involved, preparation for requests from donors, and early interventions, if that is what is indicated. Even if an agency does not expect to provide services until the rehabilitation phase, conducting an initial in-depth assessment still often is indicated, because obtaining approval, recruiting, developing materials, and establishing necessary agreements to implement programs often takes several months. Also, major funding decisions are usually made within a month or two following a disaster, thus necessitating prompt assessment and planning. It is important to recognize that, as major unexpected developments often occur following a disaster, longer-range plans requires more flexibility and adaptation.

Sometimes an initial program proposal will include long-range educational or organizational development services. If this is the case, then a later, more refined needs assessment specific to those goals is often helpful. This is for several reasons. First, during the first few weeks, especially of an emergency phase, local and national organizations with whom we may work on a long-range basis are not in a position to spend—nor are particularly interested in spending—much time identifying long-range organizational or educational needs, being more concerned with immediate postdisaster demands. Second, an accurate assessment of capacity building, organizational development, or community development requires considerable time and rather specialized expertise. The establishment of some general goals in these domains can likely be done in the initial assessment and planning, but an accurate assessment can only occur at a later stage; thus, it is important to allow for that later stage more in-depth needs assessment, usually somewhere midway into the rehabilitation phase. A psychosocial assessment of possible reconciliation interventions following conflict may even occur later.

The timing, then, for psychosocial needs assessment is dependent on many variables, as addressed above. The key principle in this regard is to be as flexible as possible both as to when, as well as how often, following a disaster, it will be best to conduct or reconduct a psychosocial needs assessment. We can now move on to discussion of where it is best to conduct a needs assessment.

Where Is It Best to Conduct a Needs Assessment?

Several principles will guide decisions about where to conduct the needs assessment and planning. Obviously, going to where the people are who have been most affected by the disaster is essential for accuracy, comprehensiveness, authenticity, and trust. If involvement of the affected population in its own recovery is a given premise, then being there is required. Similarly, if part of the process is to partner with a local counterpart, then there is no better way than to be there with that person. If another premise is that providing some crisis and emergency services while conducting the assessment is helpful not only to the recipient of the services but also to other responders, then all the more reason to be with those affected. Also, if the information-gathering model involves using staff from other service functions, it is necessary to work well and closely with those personnel and to value their contributions.

The assessment team should gather as much information as possible before traveling from home or their place of origin. As a consequence, determining the "where" of an assessment will require a succession of informational contacts and typically includes stopping off at a national or international headquarters before heading to the disaster site. Similarly, there may be some final information gathering, planning, and reporting to be completed after your work at the disaster site, back at the national or international headquarters, and anticipating as well as scheduling those return visits is helpful.

The psychosocial assessment team often finds it best to base out of an organization's on-site headquarters. This allows for cooperative information gathering and planning as well as sharing of resources. Communication with other staff and other organizations during the assessment and planning stages is critical, and having a base site expedites this need. Cell phones have reduced reliance on a central communications base, but in the emergency phase, cell phone systems are often not functioning reliably yet. Assessment staff also need places to eat and sleep, and in international response, those resources will often be in the same physical setting or compound as the headquarters facility.

Many crisis situations will result in displaced or refugee populations, so one will of course go to where those people are, even if that is not the site where the disaster originated. Sometimes both circumstances will be present, where some people are living in or proximate to the disaster site while others have moved a significant distance away. Depending on the organization's mission, both settings may need to be visited. This also depends, of course, on safety, security, and access factors. Often, especially in conflict situations, an assessment is not able to be provided in the locales where conflict still is occurring. This presents a timing as well as a location challenge because assessment and planning likely will need to be conducted for the displaced or refugee population, as well as, at some time, for the areas directly affected by the disaster and the remaining and returning populations. Again, flexibility and expectation of change is essential.

Some time typically will also need to be spent at the offices of other state- and national-level agencies and organizations. This may include ministries of health or education, national offices of humanitarian and religious organizations, universities, and international organization offices in the affected country. As a consequence, at least a couple of trips will occur between the disaster site and state and national capitals, during both the assessment as well as planning stages.

It is conceivable that a coordinated assessment could be conducted between an outside consultant experienced and trained in that process and an in-country counterpart. This might work in conflict situations in which e-mail is functioning and there is a professional staff person locally who is still able to work in the affected country. This may not be as ideal as the on-site model, but it is perhaps the best that can be done under severe security restrictions or budget limitations.

What Information Do You Need to Gather?

One would think that a standard set of questions and boxes to fill in would uniformly apply to a well-conducted psychosocial needs assessment. A few protocols have been developed that are consistent with that concept, and later in the chapter I will provide a protocol model that I have designed and applied constructively in international disaster settings. However, several factors will influence what is the most important information to gather, how to find that information, and how to evaluate and present the findings.

In the ideal world, following a major international disaster there would be one group or organization identified to conduct the necessary psychosocial needs assessment and to provide that information to all other humanitarian organizations involved for their planning purposes. Many of your basic questions may be asked and answered by others. As a consequence, some of the first information one gathers is the names of other nongovernmental organizations (NGOs) and agencies involved, locations, contact persons, and so on. United Nations High Commissioner for Refugees, the World Health Organization, and governmental agencies typically provide useful basic information, but data more specific to accurate psychosocial planning are not usually available, especially in the emergency phase. Information sharing among NGOs, however, is improving, and this helps greatly. It is important to know whether a coordination forum has been established for sharing information, and if not, to establish as effective an intergroup communication system as soon possible.

Other important influences on the information one will choose to gather are the scope, mission, and service emphases of the sponsoring agency. For example, if the organization you are representing will be limiting its services to children in conjunction with educational programs, you will not want to bother gathering much information on needs and services for vulnerable adults. That information may be critical for another agency, and your awareness of their emphasis will be valuable for comprehensive response coordination, but you can concentrate on gathering information consistent with service possibilities. This principle may be obvious, but it is not uncommon for assessment personnel to be needlessly diverted to nonessential activities because of scheduling ambiguities, confusion, and well-intended requests or suggestions.

Many organizations have a generic assessment and planning format to be used across functions. This is very helpful for administrative coordination, monitoring, and evaluation. Being well acquainted with that format before starting the psychosocial needs assessment will guide the form and content of your information gathering. Similarly, you will want and usually have what is called a "terms of reference," which will specify what you will be expected to accomplish in the needs assessment and how you will be permitted to carry this out. This should be well enough written to aid you in knowing what is most important to emphasize in your assessment activities, and you should be invited to comment on the feasibility of the terms before acceptance. It is the most essential document guiding your work. Ideally the policy and practice applicable to any potential needs assessment an organization may conduct will be preestablished; but the reality is that such agreement is often negotiated in a rushed and incomplete manner at a stopover at headquarters before heading overseas.

What we already know based on theory, literature, and clinical and community competence will influence our information gathering. Professional and scientific credentials are important for effective needs assessment as well as planning. For example, if we know the relative effect of severity and types of disasters, or identifiable support systems, we will be able to focus and prioritize our information gathering. This is one reason why there is still considerable disagreement over what information to gather. We do not know with a high degree of accuracy the best identifiers of psychosocial damage or predictors of outcome, or correspondingly the most beneficial methods of intervention. It is easier to determine how many tents or cooking kits an affected population may need. The room for error in psychosocial assessment and planning is large, so it is all the more important to be well grounded in what is known as well as what is not known. It is also correspondingly important that we explain and defend the need for professional judgment in the psychosocial needs assessment process, so that information gathering is as accurate and correctly weighted as possible. A "fill in the boxes" protocol may give you some useful base data, but correct interpretation of that data is essential for a well-conducted assessment.

Ethics also influence what we ask and how we ask questions. There are basic humanitarian worker ethics, often additional organizational principles of behavior, and professional ethics to apply. Privacy, respect, and autonomy ethics certainly need to shape and limit our assessment methods. Asking intrusive questions can be harmful and should not be done unless the information to be gathered through these questions is essential to the needs assessment and planning and the person feels fully free to decline being interviewed. Such probing and personal questions should also only be asked if there are psychosocial services available at that time to help the person being interviewed. Furthermore, a psychosocial needs assessment can be as or more effectively conducted without using individual screening or assessment procedures and is more culturally respectful when performed in this manner. This is especially appropriate in the emergency phase planning; if a program will involve longer-term rehabilitation and sufficient services can be in place at that time, individual symptom-based screenings may be conducted, with certain limitation.

The section later in this chapter addressing needs assessment protocols will examine the types of information that are important to gather under most circumstances. However, the responsible and competent assessment team will have a good understanding of the above principles before designing the assessment format they will use for any given disaster.

What Psychosocial Materials to Take Along

The key here is what type of assessment you will be conducting, it being primarily based on the present phase of development and what services will realistically be considered. You will likely limit yourself to how much you can carry on the plane, so tough choices have to be made. In emergency phase assessments, unfortunately, you have little time to read up on much before you leave. The sponsoring agency may be able to e-mail you some situational reports, and you can download basic country-wide information from the CIA Web site or other sources. Try to obtain relevant maps, a basic language book, and a book on the history and culture of the country if you are not well acquainted with that information, and in general assume that it is your responsibility to orient yourself to country, culture, conflict, and other basic information. You will have some time to read on the plane and while waiting for your visa. This material will also serve as a good reference library while you are on assignment.

Specific psychosocial material may also be needed. If the assignment is for an emergency-phase assessment and planning, consider bringing the following: assessment protocol, disaster psychology literature summaries, relevant cultural summaries if available, and basic handouts for beneficiaries, staff, and local professionals. If your planning will depend on using specific incidence and probability estimates, be sure to bring those references along. Keep in mind that assessment and planning will be your primary responsibility, but that you may also be expected to and wish to provide some crisis intervention as well as limited educational services to staff and beneficiaries. Doing so can be helpful to an effective assessment and initial service and capacity development, as well as for establishing trust, cooperation, and authenticity, as mentioned earlier. If you are going out as part of a team, you can certainly discuss among yourselves who can bring what, so you end up with the necessary minimal psychosocial supplies while avoiding duplication. It is best if you bring material that you may want to have duplicated on disk, as well as hard copies. You likely will not have time to have material translated before you leave, but knowledge beforehand of what professional material already has been properly translated is a professional responsibility. After learning the hard way, I have also in more recent years learned to take along a few summary handouts on psychosocial services for inclusion in press releases.

The sponsoring agency will inform you of what the conditions and accommodations will be like, what personal items to bring, and what office supplies and electronics will be available for use. Be sure to check to see whether you will have access to e-mail, a portable computer, and mobile telephones. Often in early assessment days these may not be immediately available, but may be there in a week or so. If you bring your own electronics, be sure you have the correct adapters and voltage converters. The personal items lists issued by the sponsoring agencies are very helpful. Also, consider bringing basic writing materials, a small calculator, a headlamp, and a personal journal. A "light-reading" paperback and a small short-wave radio can be quite relaxing during short breaks and before going to sleep at night, even after a typical 16-hour workday.

What Can One Expect to Occur during the Assessment and Planning Period?

Clearly there is no one list of expectations consistent with all or even most psychosocial needs assessment assignments. This section identifies the usual steps involved in many international psychosocial needs assessment assignments. Descriptions of selected assignments and the recommended protocol, provided later in this chapter, will hopefully promote fuller understanding.

Standing Agreement

Whether an employee of, consultant to, or volunteer for an organization, typically there is an agreement of likely availability of a mental health professional to conduct a needs assessment should the need arise. Most agencies now have such arrangements established, based on competence, interest, and often prior working relationships. If an emergency-phase assessment may be needed, larger agencies may have a roster of professionals available at short notice with such commitment perhaps for two or three months each year. Other agencies, if they have psychosocial staff already providing psychosocial services on another project, may draw those people off for a short-term assessment assignment. These prior agreements allow for more timely response by qualified staff and cause less confusion and disruption than clamoring for someone at the last moment.

Preparation

Previous sections have addressed what qualifications are needed as well as what one takes along—both of these areas being aspects of preparation. Having existing personal and professional matters in order is the other major preparation consideration. Most of these are obvious, such as having as much as possible up to date, including who will take care of your personal and professional responsibilities while you are gone, and that there is an understanding and hopefully agreement and support for your pending assignment with those people most important to you in your life. Distraction and damage can occur without these preparatory steps. It is also helpful, but not always possible, to have some plan for periodic contact with family and place of employment while you are away. In the absence of this, at least emergency contact information should be in place.

Initial Team Coordination

If you are going to be part of an assessment team, then communication among team members before leaving home is helpful, especially if you have not worked together before. Typically, a team leader will be identified by the sponsoring agency or agencies, and that person will contact the other members to establish schedule, roles, and team expectations. Most of this will be worked out when the team gets together, but these initial e-mail or telephone contacts are extremely helpful. Also, if the plan is for team members to be arriving on-site at different times, then it is even more important to have prior communication.

Administrative Briefings

Usually, before the individual consultant or assessment team heads out to the disaster site, there will be an administrative briefing, typically at a national headquarters or an international organization site. This briefing will provide for the establishment of a contract or terms of reference, orientation to the assignment, travel and accommodation arrangements, health and visa clearances, equipment issuance, communication arrangements and contact information. If more than one organization is sponsoring the needs assessment, then a similar briefing may occur at the second organization, especially if that stop is convenient to time and travel limitations. The team will usually convene at one of these administrative sites. Occasionally, time and logistics do not allow for these face-to-face administrative briefings. In this case, matters will be handled as well as possible by phone, fax, and e-mail, and you will travel directly to the disaster site.

Travel to Disaster Site

The travel time allows for some additional preparation reading, team assessment planning, and rest, if you adapt quickly to time zone changes and sleep well on airplanes. If not, and if you will have been awake for too many hours, it might be prudent to get eight hours of sleep at a hotel where your plane lands before trying to put in a first full day of work without adequate rest or beginning what might be a long, rough road trip. Anticipation, adrenaline, and just wanting to get started tend to interfere with sensible self-care at these times, so it is important to know your capacity and pace yourself accordingly. The assignment will necessitate a healthy diet as well as adequate sleep.

On-Site Orientation

Typically, if you are part of an organization that is offering several services, there will be someone in charge of logistics and a head of delegation, and perhaps a health officer with whom you will meet on arrival. Your terms of reference may have already arrived by fax, so in the best of worlds there will be a general sense of what you will need and what you will be doing. If you are on assignment for a small organization, then you may be the first on the scene from that organization, but hopefully you will have someone designated to orient you and assist you in getting started. More often than not, however, because everyone is so busy, you will need to request and advocate for what will be necessary for you to get started, such as a vehicle, accommodations, and an interpreter. If you have a local professional counterpart who is also fluent in your primary language, this can be immensely helpful. You can also do well with an interpreter who has good local knowledge and good human relationship communication skills, such as a teacher or health care professional. Ideally, for mobilization and capacity-building purposes, if your interpreter can also be your local organizational counterpart, you will have a head start on these objectives. Occasionally, drivers can also serve as interpreters, but usually it will be better to have both if you have that option.

Gathering On-Site Information

The information-gathering phase is explicitly addressed in the protocol section, and many of the principles discussed above also apply here. A practical first step is to identify and, if possible, meet with others who may already have gathered or have easy access to some of the information you need. Also, if you are working with a local counterpart, that person will need to participate in the information-gathering process decisions and can be extremely helpful. Although it can at times be cumbersome, the more extensive the participation of the beneficiaries in input, planning, and decision making, the better.

Another key principle is to be flexible, allow for changes and delays, and have backup plans for when trips and meetings need to be postponed or canceled. Knowing from the beginning what methods of information gathering are culturally acceptable or not is also an initial responsibility. Correspondingly, because of cultural, linguistic, and logistic limitations, it is important to be ready to have more than one method available to obtain the information you need, and certainly to know what is the most important information to gather. The relative importance of data will vary significantly from disaster to disaster. It is presumed that the assessment team will have the disaster psychology knowledge and experience base to decide as accurately as possible what information is the most important to obtain for assessment and planning purposes, given the specific characteristics of the disaster on hand. The protocol discussion will identify the generally most important areas of information to gather.

Intervention Planning

Intervention planning begins from the first day but is refined as information is gathered. It is a narrowing-down and selection process from a range of possibilities known to be helpful following disasters. Some possibilities will be eliminated because they fall outside of the organization's mandate, others may be culturally unacceptable or not feasible from expenditure or logistic considerations, and many services will be provided by other local, national, or international resources. Furthermore, circumstances change rapidly and significantly, so good planning will have sufficient flexibility to adjust to these changes. What if another typhoon hits soon, or the refugee population is able to move back home, or expected funding from another concerned government is not granted for a complementary project? The challenge then is to be as precise and as accurate as possible in planning under often confusing, changing, and sometimes conflicting and politically charged circumstances. Emergency-phase planning requires the greatest expertise, whereas interventions developed at later stages are able to be less exact and are not as subject to confounding influences.

Report Development

The sponsoring agency may well have an assessment and planning format with which you will need to work. Your report may even be incorporated into a larger comprehensive health or social welfare services proposal, especially if the intent is to channel psychosocial services through other functions. It is best to find out before traveling to the disaster site what report format is expected, as well as the timetable for reporting. It is also helpful to know whether you will have administrative advisement available when considering staffing, materials, and expenditure aspects of your intervention plans; whether you will be able to turn that portion over to someone else totally; or whether these aspects will be primarily your responsibility. Another key variable in intervention planning is knowing whether there will be a significant delay in approval, recruiting, and initiation of the plan. Some planning allows for smooth transition into implementation, but others require weeks or even months before something can happen. Obviously, this will significantly influence what is recommended.

Report Writing and Presentation

If the report writing is a cooperative effort with a local agency, another international organization, or both, then establish early on what everyone's review and revision roles and responsibilities are. If an assessment team is dispatched, typically the team leader has had prior experience with at least some of this process and will usually be the principle guide and author. I also suggest the reading of completed psychosocial needs assessment reports from previous agency assignments.

In addition to knowing the expected format and timetable, understanding the interests, background, and responsibilities of the readers and audiences will guide your report development. Typically, I find it helpful and often expected to have an executive summary and certain appendices, attachments, and references available. These may include reports in support of your findings and recommendations, educational or other intervention models, recruitment and staffing suggestions, descriptions of highly relevant local programs or characteristics, suggested evaluation design, and the like. To the extent that many of the decision makers and other initial readers of your report will not be mental health professionals, terminology should be chosen accordingly. At a later stage, you may wish to develop a more professional or scientific presentation or paper. The key is to provide sufficiently objective and understandable information that supports the identified needs and the appropriateness of your recommended interventions.

There may be several stages or levels of report presentation, comment, revision, and approval opportunity. The sponsoring organization will typically have periodic discussions during the planning process to advise what likely will be feasible and supported from an administrative position, and there may be opportunities to e-mail or fax initial drafts to that organization's potential decision makers. On the local, state, and national levels of the disaster-involved country, if any group or organization is likely to be involved in the program implementation, they should be provided an opportunity for a review before the team leaves the affected country. Timetable and resource limitations may necessitate that these initial presentations are in outline and oral format, with a full report to be completed later and at a different site.

Assessment and planning reports are sometimes written in the field, at some quiet place removed from the disaster site, or back at the headquarters of the sponsoring agency. There are advantages and disadvantages of each arrangement, and circumstances may dictate which setting to use. This should be determined to the extent possible before traveling to the disaster site, but again flexibility is necessary. If there is an option of spending a day or two in some quiet place away from both the disaster site and national or international headquarters, this can allow the best setting for report writing. When the report is complete, it is then usually presented in writing and in conference with decision makers at the national and international headquarters of sponsoring agencies. In turn, that organization may present the plan, in an abbreviated form, at a donor or interorganizational coordination meeting. Opportunities may arise at a later time to present the findings at a professional forum or in an article or journal format, thus hopefully advancing the knowledge and resources of interested disciplines.

Relevant Personal Experiences in Psychosocial Needs Assessment

This section briefly describes psychosocial needs assessments that I have conducted, along with the most important lessons learned from those assignments. Each instance has had its own differences and specific demands, so it should be noted that "best practices" in some settings may be counterproductive in others. Most of the variable influences in this regard have been mentioned earlier. Please keep those in mind as you read through the assignment descriptions below.

The first international psychosocial needs assessment assignment that I took on was identifying the mental health needs of humanitarian NGO staff in the former Yugoslavia during its recent war, requiring that I travel there between 1991 and 1996. This involved assignments in Slovenia, Croatia, Bosnia, Serbia, and Macedonia, interviewing and consulting with indigenous and ex-patriot staff. I will not present my general findings from those assignments here, as that is of a different focus and is available for review elsewhere (Dodge, 1998). What I primarily learned was that identifying staff needs and effective means of meeting those needs is relevant to most, if not all, assessment assignments, as maintaining emotionally healthy staff is essential to the success of the services being offered. Well-developed interviewing skills, especially in being able to establish trust and in being flexible with the process, are critical. The assessment process and its results need to be important to the people you are interviewing for you to obtain sufficient cooperation. Be sure to share your findings with those you interviewed. Take the time to become acquainted with each organization's culture and characteristics. There are differences in what is helpful to indigenous and expatriate staff. Perception of greatest needs will vary significantly among persons involved even in the same setting. The obvious is not always the most important, and differences between natural disaster- and war-related effects also became much more apparent to me.

The next international psychosocial needs assessment was in response to the Kosovo crisis. I was assigned by the American Red Cross to join two other team members from the Danish Red Cross, and we were coordinated through the International Federation of the Red Cross. This occurred in April and May of 1999, and the focus was to identify and plan for the psychosocial needs of the refugee population who had left and were continuing to leave Kosovo. This was an early emergency-phase assignment, but with the expectation that there was the possibility of some short-term as well as longer-range planning for the refugee population. I learned several additional important assessment lessons from this assignment. Having an assessment team, with its members of differing background and skills, provides for more advantages than disadvantages than does conducting the assessment by oneself. However, the team needs sufficient time before being in the thick of it to establish an effective working relationship, because support, consensus, and trust within a team will be thoroughly tested in such intense assignments. We were very fortunate in this regard—I have seen other assessment teams in misery being rendered ineffective because of internal maladaptive behavior. To the extent possible, choose your teammates wisely.

Another lesson from the Kosovo assignment is that one needs to be self-reliant and sufficiently assertive to get work done in a thorough and timely manner. This applies not only to arranging interviews, meetings, and field trips but also with such basics as obtaining accommodations or a vehicle. This does not mean that patience, flexibility, and good humor are not also important, just that assessment work is not for the timid. Similarly, although the sponsoring agency is supposed to address safety and security matters, this is somewhat relative and many matters are not predictable. Be responsible for your own safety, but be able to tolerate the effects of disaster and war, or even thrive on some degree of hardship and danger. Actually, a self-selection process seems to take place among those involved in disaster work, and most responders in these settings are quite resilient and are able to work long, hard hours under hardship conditions even for several weeks. Knowing how to pace yourself while adapting to difficult and unfamiliar conditions is a crucial skill. Later-stage assessments are typically less intense and demanding.

An important lesson learned from the Kosovo assignment is that assessment and planning has to have contingencies. We developed what was regarded as a good plan for the refugee population with the understanding that services would be able to be implemented within a few weeks, and that most of the beneficiaries would still be in refugee camps and with host families in Albania. As it turned out, about the time services were ready to be initiated, the refugees were able to return to Kosovo, and a reassessment of needs and planning had to occur to provide relevant services in Kosovo itself. Much of this was unavoidable, but in hindsight we should have included an "in the event that" section in the plan to readily allow adaptive changes to be implemented.

Probably the most important outcome from the Kosovo assignment with regard to the purpose of this chapter is that it afforded an excellent opportunity for the beginnings of the development of a psychosocial needs assessment protocol, at least for emergency-phase involvement. Too many times documents are drafted from an armchair view without being tempered by experience. With no protocol to go by, we fashioned our own and found it highly beneficial to take advantage of real-life experiences. These often prove the best beginnings of useful guidelines because there is a necessary grounding in reality.

The next international needs assessment assignment also involved a conflict situation, but it was one of terrorism rather than all-out war. This was in response to the bombing of the American embassy in Nairobi. Another variation with this assignment was that my initial trip was a year after the bombing occurred. The request was to assess the overall mental health interventions that were occurring under a USAID program and to provide training and consultation consistent with the system development needs at that stage of intervention. Focusing on organizational capacity, interorganizational relationships, staff competencies, and documentation were a larger part of the assessment than is seen in emergency-phase assignments. Being able to assess the longer-term effects of such an incident, with all of the economic, political, dependency, and compensation ramifications, also became more apparent to me, and I realized that awareness and some planning for those influences are important at earlier stages, but that often a formal reassessment a year or two into a long-term project is still highly helpful. What also struck home to me on this assignment was the importance of identifying the psychosocial effects as best as possible in terms of how they interfere with daily functioning. Emphasizing clinical symptomology is often inadequate and culturally unacceptable. In my return trip to Nairobi six months later, we had the opportunity to work on locally acceptable descriptions of functioning in urban and rural settings, so that more practical measurement of improvements could be made.

The next major international psychosocial needs assessment assignment was in response to the Gujarat earthquake in India. This occurred in January 2001 and killed more than 20,000 people. By this time, I had completed a review of literature regarding psychosocial assessment (Dodge, 2000a) and had developed a *Protocol for a Rapid Psychosocial Needs Assessment* at the request of the American Red Cross, International Services Department. This allowed me an excellent opportunity to field test the protocol in an early emergency-phase mass casualty setting, and we found that the protocol served us very well, in terms of both assessment process as well as content of findings and recommendations. One potential complication that ended up being beneficial happened when I arrived at the disaster site nine days before the other team member was able to arrive, by which time I had completed most of the data gathering and an initial draft of the recommendations. The newly arrived team member, however, was able to stay on several days after I completed my work, and this allowed him to more accurately identify mental health professionals who might become project staff and to refine some of our rural village needs and resource data. This suggested to me that a staggering of assessment, planning, and early-intervention staff can be workable. We certainly have effectively used that model in domestic disaster responses within the United States. Another advantage of this particular team member was that, as an Indian psychiatrist, he provided a complementary broadening of the team's knowledge and cultural insight.

Another important finding from this assignment was that use of competent local resources is essential. I was fortunate enough to have two local physicians available to me as drivers and interpreters. Because of the destruction of the local hospitals and clinics, they were not able to return to their practices yet, and had volunteered to the Indian Red Cross Society. They not only understood much of mental health terminology and concepts, and had excellent rapport skills for interpretation in survivor interviews, but also spoke English well, were well respected locally, and were well acquainted with local communities, resources, language, and culture. One cannot always be this lucky, but taking the time to try to obtain the best interpreter possible is highly recommended.

Managing one's time well is of course essential, especially in early-phase assessment with 14- to 16-hour workdays. I did find it helpful, though, to provide limited consultation and individual assessment on critical cases. From a needs assessment perspective, this provides a more in-depth understanding of some of the disaster effects, an understanding of who is really responding to mental health crisis needs, and an opportunity to begin establishing working relationships with the other disaster response services.

I also found in this assignment that it is best to learn how to write reports in the format requested by the sponsoring agency, as well as in a more traditional disaster psychology narrative form—the latter better serving discussion and justification of recommendation purposes. Because of this realization, some changes have occurred in how I now think it best to format an assessment narrative report, and this is outlined in the next section of the chapter. An example of that format use is the report we wrote for the Gujarat earthquake assessment and planning (Dodge & Jha, 2001).

My most recent psychosocial assessment and planning assignment was for the American Refugee Committee (Dodge, 2004). This involved working with Burmese refugees in three camps in Thailand not only to assess their current mental health needs but also for future planning, should they be repatriated back into Burma or resettled into another country. Because most of the camp residents had been refugees for a number of years, this allowed me the advantage of working with established indigenous as well as NGO resources and groups. In this setting, I came to better understand and appreciate the benefit and strength of active and full participation of the refugees themselves. In addition, this assignment demonstrated to me that needs as well as resources change significantly over time. The most meaningful lesson learned from this assignment for me was the feasibility and benefit of focusing on community and sociological models of assessment and intervention.

Certainly, domestic disaster psychosocial assessment experiences are helpful to international assignments, and the reader is encouraged to develop and draw on that work too. For all of the domestic disaster work that I have done, psychosocial assessment always plays some significant part. The key mass casualty domestic assignments that I have worked on were the Korean Airline crash in Guam and the World Trade Center attack in New York City, both of which I worked on in the early-emergency phase. Relative to psychosocial needs assessment, these two assignments helped me identify more accurately the similarities and differences of disaster effects relative to numbers and types of causalities, that one can conduct assessment and planning as well as oversee interventions at the same time, and that working with and through other staff, functions, and organizations is the most effective approach for all of these responsibilities. My domestic as well as international disaster work has consistently reassured me that my community psychology premises are well founded. I have seen the relevance of these principles in longer-term, recovery-phase domestic disaster work also. The most relevant personal example of this is likely when I conducted a needs assessment one year following the Red River Valley floods, with significant depression identified that was not very reachable through clinical resources, but better approached through community support and reintegration methods and systems.

Protocol Designs, Choices, and Uses

When I conducted a literature review before the development of a psychosocial assessment protocol a few years ago (Dodge, 2000a), I found no formalized protocol that was being used by any internationally involved organization. The most useful suggestions were found in Kalayjian's publication (1995), but as with most professional manuscripts, this had not been brought to the attention of administrative decision makers. This is not to say that there is no highly relevant literature available, and I strongly encourage anyone interested in conducting psychosocial assessments to stay current with a broad range of relevant articles and reports.

During the same time period that I was developing *A Protocol for a Rapid Psychosocial Needs Assessment* (Dodge, 2000b) for the American Red Cross International Services Department, others were pursuing similar objectives. The Disaster Mental Health Institute at the University of South Dakota was working with the International Federation of Red Cross and Red Crescent Societies and the World Health Organization to develop a "tool" for similar purposes, titled *Rapid Assessment of Mental Health Needs of Refugees, Displaced and Other Populations Affected by Conflict and Post-Conflict Situations* (Petevi, Revel, & Jacobs, 2001). Although the World Health Organization document was developed for conflict and postconflict situations, these two documents have many more similarities than differences. At the time of the writing of this chapter, I do not think that the World Health Organization "tool" has yet been field tested. Among the potential strengths of this document is an emphasis on gathering thorough information about the host communities, as well as on the refugee population.

For those unacquainted with participatory methods of assessment, the United Nations High Commissioner for Refugees has a useful publication. This is the *People-Oriented Planning at Work: Using POP to Improve UNHCR Programming* (Anderson, 1994). It is a basic workbook on refugee participation in problem identification and solution development that can be applied across a variety of service areas.

The protocol presented below is a modification of one developed for the American Red Cross International Services Department (Dodge, 2000b). That protocol was written to include explanations for what was important to include or exclude, and thus was presented in a narrative form rather than a checklist model, as the others mentioned above are. In this chapter, I do outline the protocol, but I limit it to a field assignment instrument, with the presumption that whoever may use it will be acquainted with the background information, concepts, and premises already presented in this chapter, and with disaster psychology principles and practices in general.

On the basis of the additional knowledge we have gained about psychosocial assessment and intervention over the past few years, we are in a better position to identify what are likely to be the more important areas to address in an assessment. The reader is cautioned that, although weighting of disaster assessment and intervention variables provides a rudimentary approximation of their relative importance, it must also be adjusted for all of the political, programmatic, policy, budgetary, and other influences referred to earlier. Nonetheless, the modified protocol below does highlight what usually are the most important variables to examine.

Another modification to the original protocol is the identification of key variables relevant to conflict situations, in addition to those necessary for non-conflict disasters. Most of the information to be gathered in both circumstances is the same, but there are some important differences in what to emphasize, as well as how to assess and plan. Depending on these variables and the information gathered, a more precise estimate of needs, based on predictive criteria, can be applied.

Most psychosocial assessment models used in the emergency phase do not include individual screening for psychological effects of disaster. Depending on what models of intervention are decided on for longer-term programs, however, some clinical or functioning-based screening instruments may be appropriate for participant selection and evaluation purposes. As always, this hinges on whether they are culturally acceptable. Discussion of potentially useful screening instruments is not included in this protocol because that selection and decision, although occasionally appropriate to program implementation purposes, is not necessary for psychosocial assessment and planning.

The protocol below also assumes that a disaster has occurred with sufficient damage or death to warrant a psychosocial assessment, and that there is potential to offer some level of psychosocial services. In most circumstances, the major initial psychosocial assessment will occur within the first month—perhaps even within the first week—but often two or even three weeks will have passed. Although the protocol below can constructively be used at a later phase of a disaster, its emphasis is on the above-stated context, and postrecovery assessment and planning will need to reoccur at a later time, and with greater emphasis on organizational capacity-building and sustainability variables.

It is also important to keep in mind the availability of certain specialized frameworks in the literature that can supplement a protocol under certain circumstances or be incorporated into a later-stage needs assessment. For example, if a later-stage intervention is being considered in a postconflict situation, the use of a conflict resolution analysis and predictor (e.g., Coleman, 2003) might also be used. In short, one size does not fit all.

Protocol for a Psychosocial Needs Assessment— Revised, 2004

Introduction

This protocol is an outline of the essential areas of information gathering and report writing. It is assumed that the user of this protocol has also read the previous portions of this chapter or is knowledgeable and experienced in the topics addressed in those pages. Areas that I consider to be of high importance are so identified, with the other areas still being of importance but perhaps needing less attention, especially under time constraints. Where the word "disaster" is used, it is assumed that this can include conflict situations.

A. Preparation questions:
    1. What is the purpose of the psychosocial needs assessment?
    2. Will you be conducting the assessment in conjunction with any other organization?
    3. What information-gathering methods will you be using?
    4. When does your assessment need to be completed, written, and presented, and to whom?
    5. In addition to reporting results, do you also need to present program recommendations?
    6. In what formats will your reports need to be written?
    7. How soon can you expect that program recommendations could be initiated?
    8. What are the likely program limitations in terms of duration, expenditure, and service models? (**highly important**)
    9. Do you have all of the essential reference information along for accurate assessment, analysis, prediction, and planning? (**highly important**)

B. Predisaster characteristics (Note, if this disaster involves refugees or internally displaced persons, then locale descriptions should include place or country of disaster as well as places where the survivors currently reside, and where they may reside in the future months.):
    1. Key sociopolitical, language, educational, economic, religious, and other cultural factors.
    2. Mental health resources, attitudes, knowledge and training levels, traditional approaches, leadership persons, and acceptability or otherwise of Western-style methodology, especially with grief, loss, and trauma experiences. (**highly important**)
    3. Cultural and political opinions, attitudes, and beliefs of the populations involved regarding trauma and disaster. (**highly important**)
    4. Prior disaster experiences of note, and if so how and to what extent the population affected responded and recovered.

C. Disaster characteristics:
    1. Nature and characteristics of the current disaster.
    2. Duration, proximity, and severity of the disaster for the identified population-dose effects. (**highly important**)

3. Number of deaths and serious injuries. (**highly important**)
4. If conflict related, a description of the nature and extent of threat of violence, torture, physical and sexual assault, and imprisonment, in terms of direct experience as well as witnessing.
5. Nature and extent of infrastructure and other resource losses, such as employment, schools, places of worship, governmental structures, community gathering places, and other supportive settings. (**highly important**)

D. Postdisaster characteristics (Note, in some conflict situations as well as in some natural disaster circumstances, acute disaster aspects may be ongoing. If such is the case, portions of this section and the one above become combined in description.):

1. Nature and characteristics of any residual disaster dynamics (e.g., aftershocks, number and percentage of homes destroyed, famine, civil unrest).
2. Level of basic needs being met. Include here a description of the degree of stress present resulting from crowded conditions, noise levels, and disruption of familiar surroundings.
3. Status of family reunification. (**highly important**)
4. Extent or absence of social support systems. (**highly important**)
5. General demographics of the survivor population, population figures, gender, age, and so on; proximity to epicenter; or major death and destruction sites.
6. Information, if available, on high-risk and special-needs groups within the survivor population, including the mentally ill, physically handicapped, developmentally delayed, orphans, single heads of household, elderly, demobilized child soldiers, active and deactivated military personnel, current and former detainees and prisoners of war, and torture victims.
7. General locations and accommodations of the survivor population
8. General expectations, degree of hope, and capacity to cope among the survivor population.
9. Ongoing or soon-to-be-initiated social and community activities and involvements among the survivor population that provide emotional healing, mobilization, strengthen resilience, self-sufficiency, and purpose. (**highly important**)
10. Extent of conflict or cohesion among the survivor population and between the survivor and host population with reference to ethnic, political, religious, class, and other dynamics.
11. If this is a war or other conflict situation, the attitudes, experiences, and expectations of the parties involved with regard to matters of justice and reconciliation.
12. If the survivor population is currently located in a host country or countries, what are the relocation or repatriation plans or expectations?

13. General demographics and characteristics of the host population if this is a refugee or internally displaced person (IDP) situation.
14. General educational, social service, health, religious, recreational, occupational, and other local resources available to the survivor population.
15. The extent to which there is opportunity, accommodation, and approval for natural, spontaneous, and culturally bound rituals for grieving, cleansing, healing, burials, and memorial ceremonies.
16. Local mental health resources available to the survivor population, to be described in terms of numbers, location, skill level in working with disaster survivors, and acceptability to survivors.
17. What other services are your sponsoring agency providing or planning on providing? (**highly important**)
18. What of the above or other helpful information can you obtain from or exchange with other involved local or international organizations?
19. What services are other organizations planning on offering?
20. What are the current and anticipated staff occupational stress management needs? This should include the on-site staff of the sponsoring agency as well as the staff of any likely local host or collaborating agency.
21. What resources are there available for staff care?
22. Key information on practical matters that may influence planning and service provision such as geography, accommodations, weather, and communications.

E. Useful sources of information (Some of this has already been discussed in previous sections of the chapter. Contained below is a listing of typically helpful sources of information to consider either before going out or while out on a psychosocial assessment assignment.):

1. Colleagues.
2. History, language, anthropology, political science, and mental health faculty both in home country as well as in the affected and regional countries.
3. Internet.
4. Disaster psychology writings.
5. Sponsoring and cooperating organizations, internationally and on-site.
6. Other NGOs serving the site or with relevant experiences.
7. Governmental agencies serving the area, especially ministries of health and education.
8. Professional mental health, health, and social service staff serving the area and responding to the disaster.
9. Religious, political, and other formal and informal leaders of the survivor population and host country.

10. Host families of survivors, if they are already in place.
11. Refugee camp managers.
12. Focus groups or informal discussion groups among survivors.
13. Other identified key informants.
14. Information gathered while providing crisis intervention and case consultation services.
15. Observation.
16. Talking with drivers and interpreters.
17. If available and capable, reading local newspapers and listening to local radio and television.
18. Living in or near and helping, listening, and otherwise interacting with the disaster survivors and those who are assisting them.

F. Report writing (On the basis of the above information, knowledge of the comparative influences of variables on postdisaster recovery, and efficacy of different interventions in accelerating or otherwise improving that recovery, findings and recommendations can be made. You already will be advised as to what format to use if the sponsoring agency wishes that. In terms of a generic psychosocial format, I recommend the following.):

    I. Title—Psychosocial Needs Assessment of _____

    II. Authors—Assessment Conducted by _____

    III. Date of Report

    IV. Introduction—Purpose, sponsoring agency, dates of assessment, primary methodology

    V. Predisaster Characteristics

    VI. Disaster Characteristics

    VII. Postdisaster Characteristics

    VIII. Resources Available

    IX. An Estimate of the Prevalence of Disaster-Related Psychosocial Difficulties

    X. Special Needs Populations

    XI. Priority of Service Needs—Short-, Intermediate-, and Long-Term

    XII. Staff Care Needs—Short-, Intermediate-, and Long-Term

    XIII. Service Plan—Short-, Intermediate-, and Long-Term

Appendices:

    A. Training Recommendations

    B. Program Evaluation Recommendations

    C. Staffing Recommendations

    D. Review of the Needs Assessment Process/Mission Statement

Hopefully, the reader of this chapter is now better able to decide whether he or she will want to conduct a psychosocial needs assessment, and if so how better to do so. The opportunities to conduct such an assessment do not come along all that often, but if you do have the chance I recommend it highly. The real-life challenge to one's professional, scientific, humanitarian, and personal capacities is both exhilarating and humbling, and well worth the occasional discomforts and inconveniences involved.

References

Anderson, M. B. (1994). *People-oriented planning at work: Using POP to improve UNHCR programming.* United Nations High Commissioner for Refugees [UNHCR], Geneva. Retrieved January 26, 2005, from http://www.unhcr.ch.

Coleman, P. T. (2003). Characteristics of protracted, intractable, conflict: Toward the development of a metaframework I. *Peace and Conflict: Journal of Peace Psychology, 9,* 1–37.

Dodge, G. R. (1998). *Meeting the mental health needs of refugee staff working in Yugoslavia.* Paper presented at the International Society of Traumatic Stress Studies Conference, Washington, DC.

————. (2000a). *The development of a rapid psychosocial needs assessment: Literature review.* Washington, DC: American Red Cross.

————. (2000b). *A protocol for a rapid psychosocial needs assessment.* Washington, DC: American Red Cross.

————. (2004). *Psychosocial needs assessment and recommendations for the refugees in Ban Don Yang, Nu Po, and Umpiem Mai Camps.* Minneapolis, MN: American Refugee Committee.

————, & Jha, S. K. (2001). *Psychosocial needs assessment report: Gujarat Earthquake.* Geneva: International Federation of the Red Cross and Red Crescent Societies, and Washington, DC: American Red Cross.

Kalayjian, A. S. (1995). *Disaster and mass trauma: Global perspectives on post disaster mental health management.* Long Branch, NJ: Vista.

Petevi, M., Revel, J. P., & Jacobs, G. A. (2001). *Tool for the rapid assessment of mental health needs of refugees, displaced and other populations affected by conflict and post-conflict situations: A community-oriented assessment.* Geneva: World Health Organization.

CHAPTER 6

PEACE-BUILDING, CULTURALLY RESPONSIVE MEANS, AND ETHICAL PRACTICES IN HUMANITARIAN PSYCHOSOCIAL INTERVENTIONS

Deanna R. Beech

> I have become far more cynical about the role of the international community as a result of this work. I feel that it will only be through a long-term, integrated, community-based approach stewarded but not completely controlled by foreigners that such communities will recover— more than recover—and go on to develop. With the current approach, there's great danger that the programs will not be effective and will, rather, make matters worse. There seems to be an extreme shortsightedness on the part of those making policy both at local and international levels.
>
> *—A response to the Psychologists of Social Responsibility survey of field workers*

Humanitarian assistance that addresses the emotional well-being of communities affected by ethnopolitical conflict has become an accepted and expected aspect of aid programming. From community-based programs promoting reintegration of subgroups to more traditional mental health interventions such as individual or group therapy, the interventions and programs implemented to address the psychosocial effect of conflict vary widely. However, regardless of the type of intervention proposed, defining characteristics of the work are consistent: people are in urgent, often critical, circumstances. In these crises, there is little time or space available for those providing assistance to share experiences and learn from each other. In the forums created to provide the time and space for improving the practice in the field, such as conferences and training programs, providers of similar theoretical/philosophical orientations tend to talk to others with the same view. As a result, little sharing of information across disciplines and orientations has taken place. It has also been difficult for those designing and implementing programs in the field to take the time to write about what they find effective and the lessons they have learned. These factors have resulted in a significant gap between theory and application (Psychologists for Social Responsibility [PsySR], 2002; Psychosocial Working Group, 2003; Valid International, 2002; Psychosocial Working Group [PWG], 2003). Further, given the urgency of these situations, little research has been done to determine the appropriateness of the assessments conducted or the efficacy of the programs/methodologies implemented (PsySR, 2002; PWG, 2003). In short, little is known about what may be working and why. Serious concerns have begun to be raised about the possibility that harm may be done by well-intentioned international workers (Beech, Levitt, & Wessells, 2003; Bjorn & Bjorn, 2004; Giller, 1998; Summerfield, 1998).

As a nonprofit organization whose primary mission is to draw on the research, knowledge, and practice of psychology to promote durable peace and social well-being at the community, national, and international levels, PsySR is committed to bringing clarity to this complex scene. To do this, a series of invited conferences was initiated, the *Clara* conferences, dedicated to one of PsySR's founding members, Clara Rabinowitz. This conference series has brought together professionals experienced in the design and delivery of psychosocial programs in areas affected by ethnopolitical conflict that represent a wide range of disciplines and orientations, and has successfully established an open dialog in which these professionals have been able to critically reflect on their work.

The first conference (*Clara I*; PsySR, 2002) was designed to share and compare approaches to the assessment of community needs and the implementation of culturally appropriate programs that facilitate and accelerate the restoration of functioning during humanitarian crises (Levitt & Beech, 2002). The outcome of the small-group discussions showed that there is as much disagreement as agreement over what constitutes good practices. Even more salient was the recurrent focus on issues of ethical, practical, cultural, and political concerns that were raised over the course of the conference.

To address these concerns, and to gain a deeper understanding of the differences and assumptions that underlie this work, it became evident that the discussion needed to move from theory and self-reflection to practical application. Thus, the participants requested that a second conference be organized to provide concrete scenarios to facilitate a comparison of approaches. Again, the conference work was primarily conducted through small working groups. The task of these groups was to assess the situation presented in the scenario, design a program, and discuss how it would be evaluated. The scenarios were based on the actual field experiences of some of the participants.

The following is a review of the ethical concerns that have been raised in the course of these conferences, as well as in the literature, about the process of providing psychosocial aid in situations of ethnopolitical conflict. For the sake of organization, these concerns will be discussed in the following order: assessing the situation, program design and implementation, and monitoring and evaluation. Examples and personal experiences will be provided to illustrate the issues presented. This will be followed by a discussion of the overarching ethical concerns raised in the second conference (*Clara II*; PsySR, 2003), regarding the motivations and agendas of those who are providing aid, and what allows us to assume that we know what people in another culture need.

Assessing the Situation

Ethical dilemmas begin to arise whenever representatives from international nongovernmental organizations (NGOs) arrive on the scene to assess the situation. The goal of the assessment is usually to determine what the needs are and the locations that are in greatest need. But these disasters are replete with overwhelming unmet needs and untold numbers of individuals and families with intense needs. When an NGO vehicle arrives with aid workers to do an assessment, people naturally assume that something will be done about their situation—aid workers need to be mindful of the implications inherent in the assessment process, so that expectations are not unduly raised.

What to Assess?

Before meaningful data can be collected, a dilemma with ethical implications must be faced regarding what to assess. It has generally been agreed that those who have suffered tragic events in situations of ethnopolitical conflict are not necessarily clinically disordered. This position has led to the often-repeated statement that "post-traumatic stress disorder (PTSD) reactions are normal outcomes to abnormal experiences." Although this phrasing appears to be a nice way of normalizing the difficulties that people experience as a result of ethnopolitical conflict, it is still saying that trauma invariably results in psychopathology (Shalev, 1996). It also assumes that the stress reactions are present even though the stressful event (trauma) is in the past, but in situations of ethnopolitical conflict the stressors are numerous and often chronic.

Asset-Focused versus Deficit-Focused Assessment

Describing a community as "traumatized" imposes a Western psychiatric perspective on individual and community reactions (Bracken, 1999), thereby focusing the assessment on clinical symptoms. This emphasis on symptoms of psychopathology has been described as being deficit-focused because it only addresses the presence of pathology (PsySR, 2002). That is not to say that the traumatic experiences do not have the same effect on individuals in other cultures. On the contrary, there is a growing body of evidence to support the theory that trauma affects people physiologically, as well as psychologically (Levine, 1997; Rothschild, 2002; van der Kolk, 1996). However, the presence or absence of these effects does not necessarily correspond with individual functioning because the meanings given to these symptoms are mediated by numerous variables, and especially by their sociocultural context (Boyden & Gibbs, 1997; Bracken & Petty, 1998; Green, 2003).

The majority of those who have been affected by armed conflict are able to cope with their experiences and integrate them into their individual and cultural identities without becoming psychologically disabled or developing long-term psychological symptoms (McFarlane & de Girolamo, 1996; Smith, Perrin, Yule, Hacam, & Stuvland, 2002). The strength and resiliency of those who have suffered great pain and loss should not be underestimated. For example, one young Albanian who was a Kosovo refugee staying in Montenegro during the war reflected that despite the atrocities she had been through, not all of her experiences were bad. She explained that she had made many new friends that came from all over Kosovo—people she would never have met under normal circumstances.

Of course, there is a small but significant percentage of the population that will experience severe levels of distress, but Giller's (1998) observation of the Ugandans illustrates how the presence of clinical symptoms does not necessarily translate into impaired functioning. As part of her efforts to establish a Center for Victims of Torture in Uganda, Giller set out to determine the areas in greatest need of services. She states that she was forced to go out and look for the "trauma victims" because everyone she met and observed had real physical and medical needs but otherwise appeared to be coping well in extremely difficult circumstances. For example, extended families had taken in the orphaned children, and the community helped those with disabilities.

To assess trauma levels, Giller had two Western-based PTSD scales translated into the local language, despite her concerns regarding cultural relevancy, and had them administered to the villagers by her interpreter. Although this practice fails to consider the fact that the tools were not validated and normed for the culture (a practice that does happen in the field), Giller did find symptomatology that showed that the people were experiencing the neurophysiological effects of trauma despite the fact that they were not reporting or exhibiting any observable manifestations of traumatic stress reactions. With these data, she could have designed a program that would give the people a greater awareness of and attention to their symptoms and the underlying traumatic memories, but to what end? The people were coping resiliently. Instead, Giller chose to foster this resiliency by working with the natural community networks of women in the villages. She offered a safe place for the women to talk about their experiences of being raped by soldiers, provided gynecological exams, and educated them about the sexually transmitted diseases they had acquired as a result of the rapes.

Observations such as this have led many who work in this field to shift their focus for assessment from a deficit model (symptoms) to a wellness model. Although this shift in focus has spurred the development of quantitative measures for resiliency (Hubbard, 2004), these instruments are still in the development process. Thus, many of the data regarding coping and resiliency are presented qualitatively. This can create a problem with funding, as many Western NGOs and funding organizations have a preference for, and tradition of reliance on, standardized instruments, such as the Harvard Trauma Questionnaire (Mollica et al., 1992). However, any instrument, even one that has been translated into as many languages as the Harvard Trauma Questionnaire (Kleijn, Hovens, & Rodenburg, 2001), may still encounter difficulties in application resulting from variability across dialects and nuances use of words. Administering such instruments with standard paper and pencil procedures can also present challenges. In cultures with low literacy rates and little access to writing materials, a majority of the population will be confused by or unable to complete the instrument. Further, if a translator is used to facilitate the completion of the survey through an interview, additional complications arise, such as under- or overreporting of symptoms and censoring their responses to ensure cultural acceptability.

Effect of Assessments

Another aspect of assessments that may be overlooked is the effect that this procedure can have on those who participate. Regardless of administration procedures, if symptom-based checklists are used, the material brought up by the questions necessitates the recall of traumatic events. This can cause retraumatization at a point in time at which people are clearly under excessive stress. When taking the surveys, people recall their painful experiences, but this is not done in the context of an ongoing supportive process. After the assessment, the individual is left to cope on his or her own or to rely on his or her already taxed internal coping strategies and the transient social supports established in collection centers. This practice is particularly concerning when the assessment involves sexual violence and violence against children. Such data may also constitute testimonials to human rights violations and war crimes, which can quickly bring the psychological work into political arenas, where it is often difficult to determine whose interests are being served by the data collected (Wessells, 1998).

How Much to Assess?

The next dilemma relates to the breadth of the assessment, or the question of how many levels of interaction should be assessed. The use of symptom-focused assessments described above inherently narrows the scope of focus to individual reactions. From this approach, little can be said about the community's functioning, other than listing symptom prevalence rates. Knowing about how families and communities are functioning is obviously important, as we exist within a sociocultural context (Bronfenbrenner, 1986; Vygotsky, 1978). In situations of humanitarian disaster, there is growing agreement that it is necessary to view the needs of individuals in the context of their household and the family's position within the community (PsySR, 2002; Psychosocial Working Group, 2003). This context is further complicated by the additional levels of interaction that must be added to consider the effect of the aid worker and his or her culture; his or her relationship to the agency he or she works for, and its culture; that agency's reputation in the community; the community's relationship to the agency's country of origin; and the community's perception of the international aid system and its efforts.

In the face of such complexity, it can be anxiety reducing to focus on specific measurable variables, such as an individual's symptom profile—it reduced my anxiety as I faced my first camp assessment in Montenegro during the war in Kosovo. On my way to the camp, I was talking with a colleague who was going to do a health assessment. I remember envying her nice checklist with clearly laid-out guidelines, such as the maximum acceptable ratio of people per toilet. I had done my homework and was planning to develop "culturally integrated" programs, though I must admit that it was still a vague concept to me. Looking over her list, I easily recognized the indicators of depression, anxiety, and PTSD. When I got to the camp, everyone was very eager to answer my questions and thankfully offered more information than my questions would have produced. I quickly learned that the people in the camp, with the assistance of the lead NGO, had organized themselves to take care of the main activities such as cleaning and cooking. They had even created a governing structure. There were several people appointed to oversee the needs of specific areas in the camp. These area leaders coordinated with the camp representative. The representative served as the interface between the camp and the international community—how resilient! As with Giller, it was easy to identify symptoms that would fit into diagnostic categories, but what became most evident walking around the camp was that the lack of productive activity and shear boredom were bothering people the most. They had nothing to do all day but sit with their fears and grief. The adults needed something to do that would support their naturally resilient efforts to help themselves, and the children needed to play (Beech, 2001).

In addition, in the process of determining how much assessment to conduct, it is important to be aware of the constraints of your resources and the proposed funding objectives. It would be ethically questionable—and could be potentially wasteful—to do an exhaustive assessment if you know from the beginning that your resources are limited (PsySR, 2003). This can be a difficult balance to achieve. How do you get enough data to ensure a good understanding of the system so that the programs implemented can be as effective as possible, while only getting the data necessary to formulate this answer?

Program Design and Implementation

In protracted conflict situations such as the chronic conflicts of the Sudan, Sierra Leone, and Uganda, possibly the greatest psychological benefit that may be offered is the relief of knowing that you are safe and that your basic needs will be attended to (Christie, 1997; Pilisuk, 1998). People in these settings are devoting the sum total of their mental and emotional energies to coping with their present situation.

Refugees and displaced persons (R/DPs) who have been able to flee the conflict to the relative safety of a collection center continue to endure extremely stressful conditions. These difficulties often compound the stress of their recent experiences and their fear for the safety and well-being of family and friends. As time wears on and the R/DP's status remains the same, his or her psychological situation changes. Given that the demands on the local system and on the resources of the host community continue, that community is liable to become resentful of the strain on their already-limited resources. They may even perceive the R/DPs as being better provided for by the wealthy international groups while the local community suffers. As a result, R/DPs have become targets of discrimination, marginalization, and assaults on their culture (Wessells, 1998). Although it sounds appealing to provide aid for both the R/DPs and the host community, aid funding often targets only the emergency needs of the "affected population" without regard to the needs of surrounding communities. A host community that was poor before the arrival of the R/DPs has not changed its need status. As a result, the international community, by aiding one population and not the other, may inadvertently be contributing to the negative projections and power asymmetries in the region.

If the situation progresses to the point of returning the displaced to their own territory, the variety of potential troubles facing returnees is not easily foreseen. For instance, in Montenegro, the Albanian refugees were excited about returning and fantasized that their homes and lands were still intact, or at least salvageable. Despite the uncertainty about what they would encounter on their return, they optimistically underestimated the difficulty of rebuilding. When the war ended, everyone rushed back in a flurry of excitement and anxiety as the camps emptied out. In the first week after the war ended, more than 1 million people flooded back into Kosovo, where they were met with the immense destruction that had been carried out by Serbian forces. Fortunately, the strong extended family networks in Albanian culture and the international aid agency's rapid development of distribution networks quickly provided for most of the basic needs.

In Bosnia-Herzegovina, the situation was mired in the complex cultural and interethnic tensions and the extensive problem of "squatting." Even if a family wanted to return to their home, they might not be able to because another family was "squatting" in their house, and these squatters in turn were not able to return to their home because someone else is "squatting" there. In situations like this, in which return becomes difficult and slow, Westerners often assume that the R/DPs are trying to better their circumstances by living off the host community/country. This assertion is clearly an oversimplification, but it is perpetuated by governments and aid agencies alike.

Culturally Integrated Approaches versus Western Models of "Therapy"

Given the complex nature of these situations, with the urgent and overwhelming amount of need in the population, security issues, grant proposal deadlines, and NGO competition for exposure and funding, programs have to be designed and implemented quickly. One way to accomplish this is to use "canned" programs or Western-based clinical treatment models, some of which include the direct provision of therapy by international "experts." These treatment-focused interventions emphasize the individual's experience of the trauma and assume that the "victims" need to "work through" their experiences by talking about them (Giller, 1998; Summerfield, 1998). The assumption that trauma and grief could easily and quickly be benefited by traditional psychotherapy is unusual, even from a Western clinical perspective. For instance, no one would expect a woman who was hospitalized for injuries from an automobile accident to work through the death of her husband while she is in the hospital.

Further, when expatriates provide therapy in the field, a therapeutic relationship is established. Not only does this therapy bring up intensely painful issues of loss and trauma in a short span of time and under stressful conditions, the provider often has to leave at given intervals regardless of whether or not treatment is complete. This practice is not only unsustainable but raises the ethical concern of patient abandonment, which may compound the suffering (Summerfield, 1998). This type of situation raises questions regarding the fairness of asking people in such situations to "emotionally ventilate" about their traumatic experiences when they lack the luxury of time and the spare internal resources needed to address their feelings of loss, grief, and traumatization.

A growing body of evidence is beginning to indicate that such methods are not beneficial and can actually result from reducing the individual's capacity to function (McFarlane & de Girolamo, 1996; van der Kolk, McFarlane, & van der Hart, 1996). An example of this change was evident in the programs established in Montenegro for the Kosovo Albanian R/DPs. One of the NGOs brought in psychoanalysts from Europe and conducted individual and group psychoanalysis for approximately 10 hours every day. The mother of one of the adolescent girls who was being seen by this group came crying for help because her daughter had become very withdrawn. The girl was initially referred for treatment because she had been abducted by a squad of the Serbian paramilitary and raped by many of its members. Before analysis, the girl had been actively and happily involved with the camp's community center, where she had made many friends. It was summer, the camp was located on the beach, and camp conditions were improving. No new bad news had reached the family, the United States had entered the war, and her peer group's functioning remained high. Her deterioration at repeatedly discussing her trauma in an already stressful situation was apparent. She stopped speaking to others, would not see her friends, and would only lie in the tent, staring at the wall.

This trauma saturation was also observed to have a negative effect on the psychoanalysts. Several of the providers reported difficulty sleeping, exhaustion, and feeling overwhelmed. At least two of the providers became so physically sick that they had to be rotated out prematurely. They explained that they must have caught bad colds, but it was summertime and no one else was sick.

This situation not only illustrates that allowing the compulsion to repeat traumatic experiences free reign can reduce functioning but also raises the question, "What does it mean to design culturally integrated and sustainable programs?" The psychoanalysts described above felt that their approach was among the most culturally sensitive of the programs being implemented because their work was nondirective.

An example of a clearly culturally integrated, sustainable, multilevel intervention can be found in the work done by Christian Children's Fund in Angola. After the conflicts of the early 1990s, the government of Angola had adopted a policy of placing unaccompanied minors and orphans in orphanages. Christian Children's Fund worked with other NGOs and the Angolan psychological staff to advocate in policy meetings with governmental officials that they scale back on the institutionalization of children and divert some of these funds to documentation, tracing, and family reunification. As a result, relatives for many children were identified, and Christian Children's Fund coordinated their return by working with the indigenous healers to create cleansing rituals that would allow these children to be accepted back into the community (Wessells & Monteiro, 2003). This successful culturally based approach led to a national de-emphasis on the institutionalization of children (Wessells, Schwebel, & Anderson, 2001). Unfortunately, conflict returned before the end of the decade, and although the new 2002 agreement between government forces and the largest opposition group brought peace, this time it did not include provisions for children, particularly the demobilization of the child combatants (Human Rights Watch, 2003). Efforts by international agencies are again focusing on advocating for these children.

One way NGOs often attempt to create culturally integrated and sustainable programs is to use the "train-the-trainer" model. This process uses a pyramid structure in which the expatriate experts train and work with a group of community leaders, teachers, and healers. These indigenous providers then train and work with groups of people in their communities. In theory, this appears to be an exemplary approach that would meld the tools and techniques of the international with the local culture, and in some instances it works, but in others it is not adequately implemented or supported. For example, this approach was widely implemented in Bosnia, where training was often based on Western clinical models of trauma and psychotherapy. The trainings were conducted, the programs were implemented, and then the expatriate experts left. Additional training and supervision was rarely received, and 5 years after the end of the war, UNICEF was only able to identify one NGO that evaluated program effectiveness (R. Stuvland, personal communication, 1999). In addition, when the funding ran out, the programs ended, and the indigenous providers were left with no place to take the painful feelings brought up by the "victims" by the Western-based treatment models that were implemented. As a result, it is not uncommon to find indigenous providers in this region who experienced burnout as a result of frustration and secondary traumatization.

Humanitarian interventionists are ethically obligated to conduct themselves in ways that are humane to all and that do not leave either indigenous or expatriate staff feeling depleted, dejected, or misused. Moreover, they must make adequate use of every opportunity for encouraging and empowering local communities to take the lead in implementing modes of healing that are congruent with their beliefs, customs, and cultural systems of meaning. Finally, intercultural partnerships should foster improvements in the local capacity for meeting psychosocial needs that are sustainable once the temporary surplus of external resources is withdrawn.

Power Asymmetries and the Devaluing of Indigenous Cultures

It is important to remember that the humanitarian assistance process places individuals, families, communities, and societies in relatively dependent and passive positions, creating an asymmetry of power favoring the aid provider over the recipients (Wessells, 1998). The dynamics that this process can lead to the international NGO staff, who represent wealth, knowledge, and power, being viewed as the "heroes" who will rescue the R/DPs from their troubles (Wessells, 1998). From this perspective, as people begin to receive aid, they become hopeful and excited that their situation is going to improve. For example, Albanian R/DPs in Montenegro believed that the United States was fighting with them against the Serbians. This perception led to a fantasy in which, with the help of such a powerful ally, they would not only end Serbian brutality but would also liberate Kosovo from the Federal Republic of Yugoslavia.

Dynamics such as these will be present even if these savior projections are not reinforced by the expatriates themselves, because the expatriates will be assumed to have superior knowledge. In developed countries in which education is limited, this deference to the "experts" is often a pronounced feature in the interactions between the expatriates and the indigenous people (Wessells, 1998). Giller reflected on this dynamic by stating that she "felt that she should be 'sitting at the feet' of local knowledge, but her very presence silenced that knowledge and privileged her inexperience" (Wessells 1998, p. 128).

This privileging of expatriates can interfere with efforts to gain an understanding of the indigenous practices and rituals that could benefit the community's resiliency. Local understandings and customs are put aside in favor of the programs and products offered by the international organizations (Wessells, 1998). It also creates a significant interpersonal gap that can make the establishment of a working alliance with agents from the local culture difficult, thus impeding efforts to develop culturally sound programs. If in the process we have played into the projections by "acting on" the community rather than "acting with" the community, our efforts are less likely to take root, and we run the risk of being scapegoated when the difficulties are not quickly or easily remedied. For example, in Bosnia many teachers who were providing support to the children affected by the war completed weekend training workshops designed to instruct them on the treatment trauma. They concluded that they were now fully trained in "trauma therapy," and they proudly displayed their certificates of attendance. However, as these providers tried to address the difficult and painful issues that the children shared, they felt inadequate and unskilled. They did not have the training necessary to practice Western-based therapy and felt less capable than before in responding to these children as a teacher within their culture.

Wessells (1998) discussed another power asymmetry that is created by the necessity for donors to provide assistance directly to the people affected by the conflict because the indigenous infrastructures have either been damaged or destroyed by the conflict. When this happens, donors must create distribution networks and shelters, bypassing local processes and channels of influence. Although this is necessary, it further marginalizes the local governance and fosters dependency on international resources and expertise. Moreover, aid is not distributed equally and is often used as a tool to pursue political interests (Anderson, 1996; Wessells, 1998). Humanitarian groups, trying to avoid becoming embroiled in the political agendas, adopt a stance of impartiality. However, this may inadvertently perpetuate inequalities because the greatest needs tend to be on one side—often the losing side (Wessells, 1998). Such inequities in the distribution of resources, both during and after the conflict, can serve to worsen feelings of hatred and animosity toward those who are perceived as benefiting from the war.

Target Populations

Certain groups are often identified as being the most vulnerable or at risk for developing psychological disabilities as a result of ethnopolitical conflict. Unaccompanied children and women, particularly mothers, typically receive significant attention in the literature and considerable program funding in the field. Of course, these are important and vulnerable groups that need aid. Additional priority is often reportedly given to former soldiers and child soldiers. With these subgroups, the notion of vulnerability is broadened to include vulnerability to perpetuating violence. These groups have been actively acculturated to violence, have access to weapons, and are thus particularly at risk of perpetuating and escalating the conflict. Yet, although most experts in the field will agree that developing ways to work with these subgroups to prevent further violence is a primary goal (PsySR, 2002), in application the issues are difficult to address, and the needs of those suffering physically and emotionally appear more urgent and thus get the bulk of the attention (PsySR, 2003).

Adolescents, especially young men, are also vulnerable to being brought into the perpetuation of violence while living in the collection centers. Camp life is dull and tedious, leaving people with little to do and a lot of time in which to do it. Tension and boredom are pervasive. Adolescents, even when programs are targeted at them, are often not reached. For example, in Bosnia and Montenegro the adolescents found that camp life led to a significant reduction in parental control and cultural norms. As a result, it could be observed that the adolescents were engaging in behaviors that would not have been permitted in their normal cultural settings, such as staying out late without adult supervision and becoming sexually active.

In Montenegro, adolescent boys were supported in their assumption of adult behaviors and roles by the groups of men who would sit together at length, discussing what they had been through and exchanging fantasies of revenge. The boys were encouraged to join these discussions. In the process, they eagerly identified with their role models' fantasies and expectations. The intensity of the emotions stirred in this process provided fertile grounds for recruitment into the Kosovo Liberation Army. This type of dynamic has been noted in other conflict settings (Natsios, 1997).

When we move to the notion of preventing the recurring cycles of violence, another primary concern is the socialization of children both at home and in the community. Klaine (1998) describes the recounting of past family traumas to each new generation as a process that keeps the trauma alive through secondary traumatization. Requests to the children to avenge these injustices are made both implicitly and explicitly, resulting in indoctrination into a culture of violence. In Montenegro, the Albanian women were observed not only spurring the men on in their animosity, but actively participating in the culture of violence. One woman explained that she knew she would lose some of her sons to the fight for liberation so she had more children. When this process is supported by the community's institutions, the groundwork is laid for the next conflict.

Monitoring and Evaluation

As stated above, little is truly known about the efficacy of the various methods, tools, and approaches used in the field. Outcomes research has been limited for understandable reasons. However, as psychosocial programs have become a standard part of humanitarian aid, we have an ethical responsibility to determine the efficacy of our work. How this is best done is again a matter of controversy. As discussed in the assessment section, use of Western clinical tools such as PTSD inventories has come under scrutiny, yet the Western worldview places significant weight on being able to quantifiably demonstrate effectiveness. This in turn raises questions regarding the meaning of effectiveness and how it can best be measured. For instance, does a study suggesting individual benefits from a program also mean that these benefits generalize to the whole community? And, if we tried to address the collective impact how could this be measured and quantified?

Triangulated Methodology Using Action Research

While the jury is still out on what constitutes best practices in studying efficacy, triangulated research methodologies that utilize an action research method are showing promise (PsySR, 2003). Action research is the process of gathering data at regular intervals during the project, reviewing it, and using the information gained from the review to improve the efficacy and impact of the project. Wadsworth (1998) describes it as a "cycle of action, reflection, raising of questions, planning of 'fieldwork' to review current (and past) actions that characterize all research endeavors" (p. 4). In a triangulated methodology the subject of investigation is looked at from more than one perspective, most often quantitative and qualitative, thus facilitating a more complete view of the subject under investigation (Denzin, 1978; Jick, 1983). Further, including the qualitative measures may promote a more self-critical stance as it can be an effective tool for observing impact both immediately and over time (Caroleo, 2002).

The quantitative aspects of the evaluation could utilize one of the emerging instruments that address both the resilient aspects of the individuals along with the symptoms they are experiencing (Jew, Green, & Kroger, 1999; Masten, Hubbard, & Gest, 1999). Alternatively, it could be designed in a culturally integrated way by obtaining information from the community. For example, in designing a project to improve reconciliation in a community with a history of ethnopolitical violence it could be asked, "How would you know that people of varying ethnicities were getting along better than before?" From this information, surveys that utilize a Likert scale format could be created, and the qualitative and quantitative questions could be linked providing rich information for monitoring and evaluation (PsySR, 2003).

Because the ideal world of academic experimentation does not exist in the field, there will be times when necessity and urgency preclude the implementation of a culturally appropriate research design. When this happens it is generally recommended that at the outset of program initiatives, daily notes including observations and personal reflections be written down so that at least a qualitative/process review can be done later (PsySR, 2002).

Evaluation for Rejuvenation or Perpetuation?

Another ethical dilemma with program evaluations is the fact that they are often used to perpetuate programs rather than transform them. This occurs for many reasons. First, we want to believe that we have helped. We also want to continue our work and our position/pay is contingent upon continued funding, which is contingent upon demonstrating that we did what we said we would do and that it helped. The local providers we work with also want to feel that they are helping, and they also want to make sure that the project looks good in order to maintain their employment as long as possible. These motives are understandable but do not bode well for an unbiased review of the data.

Overarching Ethical Concerns

In the process of discussing the current state of this field during the *Clara* conferences, two pivotal overarching concerns became evident: (1) What are the agendas behind the work?, and (2) What lets us assume that we know what people of another culture need?

What Are the Agendas behind the Work?

Given the complex multitiered nature of the humanitarian aid system and its interaction with the complex situations of communities affected by ethnopolitical conflict, identifying the motivation and agendas of the players involved is difficult. We may not even be aware of all of our own motivations. There are the motives that are easily discussed, such as wanting to help others, and those that are less politically correct such as excitement-seeking (Ehrenreich, 2005). As is true of all actions, the choice to do this work is likely to be multiply determined. The motivations of the aid agency for which you work must also be considered along with their guiding philosophy (religious affiliation, humanitarian focus, etc.), and their evident, yet often unspoken, need to compete for funds and increase their visibility. Further, in order for agencies to provide aid they must secure grants from donors who have their own agendas. When the funding source is governmental, political agendas and foreign policy become engaged in the aid process, along with the possible historical contributions of these governments to the suffering that is being addressed. For example, a Norwegian NGO working in Afghanistan with a European Community funding banner on their door will likely be perceived differently by the community than a U.S.-based NGO sporting a USAID banner.

The mix of motives and agendas presents opportunities for incompatibilities to arise (Ehrenreich, 2005). Following the example above, imagine being a U.S. aid worker in an Afghanistan community where the U.S. bombed the home of a local family killing men, women, and children in the effort to get one Taliban leader. How do you present yourself to that community? How do you work with their anger, rage, and grief? How do you protect yourself? How do you answer the questions of how the U.S. can do something like that? Do you take your observations of the impact of the choice to bomb a home back to the government to attempt to effect a change in policy? It is not enough just to recognize these issues. The understanding of these relationships needs to be widely shared and followed by work to change the policy in the larger political arena (PsySR, 2002).

What Makes Us Assume That We Know What They Need?

Rony Berger, M.D., the director of clinical services at the Israel Trauma Center for Victims of Terror and War, asked at the second *Clara* conference (PsySR, 2003), "What gives us the right to decide for someone else that we know what they need, or when they should reconcile with those that have caused them such pain?" In this dialog, Dr. Berger was pointing to the fact that most of the time international agencies decide when something should be done and set up specific funding guidelines that support certain types of work and not others. By applying for these grants, the aid community could potentially be complicit with railroading a Western-based agenda over the needs and interests of the community.

The process of asking communities if and how we should go about helping requires aid workers to begin from the uncomfortable position of not knowing what they intend to implement. Imagine writing a proposal that says you will go and talk with the village elders about their needs and then jointly determine ways that the skills and knowledge you have can be interwoven with the community's strengths and resources. Ideally this would be funded as a truly culturally integrated approach to humanitarian aid. In practice, most donors and aid agencies want psychosocial programs to run like other relief programs, where there are a given number of people in need (e.g., hunger) and so you simply distribute a proportional amount of goods or services (e.g., food provisions) until those needs are satisfied. The psychosocial equivalent means estimating how many people are suffering with stress and grief reactions, and then training a preset number of people to provide treatment to those identified as suffering. As described above, programs based on Western treatment models may be preferred because they provide clear guidance regarding what to assess and which interventions to implement.

PsySR's survey of humanitarian aid worker in the field (PsySR, 2002), such as the one quoted at the beginning of this chapter, shows that externally motivated interventions based on Western models often fail. The aid workers that we surveyed typically described that over time they have shifted away from standard assessment measures and treatment models and moved to a more interactive position in which they spend time talking with people and being present in the culture.

This position moves the dialog to the notion of being "invited in" by the indigenous community. In fact, some consultants require that the community seek contact with them and ask for their collaboration. In this way they are literally "invited in" to the community. However, this requirement raises more questions such as, "How can an affected community know what is available and who to contact?" Others take the stance that we should go even if we have not been asked because we can help. Yet again, this position causes us to circle back to the question of, "How do we know that we are helping when we lack the studies to show what works and what does not?"

Summary

Ethical concerns in the arena of psychosocial humanitarian aid abound. This series has been designed to create a forum for lessons learned by those who have been doing this work in the effort to curb the continual re-creation of the wheel that takes place as new and even seasoned providers seek to offer their skills to those in desperate need, but this is just one of the many steps that are needed. To realize our potential contribution to the development of cultures of peace around the world we must first take a critical look at our own professional community. Individuals interested in this work should receive specific training that is aimed at creating "hybrid" practitioners (PsySR, 2002). These practitioners would have strong collaboration skills and be capable of addressing clinical, community, and human rights needs from interdisciplinary perspectives. Mechanisms for collaboration across disciplines and orientations need to be established that will challenge the assumptions from which we work, rather than perpetuate the "preaching to the choir" tendency that naturally exists in most institutions. And those doing the work in the field should utilize a peer supervision model to facilitate the development of programs that are culturally integrated and sustainable, check for subjective biases, and offer each other support in these difficult situations.

PsySR's survey of field providers (2002) identifies considerable and growing discomfort among experienced practitioners regarding the current approach to humanitarian assistance. Truly integrating or blending Western techniques with local healing practices is a difficult art. Time pressures and competition for funding further complicate the situation. Interventions continue to focus on short-term crisis work, with little attention being paid to prevention and long-term sustainable peace building projects. There is also a general failure to integrate the crisis work with long-term development goals and programs. This is where psychologists have possibly their greatest contributions to offer to a society struggling to re-establish itself. We can offer guidance in the development of cultures of peace. We understand the dynamics of structural violence and can educate families, communities, governments, and donors to address them. We can aid people and communities as they work through the grief and nightmares left by the conflict. Further, we can advocate for the creation of systems that support the core elements of peace—social justice, human rights, nonviolence, inclusiveness, civil society, peace education, and sustainability (United Nations [UN], 1998).

References

Anderson, M. B. (1996). Humanitarian NGOs in conflict interventions. In C. A. Crocker, F. O. Hampson, & P. Aall (Eds.), *Managing global chaos: Sources of and responses to international conflict* (pp. 343–354). Washington, DC: United States Institute of Peace Press.

Beech, D. (2001, August) *Policies for extending care to victims of ethnopolitical violence.* Paper presented at the meeting of the American Psychological Association, San Francisco, CA.

———, Levitt, J., & Wessells, M. (2003). *The negative effects of humanitarian interventions and difficulties with post-war construction.* Symposium conducted at the meeting of Psychologists for Social Responsibility, Washington, DC.

Bjorn, G., & Bjorn, A. (2004). Ethical aspects when treating traumatized refugee children and their families. *Nordic Journal of Psychiatry, 58*(3), 193–198.

Boyden, J., & Gibbs, S. (1997). *Children of war: Responses to psychosocial distress in Cambodia.* Switzerland: United Nations Research Institute for Social Development.

Bracken, P. (1998). Hidden agendas: Deconstructing post traumatic stress disorder. In P. Bracken & C. Petty (Eds.), *Rethinking the trauma of war* (pp. 38–59). London: Free Association Books.

———, & Petty, C. (1998). *Rethinking the trauma of war.* London: Free Association Books.

Bronfenbrenner, U. (1986). Ecology of the family as a context for human development. In T. Husen & T. N. Postlethwaite (Eds.), *International encyclopedia of education* (2nd ed., Vol. 3). Oxford, England: Pergamon Press/Elsevier Science.

Caroleo, O. (2002). Facing the self: The magic of qualitative methodology. *Therapeutic Recreation Journal, 36*(4), 382–390.

Christie, D. (1997). Reducing direct and structural violence: The human needs theory. *Peace and Conflict: Journal of Peace Psychology, 3*, 315–332.

Denzin, N. (1978). *The research act* (2nd ed.). New York: McGraw-Hill.

Ehrenreich, J. H. (2005). *The humanitarian companion: A guide for staff of humanitarian aid, human rights, and development projects.* Rugby, Warwickshire, UK: ITDG.

Giller, J. (1998). Caring for "victims of torture" in Uganda: Some personal reflections. In P. Bracken & C. Petty (Eds.), *Rethinking the trauma of war* (pp. 128–145). London: Free Association Books.

Green, B. (2003). Traumatic stress and its consequences. In B. Green, M. Friedman, J. de Jong, S. Solomon, T. Keane, J. Fairbank, B. Donelan, & E. Frey-Wouters (Eds.), *Trauma interventions in war and peace* (pp. 17–32). New York: Kluwer Academic/Plenum.

Hubbard, J. (2004). Tracking trauma in the field: psychosocial interventions in humanitarian response. USAID Humanitarian Debate Series, Washington, DC.

Human Rights Watch (2003, April). *Forgotten fighters: Child soldiers in Angola.* Retrieved January 26, 2005 from http://www.hrw.org/reports/2003/angola0403/

Jew, C., Green, K., & Kroger, J. (1999). Development and validation of a measure of resiliency. *Measurement and Evaluation in Counseling and Development, 32*(2), 75–89.

Jick, T. (1983). Mixing qualitative and quantitative methods: triangulation in action. In Van Maanen (Ed.), *Qualitative methodology* (pp. 135–148). Beverly Hills: Sage.

Klaine, E. (1998). Intergenerational aspects of the conflict in the former Yugoslavia. In Y. Danieli (Ed.), *International handbook of multigenerational legacies of trauma* (pp. 279–295). New York: Plenum Press.

Kleijn, W., Hovens, J., & Rodenburg, J. (2001). Posttraumatic stress symptoms in refugees: assessments with the Harvard trauma questionnaire and the Hopkins symptom checklist—25 different languages. *Psychological Reports, 88*(2), 527–532.

Levine, P. (1997). *Waking the tiger.* Berkeley, CA: North Atlantic Books.

Levitt, J., & Beech, D. (2002). *The Clara Conference process paper.* Washington, DC: Psychologists for Social Responsibility.

Masten, A., Hubbard, J., & Gest, S. (1999). Competence in the context of adversity: Pathways to resilience and maladaptation from childhood to late adolescence. *Development & Psychopathology, 11*(1), 143–169.

McFarlane, A., & de Girolamo, G. (1996). The nature of traumatic stressors and the epidemiology of posttraumatic reactions. In B. van der Kolk, A. McFarlane, & L. Weisaeth (Eds.), *Traumatic stress: The effects of overwhelming experience on mind, body, and society* (pp. 129–154). New York: Guilford Press.

Mollica, R. F., Caspi-Yavin, Y., Bollini, P., Truong, T., Tor, S., & Lavelle, J. (1992). The Harvard trauma questionnaire: validating a cross-cultural instrument for measuring torture, trauma, and posttraumatic stress disorder in Indochinese refugees. *Journal of Nervous & Mental Disease, 180* (2), 111–116.

Natsios, A. (1997). Humanitarian relief interventions in Somalia: The economics of chaos. In W. Clarke & J. Herbst (Eds.), *Learning from Somalia: The lessons of armed humanitarian intervention* (pp. 77–95). Boulder, CO: Westview.

Pilisuk, M. (1998). The hidden structures of contemporary violence. *Peace and Conflict, 4*(3), 197–200.

Psychologists for Social Responsibility. (2002, July). *Integrating approaches to psychosocial humanitarian assistance: PsySR Conference Report.* Retrieved January 27, 2005, from http://www.psysr.org/

———. (2003). *Working with communities affected by ethnopolitical conflict: PsySR Conference Report.* Washington, DC: Author.

Psychosocial Working Group. (2003, October). *Psychosocial interventions in complex emergencies: A conceptual framework.* Edinburgh, United Kingdom. Retrieved January 27, 2005, from http://www.forcedmigration.org/psychosocial/papers/PWGpapers .htm

Rothschild, B. (2002). *The body remembers: The psychophysiology of trauma and trauma treatment.* New York: W.W. Norton & Co.

Shalev, A. (1996). Stress versus traumatic stress: From acute homeostatic reactions to chronic psychopathology. In B. van der Kolk, A. McFarlane, & L. Weisaeth (Eds.), *Traumatic stress: The effects of overwhelming experience on mind, body, and society* (pp. 77–101). New York: Guilford Press.

Smith, P., Perrin, S., Yule, W., Hacam, B., & Stuvland, R. (2002). War exposure among children from Bosnia-Hercegovina: Psychological adjustment in a community sample. *Journal of Traumatic Stress, 15*(2), 147–156.

Summerfield, D. (1998). The social experience of war and some issues from the humanitarian field. In P. Bracken & C. Petty (Eds.), *Rethinking the trauma of war* (pp. 9–37). New York: Free Association Books.

United Nations [UN]. (1998). *Proclamation of the year 2000 as the International Year for the Culture of Peace.* [General Assembly Resolution 52/13]. Retrieved January 27, 2005, from http://daccess-ods.un.org/TMP/1395331.html

Valid International. (2002, May). *Meeting the rights and protection needs of refugee children: An independent evaluation of the impact of UNHCR's activities.* Geneva, Switzerland: United Nations High Commissioner for Refugees [UNHCR].

van der Kolk, B. (1996). The body keeps the score: approaches to the psychobiology of posttraumatic stress disorder. In B. van der Kolk, A. McFarlane, & L. Weisaeth (Eds.), *Traumatic stress: The effects of overwhelming experience on mind, body, and society* (pp. 214–241). New York: Guilford Press.

———, McFarlane, A., & van der Hart, O. (1996). A general approach to treatment of posttraumatic stress disorder. In B. van der Kolk, A. McFarlane, & L. Weisaeth (Eds.), *Traumatic stress: The effects of overwhelming experience on mind, body, and society* (pp. 417–440). New York: Guilford Press.

Vygotsky, L. (1978). *Mind in society: The development of higher psychological processes.* Cambridge, MA: Harvard University Press.

Wadsworth, Y. (1998). What is participatory action research? Action Research International [Online], Available: http://www.scu.edu.au/schools/gcm/ar/ari/p-ywadsworth98.html

Wessells, M. (1998). Humanitarian intervention, psychosocial assistance, and peace-keeping. In H. J. Langholtz (Ed.), *The psychology of peacekeeping* (pp. 131–152). Westport, CT: Praeger.

———, & Monteiro, C. (2003). Healing, social integration, and community mobilization for war-affected children: A view from Angola. In S. Krippner & T. McIntyre (Eds.), *Psychological impact of war trauma on civilians: An international perspective* (pp. 179–191). Westport, CT: Praeger.

———, Schwebel, M., & Anderson, A. (2001). Psychologists making a difference in the public arena: Building cultures of peace. In D. Christie, R. Wagner, & D. Winter (Eds.), *Peace, conflict, and violence: Peace psychology for the 21st century* (pp. 350–362). Upper Saddle River, NJ: Prentice Hall.

CHAPTER 7

Effective Intercultural Collaboration on Psychosocial Support Programs

Nancy Peddle, B. Hudnall Stamm, Amy C. Hudnall, and Henry E. Stamm IV

> We yu go na kohntri, if yu mit pipul dehn de dans wit wan fut, yusehf foh dans wit wan fut. Boht if yu dans wit tu fut, dehn go koht di ohda wan ohnda yu.
>
> [*When you go to a country where the people dance on one foot, you should dance on one foot as well. If you dance on two feet, they'll cut one of them from under you.*]
>
> —*Sierra Leone proverb written in Krio and English*
> *(Sierra Leone Web, 2004)*

Theories of Culture

This chapter discusses lessons learned in the crucibles of fieldwork, where preconceived notions and good intentions are subjected to the pressures of human misery and loss. Through our collective experiences, working across cultures, we have learned the importance of approaching work within a new culture delicately and respectfully. By learning key cultural norms before working in a culture and applying specific culturally sensitive behaviors while in the culture, your chances of success are greatly enhanced. This chapter applies our experiences (gained through fieldwork, telecommuting to support fieldworkers, and research) to a framework for the user to refer to in the field, including examples of how we have applied what we know. At the same time, we anticipate that readers bring their own perspectives about intercultural collaborations on psychosocial support programs. We expect this framework to be readily modified to fit the unique aspects of a given situation. Most important, though, we hope that this chapter will expand awareness of multicultural challenges and remind us all of how easily we can unintentionally harm those we meant to help. Protecting the communities in which we work by understanding their strengths and challenges from their perspective also serves to help protect us, as workers, from burnout or secondary trauma, increasing our availability in a world where interpersonal and cross-group violence is an all too frequent occurrence.

To understand the challenges of providing culturally sensitive (or culturally relevant) psychosocial services in the aftermath of a traumatic event, it is important to be familiar with basic cultural concepts posited by theorists such as Eviatar Zerubavel, Clifford Geertz, Milton Bennett, Margaret Mead, and others. Zerubavel (1997), for example, suggests that as a social being, one's thinking is affected and constrained by particular social environments—the world looks and feels different according to one's sociomental lenses. A slightly different perspective is articulated by Bennett (1998), who suggests that much of social reality is constructed through the shared patterns of beliefs, behaviors, and values of interacting thought communities. This understanding has been incorporated into the United Nations' policies on development. As stated in one United Nations Educational, Scientific, and Cultural Organization (UNESCO, 1997) planning manual, culture influences individual perceptions through beliefs and values, and culture implies its own imperatives for action.

Self-Awareness

It is not enough, however, to investigate the theoretical concepts and definitions of culture before embarking on a mission to a foreign field. One must also become aware of one's own personal orientation, "thought communities," beliefs, behaviors, values, and ways of thinking and interacting with others. To be sure, understanding one's orientation is a work in constant progress, but when it comes to working interculturally in the aftermath of a traumatic event, self-awareness greatly enhances the results. As a visiting aid worker in a war zone or disaster situation, this self-knowledge and its implications for actions can have several positive outcomes. First, it leads to a greater understanding, and possibly acceptance, of the culture(s) within which one collaborates to build healing psychosocial programs. In these situations, self-knowledge strengthens one's tolerance for living in a strange environment, and thus the skills and knowledge one brings to the work might be deployed more effectively. Second, it can help if pushed to the edge during rough times—and the rough times always come—when one might consider the option of returning home out of frustration, fear, lack of safety, or exhaustion. An additional aspect of this is the guilt or betrayal one might experience when leaving—outsiders always have the option to leave, whereas helpers within the culture do not. Good self-knowledge helps determine what the best course of action actually is. Another potential benefit is that self-knowledge can facilitate change that is more than surface deep and discourages an ideology based on what La Voy (1999) refers to as Western elites and alienated majorities.

Trauma and Culture

In addition to gaining a basic understanding of the influences and interactions between people and their cultures (including one's own culture and one's own self), it is also necessary to read and study the trauma literature and the implications of culture on traumatology. One should have an awareness of the central discourses regarding trauma and culture. There is a lively debate about the best ways to understand the interaction between trauma and culture, and even whether the theories about traumatic stress have universal applicability. Some of the authors who have written about the ethnocultural considerations of treating trauma include Bracken and Petty (1998); Marsella, Friedman, Gerrity, and Scurfield (1996); Nader, Dubrow, and Stamm (1999); Peddle, Monteiro, Guluma, and Macaulay (1999); Stamm, Stamm, Hudnall, and Higson-Smith (2004); and Summerfield (1998).

Post-traumatic stress disorder (PTSD) and its treatments are widely acknowledged concepts in Western medical literature and often are at the core of any discussion about trauma. The official definition of PTSD is found in the *Diagnostic and Statistical Manual of Mental Disorders (DSM-IV)* (American Psychiatric Association, 1994). However, some researchers view the diagnostic classifications as inadequate, especially in regard to trauma-related personality changes (Herman, 1992; Weine et al., 1998). Nonetheless, it is a definition that is widely used internationally as psychosocial programs are set up to assist those who have experienced traumatic events. An overemphasis on the diagnosis and treatment of PTSD, however, overlooks one very important aspect about reactions to traumatic events—even if the symptoms warrant a diagnosis, doing so may not be in the best interest of the client (Stamm & Friedman, 2000).

Moreover, many traumatic events are not limited to individual experiences, especially in geographic areas affected by war or large-scale natural disasters. Traumatic or horrifying events may affect local communities, regions, or sometimes entire nations (Stamm et al., 2004). Multiple examples of horrifying events happening to larger communities can be found in the international humanitarian disaster literature and typically involve war or community violence such as seen in the 1994 genocide in Rwanda. One should consider the consequences that such events can have on the community at large or, more broadly, on the culture of the individuals affected by the event. Thus, it is possible that the culture itself may exhibit the effects of stress such that its institutions and infrastructures no longer offer viable support to its individual members. As a result, although the PTSD diagnosis may be widely used as a base for therapeutic approaches, when applied to a group there are limitations on relying on the narrow definition of PTSD and the subsequent medical model of treatment.

Most of the validating research on PTSD and other diagnoses in the *DSM-IV* have been carried out in Western industrialized nations (Friedman & Marsella, 1996). Despite this, many see PTSD as the extreme end of a continuum of normal responses to an abnormal situation. Because what is perceived as "normal" and "abnormal" are social constructs, a definition incorporating these concepts poses the questions of what, precisely, are psychological wounds and what, precisely, are recovery models beneficial to victims of seemingly traumatic events in non-Western societies.

Some theorists and practitioners challenge the usefulness of the PTSD diagnoses and treatment models for non-Western cultures (Bracken, 1998; Kleinman, 1995; Summerfield, 1998; Young, 1995). They argue that the concept of PTSD is grounded in a Western social milieu in terms of both the interpretations given to seemingly traumatic events and to the community and individual responses to the events. Therefore, in non-Western societies, the social constructions of cultural interpretation to stressful events and definitions of "normal" individual responses to those events may be sufficiently diverse from Western traditions and understanding to limit the usefulness of trauma theory and treatment as expressed in the PTSD diagnosis. Yet, there may be aspects of PTSD that are universal within the context of ethnocultural variations. Authors in Marsella et al. (1996) argue that we must remain open to ethnocultural differences that do not conform to the PTSD diagnostic criteria but that may be expressions of the phenomenon. For example, after the genocide in Rwanda in 1994, Westerners began to pour into the country to provide aid. Specialists in trauma arrived anticipating that Rwandan survivors would be suffering acute PTSD symptoms. Imagine their surprise when no one was complaining of PTSD-like symptoms such as nightmares, ruminating, or flashbacks; what the one hospital in Rwanda was treating in large numbers were headaches and stomachaches. In fact, the Western practitioners finally understood that the Hutus and Tutsi did not construct concepts of emotional health and emotional responses in their day-to-day language. They expressed their reactions to stress in somatic terms like headaches or stomachaches. To help people in this culture, it was necessary for practitioners to reconsider their assumptions and to consider the responses of the people with whom they were working.

What constitutes a traumatic event and the ways in which one experiences it are related to the cultural differences that are tied to one's social construction of reality. The reactions to the event can vary considerably, yet there are almost no studies that have compared the responses to traumatic events from members of one culture or nation with those of another in an effort to understand the symptoms and their meanings across cultures (Green, 1996). The social context from which meaning is derived, combined with the stressors of a traumatic event or environment of an event—that is, the magnitude of the exposure and the extent of the exposure—is important in determining the phenomenology of one's reaction. In addition, the reactions can be influenced by previous experiences and a multitude of individual, psychological, social, economic, political, and spiritual factors (cf. Arroyo & Eth, 1996; Marsella, Friedman, Gerrity, & Scurfield, 1994; Ressler & Tortorici, 1993). Any responses received by the exposed person also influence reactions at a personal level, as well as at an institutional level, and are all imbued with the culture (Dubrow, Liwski, Palacios, & Gardinier, 1996; Green, Wilson, & Lindy, 1985; Marans, Berkman, & Cohen, 1996).

Despite cultural differences and the limitations in cross-cultural methodology, there have been a number of recent studies among non-Westernized war-affected populations that have found the PTSD diagnosis appropriate, but the culture is always a key element of understanding the situation (for a review, see Stamm & Friedman, 2000). What, then, should an aid worker posted to an unfamiliar field do to provide successful psychosocial support? The best suggestion, perhaps, is to come prepared with the best training possible, with self-awareness, and with the ability to realize that prior knowledge and theoretical underpinnings might not be adequate or entirely appropriate for the new setting. The other critical imperative is that one needs to help design and implement an aid program with the explicit collaboration and partnership of the community receiving the aid.

Creating Culturally Appropriate Interventions

There is a long history in traumatic situations of international aid organizations, the United Nations, and nongovernmental organizations sending in teams of "experts" to provide aid and restore disrupted communities. Good intentions and international funding, however, have not always led to good outcomes. What was often missing in these efforts were collaborations and partnerships with the affected communities, which frequently meant the efforts were not sustainable after the aid workers left because the community members were not consulted and had no real stake in the program. Culturally appropriate interventions, by contrast, draw from a community's experiences and knowledge to increase the long-term self-sufficiency of communities, families, and children. The interventions should encourage the community, including the children, to take active roles in articulating problems and implementing solutions. Times of crisis are opportunities to do things differently, and creating partnerships between internationals and locals for psychosocial support programs can capitalize on this openness to change.

This emphasis on collaboration springs partly from the work of ecological theory, which views traumatic events, individuals, and cultures in holistic systems. It thus provides a mechanism for understanding the phenomena of trauma in a culturally relevant way and in creating culturally appropriate interventions. For example, Harvey's (1996) ecological theory of psychological trauma, treatment, and recovery emphasizes the local social, cultural, and political contexts of victimization and uses Herman's (1992) view that the community is a major source of resiliency for recovery from trauma.

Theory, as well as reports on successful projects, may hide the "bumps" in the road of cross-cultural psychosocial support work. For example, in the Sierra Leone Kids in Distress program (KIDS), one of the authors expended a great deal of energy monitoring the program's content to make sure that it addressed the needs and languages of all the program participants as both trainers and recipients of support. Sierra Leone comprises many cultural subgroups, such as the Mende, Temne, and Creole, among others, who speak different languages and have different traditions. To add to this cultural mix were trainees from Sierra Leone's capital city, Freetown—who tended to be Western-educated urban dwellers—and those who lived upcountry and tended to be more traditional village dwellers. There were a number of times that even the native Sierra Leone trainers needed to be reminded about their own cultural differences to provide effective interventions.

A more detailed example of collaboration and culturally appropriate intervention is found in the experiences of a nonemergency psychosocial support program in Ireland. Sitting in a colorful, brightly lit hotel lounge in Kinvera, Ireland, with the local women's group, we, as international consultants, learned about a "blow-in"—a concept that anyone entering collaboration with people from a different culture should know about. We were all engaged in a participatory learning and action activity, an approach used to help people identify their own problems and options for handling them. As we became more comfortable, we bantered with one another and each others' stories filled the air. "I've been here 15 years," said one. "Oh, that's nothing," said another, "I've been here 25 years." Then a third topped that with 37 years and added, "I'm still considered a 'blow-in.'" A "blow-in" is someone in Ireland who, after many years in the community, still remains an outsider.

The women of Kinvera sent us, the "outsider facilitators," a powerful message through their story of "blow-ins." They would work with us in finding a solution to their particular dilemma, but we needed to recognize their knowledge and what they brought to our work. As we focused on their traditions and customs, the glue to holding the Kinvera community together, we were able to share some tools that allowed them to better address their problem. Moreover, this collaboration left us little room to fall into the old paradigm of being the substantive expert coming to "fix" their problem, even though the seduction of "fixer" always remains.

So are there any guidelines or rules that one should follow when the call or e-mail comes that says, "Pack your bags; you have 72 hours to travel to _____" (fill in the blank—a culturally distinct community in Europe or America, South Africa, Sierra Leone, Albania, the Occupied Territories, Indonesia, etc.)? Although there are no "one-size-fits-all" preparations, based on our own experiences, we believe there are some actions that are well worth taking. Among these is to become as familiar as possible with the history, land, and people of the designated region.

A Framework for Considering Culture

In the following section, we examine eight domains that we believe contain cultural clues that are necessary to consider. We do not think that these eight domains are necessarily exhaustive, but offer them as a starting place for structuring your thinking about culture. Some of these domains will be unfamiliar to mental health personnel but not to anthropologists. However, in this chapter we address them using a mental health lens. Although no intellectual enterprise will fully prepare you for working in a culture that is different from your own, thinking through these areas— place; time; religion, spirituality, and ceremonies; interrelated issues of health interventions; literature; primacy of the family social status; death and dying; and coming in from the "outside"—provides a framework from which to contemplate and understand different traditions across different cultures. This framework is presented more fully, and with examples across multiple cultures, in a book edited by one of the authors, with two other colleagues. The book is *Honoring Differences: Cultural Issues in the Treatment of Trauma and Loss* (Nader, Dubrow, & Stamm, 1999). For this chapter, we have summarized ideas that should be applicable to any culture. You will need to "translate" the concepts and questions to the specific culture of interest to you.

Domain A: Place

This concerns physical space, or geography, but is much more. Unlike many Western urban dwellers, where physical locale may have more economic meaning than psychological qualities, many rural inhabitants throughout the world view and imbue geography and place with far more meaning. In many regions of the world, where subsistence farming or hunter/gatherer technologies still play a role in individual and community existence, the inherited cultural knowledge of space is intertwined with how one "fits" in the world. For example, associations with ancestors, beliefs about origin, the support community, or spiritual or revered leaders may be place bound. Healing and health also may have geographical strictures, especially in cultures without access to Western-style medical practices or treatments. Healing may depend on local knowledge of plant and animal resources for their curative powers. Finally, the sense of place may be tied to spiritual well-being. For many indigenous cultures and communities, belief systems evolved in time, and the core of spirituality is sometimes contained in specific localities—the "sacred spaces"—that cannot be replicated elsewhere.

Domain B: Time

Every culture, urban or rural, Western or non-Western, has a way of measuring the passage of time and the seasons. In many ethnic and indigenous communities, time is measured in cycles (e.g., "planting time," "ice break-up time," etc.), such that time is directly related to the life and activity of the community, not to a designated work/product schedule. For others, the past is present; that is, remembering the past is not just the commemoration of famous events but also an active guide for present and future behavior. Long-ago events influence current circumstances, such that actions of heroes may be recalled to teach each generation proper behavior within the community, perceived wrongs that occurred generations ago are precedents for current and future action, and the memories of past events (or some version of memory of past events) are taken into account in maintaining or establishing relationships. Finally, one should be aware of "indigenous time," UN time, and clock time (and understand the difference). Although watches and time clocks may be used in many non-Western communities, events and meetings often take place when those who are needed are gathered together, regardless of the appointed clock time.

Domain C: Religion, Spirituality, and Ceremonies

All cultures have core religious practices and spiritual beliefs, but not all individuals within those cultural communities adhere to these practices and beliefs. Multiple practices and beliefs can also exist within relatively homogeneous communities. Moreover, traditions do evolve and generally show some change over time, especially for groups that have migrated (by choice, because of environmental changes, or because of war) or experienced protracted contact with other cultures. Gaining access to knowledge about a culture's core spirituality is not always easy. For example, indigenous ceremonies may be open only to the initiated or knowledgeable. Questions about traditions and ceremonies should be addressed quietly, and usually to a trusted elder. They should also be asked in a way that allows the elder to not answer the question should they feel that the asker is not prepared to know the answer.

Other aspects of an indigenous spirituality may be unfamiliar. Dreams and visions are important in the absence of formal written language, and the power of visions and dreams to convey religious meaning, guidance, or help in decision-making is far stronger and more prevalent than is turning to "holy writ" for such direction. Furthermore, body/mind/soul generally should not be treated as separate entities. This understanding is crucial to the successful creation of psychosocial programs—treating physical ailments often or even primarily must focus on healing "soul wounds" first. Conversely, as illustrated by the Rwanda story, "soul wounds" may be experienced as physical illnesses.

Domain D: Interrelated Issues of Health Interventions

Health care in many cultures is intertwined with other issues, and one must take these into account when designing interventions. As suggested above, the past affects the present. Wounds to culture, such as invasions, profound social disruptions, war, or other events, may markedly alter the existence of a group or culture and may affect more than one generation. For instance, generations of oppression might foster widespread acceptance of the status quo. Trauma carried over from past events may inhibit effective parenting of future generations, with remembrance of things past being stressed so strongly that future generations continue to carry those burdens (i.e., intergenerational trauma).

Domain E: Literature

All cultures possess some form of literary expression, sometimes written down, and at other times carried in songs and stories. Both oral traditions and written literature provide knowledge and insight into indigenous thinking. Folk tales, legends, and stories, for example, often contain hints about the core values and beliefs of a culture. Because of an increase in published information, traditional as well as modern literature is available. It is important not to read all books about a culture with the same eye; some books are accepted by the community as accurate and reflective of them, but others are at best fantasy versions that are loosely based on the culture, and at worst, egregiously factually wrong and an appropriation of another's culture without their permission. Using scholarly skills to assess the veracity of the author's authority, as well as talking with local people, usually helps you sort the wheat from the chaff.

Domain F: Primacy of the Family Social Status

In many non-Western cultures, the family often takes precedence over the individual. Individual social status, for example, may be determined by a family's social status, individual autonomy often is subsumed to the family, individuals act on behalf of family, and so on. Interventions for individuals may involve family in terms of dealing with family issues and dynamics first before addressing individual needs or concerns. Elders often play a key role in the family systems. Their influence can be quite powerful, and their alliance is often crucial if programmatic changes are to occur.

Domain G: Death and Dying

All cultures have developed beliefs and ceremonies regarding their dead, but these can vary widely. Many societies practice elaborate rituals venerating a person and their death; for others, the dead person's name must never be mentioned in public. In still others, newborns are routinely named after deceased family members, and in still others, only special preparations or designated persons are allowed to deal with death as a matter of respect or fear that the spirit of the dead may harm the living. Some communities practice "giveaways" or "potlatches," where the deceased relative's possessions are given away (sometimes to the impoverishment of the living relatives). Such ceremonies are part of an elaborate complex of social obligations and power distribution. The deceased may be elevated to the realm of perfection or holiness. Mourning rituals may appear "crazy" to your social construct (as do ours to other's social constructs) but are appropriate when viewed in context of the person's culture.

There is another aspect of death and dying to take into account. High mortality rates may be typical in some societies. Although this can be a source of the cultural "wound," high death rates often mean that some individuals within a culture are more accustomed or aware of the reality of death and are less susceptible to being surprised by death or perceiving it as traumatic.

Domain H: Coming in from the Outside

To be an aid worker or outside expert offering advice and service to a troubled community involves inherent obstacles (see Nader et al., 1999, pp. 145–147, 279, 280). For example, one may be seen first as part of the problem, not as a helper or solution. This makes it difficult to gain the respect and trust of key individuals within the community, but gaining trust is of utmost importance. One can adopt certain behaviors, however, that help to overcome the initial reticence. First, learn to watch and observe. Know that patience and flexibility are very important virtues. Most important, attend to the people, not to problems or events.

Sierra Leone: Cultural Collaboration in Action

In 1996, Christian Children's Fund, the United Nations Children's Fund, and the Sierra Leone government came together in a unique collaborative effort and created the KIDS project to address the psychosocial problems of children 18 years and younger throughout Sierra Leone. As a project designer, one of the authors (NP) was hired by Christian Children's Fund to facilitate the project implementation to help children cope with the stress of chronic war. The specific goal was "to increase the capacity of community-based health social service and education staff working with children and youth living in war-torn Sierra Leone," through a national training plan. Ultimately, by indirectly using the eight domains explained above, the KIDS project provided the participants with a model of exemplary psychosocial collaboration from which they could institutionalize the lessons into the new administration, and thus the society.

As a means of incorporating Sierra Leone's cultural norms, the KIDS project was based on a "train the trainers" model. In other words, full consideration of these eight domains required the active and equal involvement of

Sierra Leonean partners and nongovernmental organization members. Partners from the "outside" shared their psychosocial skills, and partners from the "inside" shared local knowledge; these two knowledge sets combined to form a successful holistic method of aid.

Over a four-month period, the partners worked out how best to implement the project, using experiences in the field to test their ideas and curriculum. This allowed them to make cultural adjustments that considered whether the children were in urban or rural areas, living in refugee camps, and so on. In other words, adapting the curriculum to fit the needs of place and what meaning place held for the children and their families (Domain A).

Local partners provided sources of healing through Sierra Leone literature, sharing regional songs and stories, drumming, and religious ritual (Domains C and E). They drew on local beliefs about family and community (Domain F). In the Economic North, the nuclear family is the most important, but even the power of family is limited. In Sierra Leone, however, the single family unit includes one's mother, father, brothers, sisters, cousins, and neighbors. Everyone in a tribal unit, a neighborhood, or community is your family, and as a member of that family, you are subject to the advice and concern—some in the Economic North might say nosiness—of this large "family." To successfully help a person in Sierra Leone, the KIDS project had to incorporate the entire family in the process, not just the mother and father, and if the child's family structure was disrupted, then the volunteers had to find ways to fill that void, or healing was not possible.

A coup d'etat on May 25, 1996, forced Sierra Leone into a state of anarchy, right at the time when farmers would have been sowing the staple crops on which their survival depended. Most farming was disrupted as rebels looted and burned homes, maiming, raping, and killing indiscriminately. Only a few of the staff chose to stay, and most of the KIDS project members were relocated to Guinea by their nongovernmental organizations. This might have meant the end of the project but for the participants' belief that this was a program that was working!

Because of its successful blending of local culture and psychological knowledge, the partners had ownership in the program, molding and shaping it to fit Sierra Leone, and in doing so, gaining a sense of individual empowerment (Domain H). They were unwilling to watch it end. After attending to their own emotional well-being, the staff began working again (Domain H). Those who remained in Sierra Leone continued to provide culturally appropriate psychosocial support while training new volunteers. The coup not only disrupted the planting season but altered other aspects of the Sierra Leone farming calendar as well (Andersen, 2004). By being forced off their land, farmers were unable, at the correct time, to complete the rituals that are believed to protect the family, determine a good harvest, and ensure the continued help of their ancestors (Domains A, B, C, and F). Knowing these kinds of concerns, and thus knowing what problems needed to be addressed and how best to address them, allowed the remaining project members to continue their work effectively.

After the coup, the entire team collaborated with Médecins Sans Frontières (Doctors Without Borders) in Sierra Leone hospitals. The physicians were tending to amputee victims, but their success rate was inexplicably low—too many of the patients were dying for no reason apparent to Western medicine. Patient belief systems are powerfully linked to healing. For example, one local belief in Sierra Leone is that bad devils must be appeased by a sorcerer for healing to occur. Once the KIDS project staff added psychosocial interventions that addressed local beliefs about medicine, healing, and death (Domains D and F), the survival rate increased exponentially: "The team could relate at a cultural level and from their new psychosocial knowledge," thus supporting the physical healing (Peddle, 1998).

The KIDS project is not officially functioning today, but the concepts and tools that the local project members acquired are still in use: "They made the knowledge connections and integrated it into their culture. The building of the capacity of adults to help children in Sierra Leone was accomplished" (Peddle, 1998).

Summary

In closing, no text can fully prepare any of us to work in a culture that is different from our own. However, as noted in this chapter, there are several things that can assist and speed the adaptation and expansion of an awareness of existing multicultural challenges. These preparations focus on the key issue with which we began this chapter; that is, reminding us of the importance of not bringing harm to those we have come to help with our trauma interventions and treatments, and of how to protect the communities with whom we work.

The key point to cultural competency seems to be not one's knowledge of another culture but one's knowledge of one's self and one's own culture. Without a referent point, it is nearly impossible to accommodate and adapt to another culture without losing one's identity and ego strength in the process. Being able to look at something that is different, compare it to one's own experiences, and then make a decision about what each means and how one responds to them is perhaps protective and adaptive, even if it is an entirely internal process. Disappearing into another's culture to fill a personal void is inevitably an awkward and sometimes dangerous process. Actually choosing to embrace another's culture, or even to join it, is an entirely different endeavor. However this is done, doing it under the intense pressure of providing aid or helping to provide aid to the members of the unfamiliar culture is a psychologically and physically intense process.

When considering other cultures and how to understand them and how to work in them without bringing harm to those we intend to assist, we have suggested using a framework to think through cultural elements. We reviewed multiple domains in which we believe that cultures may have unique characteristics. These domains include (A) place; (B) time; (C) religion, spirituality, and ceremonies; (D) interrelated issues of health interventions; (E) literature; (F) primacy of the family social status; (G) death and dying; and (H) coming in from the "outside." This last domain, coming into a community from "outside" of the community, may provide the door to understanding the other domains. Outsiders typically are integrated into a new community regardless of whether the community is of a different or similar culture, in a layered way. It may be reassuring to remember that intercultural collaboration is not dissimilar to the development of any supportive relationship—true relationships develop over years of being present in each other's lives.

References

American Psychiatric Association. (1994). *Diagnostic and statistical manual of mental disorders* (4th ed.). Washington, DC: Author.

Andersen, P. C. (2004). *Kono farm calendar.* Sierra Leone Web. Retrieved September 12, 2004, from http://www.sierra-leone.org/calendar.html

Arroyo, W., & Eth, S. (1996). Post-traumatic stress disorder and other stress reactions. In R. J. Apfel & B. Simon (Eds.), *Minefields in their hearts: The mental health of children in war and communal violence* (pp. 52–74). New Haven, CT: Yale University Press.

Bennett, M. J. (Ed.). (1998). *Basic concepts of intercultural communication.* Yarmouth, ME: Intercultural.

Bracken, P. J. (1998). Hidden agendas: Deconstructing post traumatic stress disorder. In P. J. Bracken & C. Petty (Eds.), *Rethinking the trauma of war* (pp. 38–59). London: Free Association Books.

Bracken, P. J., & Petty, C. (Eds.). (1998). *Rethinking the trauma of war.* London: Free Association Books.

Dubrow, N., Liwski, N. I., Palacios, C., & Gardinier, M. (1996). Traumatized children: Helping child victims of violence. In Y. Danieli, N. Rodley, & L. Weisaeth (Eds.), *International responses to traumatic stress* (pp. 327–346). Amityville, NY: Baywood.

Friedman, M. J., & Marsella, A. J. (1996). Posttraumatic stress disorder: An overview of the concept. In A. J. Marsella, M. J. Friedman, E. T. Gerrity, & R. M. Scurfield (Eds.), *Ethnocultural aspects of posttraumatic stress disorder: Issues, research, and clinical applications* (pp. 11–32). Washington, DC: American Psychological Association.

Green, B., Wilson, J. P., & Lindy, J. (1985). Conceptualizing posttraumatic stress disorder: A psychosocial framework. In C. R. Figley (Ed.), *Trauma and its wake: Vol. 1. The study and treatment of post-traumatic stress disorder* (pp. 53–72). New York: Brunner-Routledge.

Green, B. L. (1996). Cross-national and ethnocultural issues in disaster research. In A. J. Marsella, M. J. Friedman, E. T. Gerrity, & R. M. Scurfield (Eds.), *Ethnocultural aspects of posttraumatic stress disorder: Issues, research, and clinical applications* (pp. 341–361). Washington, DC: American Psychological Association.

Harvey, M. R. (1996). An ecological view of psychological trauma recovery. *Journal of Traumatic Stress, 9,* 3–24.

Herman, J. L. (1992). Complex PTSD: A syndrome in survivors of prolonged and repeated trauma. *Journal of Traumatic Stress, 5,* 377–391.

Kleinman, A. (1995). *Writing at the margin: Discourse between anthropology and medicine.* Berkeley, CA: University of California Press.

La Voy, D. E. (1999). *Participation at USAID: Stories, lessons, and challenges.* Washington, DC: U.S. Agency for International Development.

Marans, S., Berkman, M., & Cohen, D. (1996). Child development and adaptation to catastrophic circumstances. In R. J. Apfel & B. Simon (Eds.), *Minefields in their hearts: The mental health of children in war and communal violence* (pp. 104–127). New Haven, CT: Yale University Press.

Marsella, A. J., Friedman, M. J., Gerrity, E. T., & Scurfield, R. M. (1994). Ethnocultural aspects of posttraumatic stress disorder. In R. S. Pynoos (Ed.), *Posttraumatic stress disorder: A clinical review* (pp. 17–64). Lutherville, MD: Sidran.

———. (Eds.). (1996). *Ethnocultural aspects of posttraumatic stress disorder: Issues, research, and clinical applications.* Washington DC: American Psychological Association.

Nader, K., Dubrow, N., & Stamm, B. H. (Eds.). (1999). *Honoring differences: Cultural issues in the treatment of trauma and loss.* Philadelphia, PA: Brunner/Mazel.

Peddle, N. (1998). National kids in distress project. *United Nations Chronicle, 35,* 46–47.

———. Monteiro, C., Guluma, V., & Macaulay, T. E. A. (1999). Trauma, loss and resilience in Africa: A psychosocial community based approach to culturally sensitive healing. In K. Nader, N. Dubrow, & B. H. Stamm (Eds.), *Honoring differences: Cultural issues in the treatment of trauma and loss* (pp. 121–149). Philadelphia, PA: Brunner/Mazel.

Ressler, E. M., & Tortorici, J. M. (1993). *Children in war.* New York: United Nations Children's Fund.

Sierra Leone Web. (2004). Krio Proverbs. Retrieved September 12, 2004, from http://www.sierra-leone.org/proverb1.html

Stamm, B. H., & Friedman, M. J. (2000). Cultural diversity in the appraisal and expression of traumatic exposure. In A. Shalev, R. Yehuda, & A. McFarlane (Eds.), *International handbook of human response to trauma* (pp. 69–85). New York: Plenum Press.

Stamm, B. H., Stamm IV, H. E., Hudnall, A. C., & Higson-Smith, C. (2004). Considering a theory of cultural trauma and loss. *Journal of Trauma & Loss, 9,* 89–111.

Summerfield, D. (1998). The social experience of war and some issues for the humanitarian field. In P. J. Bracken & C. Petty (Eds.), *Rethinking the trauma of war* (pp. 9–37). London: Free Association Books.

United Nations Educational, Scientific and Cultural Organization. (1997). *A cultural approach to development: Planning manual: Concepts and tools.* Paris: UNESCO.

Weine, S. M., Becker, D. F., Vojvoda, D., Hodzic, E., Sawyer, M., Hyman, L., Laub, D., & McGlashan, T. H. (1998). Individual change after genocide in Bosnian survivors of "ethnic cleansing": Assessing personality dysfunction. *Journal of Traumatic Stress, 11,* 147–153.

Young, A. (1995). *The harmony of illusions: Inventing post-traumatic stress disorder.* Princeton, NJ: Princeton University Press.

Zerubavel, E. (1997). *Social mindscapes: An invitation to cognitive sociology.* Cambridge, MA: Harvard University Press.

CHAPTER 8

WORKING EFFECTIVELY WITH THE MASS MEDIA IN DISASTER MENTAL HEALTH

Judy Kuriansky

One of the first lessons I learned when I became a reporter for television news was, "If it bleeds, it leads." This phrase refers to how blood and tragedy easily and consistently capture the attention of the public and the news media. This is one reason why psychologists are needed to ameliorate the effect of the emotionally dangerous and deadly dramas played out daily on the public stage by either malicious design or an accident of nature. Psychologists have been increasingly involved in communication with the public, and mass media can offer the field of psychology abundant opportunities for communicating with the public about issues with emotional consequences (Kirschner & Kirschner, 1997; Schwartz, 1999). Although there have been no scientific studies performed to date documenting psychologists' collaborative role with media in times of disaster, there are many anecdotal reports from experts who agree that partnerships of this sort can be extremely valuable in the interest of public education. This chapter is an overview of how the mental health profession and the media collaborate in times of crisis, as well as an exploration of inherent problems, untapped opportunities, and recommended practices. Examples are given from the author's experiences both as a crisis counselor and as a journalist.

Importance of the Role of Mental Health Professionals in Disaster Media Reports

Unfortunately, there is never a shortage of major disastrous events, both natural (earthquakes, floods, hurricanes) and man-made (violence, murder, terrorism). These calamities exact a tremendous emotional, physical, and financial toll not only locally but across the global community. That globalized effect is, to a great extent, the product of advances in mass communication, as was evident after the 2001 terror attacks on the World Trade Center and the 2004 earthquake and tsunami in Southeast Asia. In both instances, worldwide broadcasting of these tragedies led to unprecedented offers of humanitarian aid and awareness of psychosocial needs.

Although research shows that many people recover from a disaster more quickly than might be expected, moderate and prolonged impairment in up to a third of the affected people can be expected. Clinically significant problems tend to be more severe in developing countries, where risk factors include limited access to psychosocial resources and care (Norris, 2005; Stevens & Wedding, 2004). Factors that facilitate positive outcomes include availability of information and education that help people understand normal responses to such events, encourage sharing and emotional release, and facilitate formation of family and community bonds (NSW Institute of Psychiatry and Centre for Mental Health, 2000). Being able to communicate to the public through the media gives psychologists a valuable tool for achieving important mental health goals.

The media have a dramatic and widespread influence on how people think and feel in many situations, especially after a major mass disaster (Echterling & Wylie, 1999). People receive information and guidance on how to cope through print and electronic media, and increasingly through the Internet, cell phones, and text messaging. Increasingly rapid communication has transformed our world to the point at which information about disasters can be immediately transmitted to billions of people around the globe. The effect of these messages can have beneficial or harmful psychological consequences, which is why it is imperative that psychologists learn to work effectively with the mass media. The mental health professions are uniquely well suited to provide the public with reliable information and advice about how to cope with tragic situations and should become integrally involved with the media in communicating messages that serve the public interest. Those who do this type of work are known as "media psychologists."

Talking Away Fears in a Public Arena: An Affecting Personal Experience

One of my most powerful experiences as a media psychologist occurred in 1989, when I was vacationing in Australia. While camping I learned that the worst earthquake in the country's history had struck with tragic consequences for the nearby town of Newcastle. Historic buildings were irreparably damaged, hundreds of people were injured, and 14 victims—mostly elderly—were buried in the ruins. The timing of the quake, during the otherwise joyous Christmas season, made the pain and despair all the greater. When I called my friend David Banks, a newspaper editor, to tell him I would not make it back for our meeting, he said, "File me a story and get it here by four o'clock. That way we can report on the psychological aftermath before the other papers, and from an expert who's really on the scene." Thus began one of the most powerful experiences, and lessons, I have had in using the mass media for psychological healing after a disaster.

Though as a foreigner I was unfamiliar with local procedures, a call to the chief constable explaining my assignment and offering to help led to my being whisked through checkpoints and over debris to the command post. The media liaison staff members at the site were already busy contacting newspapers, radio, and television stations to arrange interviews for me to talk about how to cope. One radio station suspended its scheduled programming to put me on air answering callers' questions about their anxieties—a previously unfamiliar format that serves to this day as a model for how psychologists and the media can work together in times of disaster.

As the phones began ringing, I answered a call from a 71-year-old woman who was in a supermarket where boxes fell on her head and was now housebound and frightened about what to do next. Next, a mother called about her nine-year-old son having nightmares, and I suggested that he draw them. Another mother worried about her older child's bed-wetting, but I reassured her that such behavior (know as regression) is an understandable and temporary reaction. A sergeant sharing his stress at being part of the victim identification team proclaimed, "Everybody leans on the rescue squad, but we need help too." I spoke with a rescue worker who was wracked with guilt over joking about accidentally stepping on body parts and a minister who called to tell listeners it was okay to be angry at God. One man chastised me by saying, "You're only making people more upset by talking about it," but many callers expressed gratitude for having a public forum to share feelings and fears.

My story for the *Daily Telegraph* newspaper ran on the front page—which is exceptionally rare for a psychological feature. Under the headline, "Talk away your fears," it offered advice about how to cope (from giving youngsters increased attention to getting back to normal routines). From sharing on the radio show to the front-page newspaper story, the media had helped spread a psychological message of healing. This example of authorities and media executives taking spontaneous innovative action in a crisis provides a model for creative programming that uses valuable psychological resources to serve the public. Given proper planning and training, local experts can employ this model of public education with very limited financial resources.

Historical Perspective on Media and Disaster Mental Health

A study of psychology and the news media showed that psychologists were minimally represented, even on shows featuring psychological content. Of 146 television news magazine and talk shows that featured psychological content, only 12 percent of the 158 experts were psychologists

(Diesch & Caldwell, 1993). Given the sensitive nature of issues related to trauma, the importance of experts' participation cannot be overestimated. Following the 2001 terrorism attacks on the World Trade Towers and the anthrax attacks in the same year, feelings of panic rose to dangerously high levels, and mental health professionals responded by helping to reduce public anxieties. Yet even after innumerable electronic and print media stories welcomed the participation of mental health professionals in the analysis and healing process, important opportunities for involving psychologists were later missed in other situations. For instance, although legal analysts and military experts flooded the airwaves during the 2003 initial stages of the war on Iraq, psychological commentary was minimal in comparison.

It is common for the media to use celebrities to comment on disasters as participants in highly publicized fund-raising broadcasts. For instance, in a recent telethon for victims of the Asian tsunami, there were frequent references to hope and healing, but a pretaped feature describing the "psychological aftermath" featured not one psychologist, and an hour-long program that followed the telethon discussed healing and interviewed relief workers but showed only one volunteer who was identified as a psychologist.

What Qualifies a Psychologist for Mass Media Expertise?

Because the news media usually look to psychologists for descriptions of symptoms and giving advice about coping, experts must keep up with the latest research and best clinical practices in the disaster field. One way to do this is to attend professional meetings of organizations like the International Society for Traumatic Stress Studies, composed of international experts dedicated to trauma treatment, education, research, and prevention. Training for responders is available from organizations like the Red Cross, as well as from centers all over the world that specialize in trauma. However, it is also important to become adept at communicating messages that are brief but informative and accessible to a broad range of people who vary in age, education, and experience with mental health concepts.

Types of Media Opportunities

There are a vast number of outlets for media coverage of professional psychological opinions and advice. These include electronic (radio and television), print (newspapers, magazines), and new media (Internet and telecommunications). Opportunities for publication include not only being interviewed but also submitting op-ed pieces, letters to the editor, or articles for community newspapers. Financial compensation is rarely given, so those who engage in these efforts must do so without expectation of material gains.

Creative collaborations and cross-promotions help get the message out. This was the case with a pamphlet developed after 9/11, called *ACCESS: Emergency Survival Handbook*, which included a psychoeducational section I wrote on emotional response, recovery, and preparedness for disasters (Edie Hand Foundation, 2002). The pamphlet was distributed to the public in collaboration with radio stations in southern states across America. The organizer then arranged for a special event breakfast for a local area chamber of commerce, where I gave a speech to help business owners and employees ease anxieties and create a safer, more anxiety-free business environment. That speech, called *Getting Back to Business in the Age of Terrorism*, was covered by a local journalist (Burroughs, 2002). Later that day, I facilitated a videotaped discussion with employees at a local dairy company, airing their feelings related to 9/11. The combined effect of these separate pieces can sometimes add up to more than the sum of their parts.

New Media

"New media," which refers to the many different forms of electronic communication made possible through the use of computer technology, is another way that mental health professionals can get their message out. The term is meant to draw a distinction between these methods and the "old" media forms, such as printed newspapers and magazines. New media make collaboration across continents and time zones easier and more effective. Articles about disaster recovery can be submitted to Web sites, particularly ones that deal with psychological or spiritual issues, or posted on a personal Web site or on one hosted by an organization. For instance, in the wake of the 2004 tsunami, mental health organizations e-mailed each other to collate information and resources disseminated in electronic newsletters and Web site postings, making that information available to vast numbers of other professionals and authorities. In this manner, professionals can assist each other in determining the best actions to take, where to contribute funds, and a plan for implementing research and appropriate interventions before making the information widely available to the wider public.

Creative use of new media formats can aid in the public role of psychology in healing. After the 2001 World Trade Center attacks, I used streaming video as a unique form of advice giving in my role as a reporter for a site called CameraPlanet. On-the-spot encounters with individuals and couples who asked questions related to their experiences and reactions to the attacks were videotaped, edited, and then posted on the Web site. The interviews took place in the streets in the area around Ground Zero. A group of teens playing ball in a school yard near the site stopped to ask, "What can we do with a friend we know is depressed as a result of the planes crashing into the towers, but does not say anything about it?" A couple strolling with their baby asked, "How can we feel good about raising our child in a world where terrorism like this happened and can happen again anytime?" People could then post comments or questions on another part of the site, communicating with others as well as with the expert. Although the technology of streaming video is still new and problematic, it is promising.

How the Media Calls on Experts

Experts on disaster can either respond only to requests from the media or proactively offer stories and reports on important information to the public. At the time of crisis, a media outlet wanting psychological commentary often calls a professional organization for referral to an expert who can address the angle of their story. Organizations should have a list of experts ready, and professionals who want to provide that service should contact their organization (usually the public affairs office) to be put on the referral list. Reporters also do their own research, searching the Internet for experts who have written on or been quoted about that subject. Over time, journalists develop their own list of experts—usually people who have been on their show before, sometimes even about a different topic—who have proven their credibility and authority and are available on short notice.

Journalists frequently refer their colleagues to sources they have used successfully. Colleagues or friends may also precipitate a story. A friend who heard about my trip to Jerusalem during the height of the second Intifada contacted a reporter he knew at the *Jerusalem Post*, who then wrote a news story about my mission of donating money to various hospitals and rehabilitation centers (Siegel, 2002). Weeks later, when I counseled the students and staff at Hebrew University after a tragic bombing, that reporter called another colleague, who in turn wrote a feature story for a magazine (Hartog, 2002). This illustrates how one thing leads to another, magnifying the effect of the original story. The media sometimes recognize the value of psychological commentary on their own; however, at other times it may be necessary to "pitch" a psychologically oriented story to the media. This more proactive approach means offering your story to a given outlet or signaling your availability to comment.

Timing of Psychological Commentary in Disasters

In rare instances, the media will seek a psychologist's commentary on the first day of covering a disaster, but more often the first concern of the media is to get the facts about loss of life, financial costs, and reactions from people involved as well as from government officials. Psychologists who happen to be on the scene may get asked for a brief comment about people's reactions and needs (called a "sound bite"). What that professional says must be chosen carefully, as it is likely to be repeated several dozen times across the 24-hour news cycle. When the media know that the public is captivated by an event, they may search for new—or even "spicy"—angles. For example, three days after a major electrical outage in New York, a major local newspaper called me to ask if when the lights go down, people's sex drive goes up.

Benefits of Working with the Media

There are many benefits to working with the media around trauma issues. Along with the professional satisfaction of doing a service to the community, there are valuable opportunities to reduce stigma by "de-pathologizing" victims and survivors of disaster, as well to offer reassurance that help is available. Furthermore, trauma experts working with the media can provide positive role models for the public on how a psychologist is helpful, in terms of giving good advice, assuaging people's fears, and alleviating anxiety by demonstrating how to stay calm in crisis. There are also personal benefits—called "compassion satisfaction"—that come from working with any trauma survivors, including increased self-confidence, sense of meaning, spiritual connection, and respect for human resiliency (Figley, 1995).

Limitations and Caution in the Media

Bad news makes headlines, but good news stories are usually buried in the back pages. Although some production groups are striving to emphasize good news, the basic goal of mainstream media as a business is to make money by selling papers or getting ratings. Psychodynamically, some people even like hearing bad news because it makes them feel their own life is not as bad. A disaster can highlight important long-standing but neglected social or psychological issues. For example, after the 2004 Asian tsunami, the media began to cover problems of orphans, child trafficking, and ostracized widows. Unfortunately, the news has a short attention span, and a story only has "legs" until the next big issue, scandal, or crisis comes along. Disaster survivors suffer when the public and media attention withdraw after initial intense interest in their lives and welfare. Ongoing coverage of child care, women's rights, or other public interest issues is desperately needed (Kuriansky, 2005b).

Although too little information can leave people suffering, too much can have an adverse effect on mental health, heightening public anxiety (Heldring, 2004). Advice psychologists gave in the aftermath of 9/11, as for other mass disasters, was to avoid media "overexposure" by restricting watching television news or reading publications about the events—advice the media, to their credit, allowed and even encouraged, even if not in their own interest. Reducing media overexposure applies particularly to children. For example, a Board of Education study after 9/11 found that some youngsters who saw many replays on television of the planes crashing into the World Trade Center buildings thought that the terrorist events were happening repeatedly. In cases like this, mental health professionals can play a role not only on-air but also behind the scenes, advising media about how to present a story. Potential misuse of terms related to disaster poses another problem. After 9/11, experts noted that terms like trauma and posttraumatic stress disorder were at times inaccurately applied and alarmed the public unnecessarily.

A major ethical concern centers on the exploitation of people's trauma, such as interviewing survivors at their most vulnerable time and eliciting extreme emotional reactions. For this reason, it is important to weigh the need for information with respect for people's privacy and emotional states. The media love controversy, and to generate a lively debate, producers may want to pit one expert's point of view against other. For example, in the wake of the tsunami, a cable network devoted several hour-long shows to debates among religious leaders about whether God was to blame. Prepare yourself for such events by speaking to the other interviewees before participating in the show to establish a sense of professionalism and common interest in the public's welfare.

To stand out from the rest, the media also highlight dramatic successes or failures. Do not be lured into overdramatizing or answering questions designed to elicit a strong response (like asking you to comment on officials' reactions). Unusual circumstances can make a psychologist a likely commentator, as happened when I was in China post-9/11 and did press interviews with the consulate about the aftermath of the terrorist attacks. In such instances, it is important to stay focused on psychological, not political, messages.

Media will always respond to stories that include major high-profile leaders and celebrities, so experts should be prepared to be asked to comment on such figures. During 9/11, I was confident about saying that Mayor Rudy Guiliani provided a good example of what the public needed in a disaster: a strong leader who was in control but who was also empathic. By being a container for people's fears, as well as an authority figure the public could respect, Guiliani represented a good "father figure" from a psychodynamic point of view. When he publicly cried at the funerals of his close friends and city employees who perished in the terror attack, I was able to point out a valuable lesson—that crying under such circumstances is not an "unmanly" thing to do (Kuriansky, 2003a).

Media vary in their interest in psychological responses, and I'll never forget (sadly) the television news director who told me, "AIDS is not a psychological issue" when I proposed in 1982 that the station do a special on the psychological aspects of the disease. More recently, when war in Iraq broke out, the executive producer of a major international television network news show said that neither he nor his host were interested in the psychological angle of that or any other story. Thus, it is important for mental health professionals to be more persistent in educating the media about the "psychological" aspects of major traumatic events and the importance of presenting these issues to the public.

What the Media Needs

The media have specific needs for stories that may or may not coincide with your own needs to tell the story. These include:

1. News: relevant, interesting information that touches people's lives
2. Expertise: compelling, interesting facts, tips, recommendations, and analysis of trends
3. Clarity/focus: condensed information, conclusions, and issues simplified to make it easy for broad audiences to understand
4. Spokespeople: reliable, credible contacts that can provide valuable information, and quotes on-air in an energetic and concise way. Although honesty (saying, "I don't know") is certainly absolutely ethical, make use of valuable time by offering what you do know about another aspect of the issue.

Tips about How to Work with the Media

As a media psychologist and disaster relief counselor, I have been interviewed about numerous disasters (SARS in China, 9/11, Hurricane Hugo in South Carolina, earthquakes in Mexico and Australia, terrorism in the Middle East, the war in Iraq, and the recent Asian tsunami). I have also reported on these events as a television reporter, call-in radio advice host, and newspaper and magazine columnist. The following guidelines on effective use of the mass media as a public mental health resource in disasters have been drawn from years of experience. These action principles are stable and can be applied in other situations, inserting the appropriate content details.

When you are interviewed:

- Ask yourself what you want the audience to know. Decide on your message and say it no matter what you are asked. Important messages for disaster recovery include "stay calm," and "get back to normal routine."
- Be to the point. Most television or radio stories are only a few minutes long, leaving room for expert comments ("sound bites") of two sentences (even if you are interviewed for ten minutes). Especially in a live television interview, say your message at the beginning, as the topic may turn in another, unexpected direction.
- Present a human interest "angle." Use personal stories to help the audience better understand and relate to the point, but preserve confidentiality by talking in generalizations, like "Usually children who have nightmares after the disaster," and so on.
- Be "reader (or viewer)-friendly." Make clear and practical points that can be presented in a newspaper sidebar or on a list on television. Think and talk in headlines.
- Be well-informed. Keep current on the facts of the situation and be equally up to date on relevant statistics and research and trauma issues. Rely on reputable books, journals, international conferences, Internet sites, and trauma experts (e.g., Stout, 2002).
- Be adaptable. Always turn a question, however inappropriate, into a valuable psychological message.

- Be innovative. The media prefer anything that sounds new or surprising. Some orphaned children who returned to Sweden after the tsunami devastation in Thailand appeared happy—a reaction that seemed inappropriate but was understandable, given that they did not yet comprehend the full effect of their parents' disappearance. Shape your advice accordingly (in this instance, listening to children instead of prompting them with questions like, "Wasn't it terrible to lose your parents?").

- Dare to be positive. Studies show that many people cope surprisingly well after a disaster. The latest focus of the psychological community is on people's resilience after crisis.

- Use visual aids and speak vividly. For a television interview about children's reactions after 9/11, I brought a teddy bear on to the set to describe the concept of "contact comfort" (how holding soft toys can be comforting to children). Such soft animals have cross-cultural value, as they were handed out to children after 9/11 at the Family Assistance Center, and also to Swedish children met at the airport, returning from the tsunami disaster. Because a picture is worth a thousand words, for an interview about 9/11 on a Chinese television show, I brought photos of the memorials that the producer could enter into their computer and insert in postproduction, as well as a baseball cap with the insignia of the twin towers that the host put on.

- Give practical advice. In a television interview about a teen who hijacked a plane and flew it into a bank building, I advised teens to pay close attention to friends' behavior and not be afraid to tell adults or authorities about unusual behavior they notice.

- Be prepared. When asked to give a media interview, ask, "What is the topic?" "Who else is on the show?" and "What is the format (debate, one-on-one interview, live or taped)?"

- Give out referral information, including your own or others' organizations, phone numbers, and Web sites. Prepare these in advance, so producers can present this information.

- Give "best-practices" advice. Advising the public is a big responsibility, especially after a disaster when people are vulnerable. Be sure to read the latest books on disaster relief and check the Web sites of respected specialization groups. Describe short- and long-term emotional, cognitive, physical, interpersonal, and spiritual reactions; survivor guilt; risk factors; and getting professional help when needed. Pay particular attention to problems of children and accepted techniques for helping kids cope with trauma.

To pitch a story and get coverage:

- Be timely. Address "Why is this report important on this day for people to hear?" Give your "pitch" in two sentences or 30 seconds. Pitch stories that coincide with special days of recognition, such as the anniversary of the event, or a national Mental Health Day.

- Be creative. The more compelling the story, the more likely it is to get covered.
- Know the media outlet, and fashion the message to fit their needs and style. Watch the television show to identify the length of segments and interviewer's style. Read the newspaper to determine if they cover psychological-type stories.
- Make the story relevant to the audience. Local media will always want to know "Who in our community has been affected?" Swedish media covered the tsunami tidal wave disaster extensively because so many Swedes vacation in Thailand, and many were there at holiday time when the tragedy happened.
- Develop relationships with reporters, whose choices of words signal interest in psychological issues, showing their receptivity to your message.
- E-mail or fax the news desk or particular reporter. Call at the right time (not right before a broadcast, when the staff is rushing to get the show on the air). One exception is breaking news, when you should call the news desk or hotline right away.
- Be willing to serve the public interest by giving background information, psychological research, and professional journal articles without being quoted or appearing on air. I often e-mail the article I wrote for an Austrian journal about personal reflections and professional experiences after 9/11 (Kuriansky, 2003a).
- Respect all types of media. Small town papers are important, so do not just focus on national outlets. Be tolerant of different levels of experience in journalism and in the topic of trauma, using patience and understanding, as you may be asked oversimplified ("What is a disaster?") or inappropriate questions.
- Create long-term relationships. Update the media on new aspects of issues, to be prepared in case of another event.
- Let colleagues—especially through professional associations—know about your work so they can refer you if the occasion arises.
- Hiring public relations representatives is expensive. Instead, develop your own contacts, give speeches at community centers, and list professional expertise in reports of available experts and through companies that provide low-cost service on the Internet, like Radio-Television Reports and PR Newswire.
- Consider different formats for a psychological message. For instance, you might develop a media kit about disaster issues containing relevant quotes, contact information, and tips that a reporter can use verbatim when in a rush. Other examples include a fully produced television story provided to stations in a form they can air with little effort or expense; a printed form of information that an organization or company wants to communicate to the public, prepared in a format that can be directly printed into a publication; or public service announcements that are given exposure free of charge.

Are You a Good Match for Media Psychology?

Just as there are psychodynamic reasons why professionals choose disaster relief work, there are reasons for wanting to work with the media in disasters. It is wise and responsible to examine one's own motivations to prevent disappointment and be able to perform professionally. Extreme needs for control or self-importance get in the way of communicating the message. Professionals most suited for media work have a healthy ego that is not overwhelmed with narcissism, so that the message is about what's happening and not about themselves.

Mental health professionals are not actors, and talking about disaster certainly requires a serious tone, but the media respond to people who come across as energetic, especially on television, where energy attracts viewer attention. It is also helpful to have surplus energy and a schedule that can accommodate early morning or late night appearances. Other desirable qualities, especially for live television or radio, are coming up with an answer quickly without leaving "dead air," and being definitive rather than excessively qualifying a point. Speak in a conversational style without self-consciousness that millions of people are listening or watching. Above all, it is crucial to be well informed about the field and to have good communication skills. Professional media training is expensive, but you can practice presentations and role playing with friends or coworkers, who can then give you feedback about your performance. You can also learn a great deal from audio taping or videotaping your performance to replay and review.

Fearing the Media

Because of the controversies that abound in the disaster field, such as the one concerning which interventions are most effective for whom and at what time (e.g., "critical incident stress debriefing" vs. "psychological first aid"), some experts are leery of responding to media. Fears include discomfort with "pat answers" or being put in a nonscholarly format, being "edited" and therefore misrepresented or taken out of context, or other ethical concerns. However, it is possible to offset the downside of responding by recognizing the value of the opportunity. Fashion and polish your message into short sentences and practice saying them clearly and with confidence, but also feel free to express any concerns to a reporter. When being taped, speak in full sentences, making your point in different ways so it can be used without editing. Do not answer if you're uncomfortable. Refer to other sources that support or clarify your comments.

Important Messages to Convey

Key messages to impart to the public include helping people feel safe, get back to their normal routine as much as possible, and seek support. Both children and adults need to be comforted. For instance, while handing out teddy bears to children after 9/11, some adults asked if they could have one for themselves. As one man told me, "I need a teddy bear, too." Some trauma reactions that can be explained to the public include how the immediate event can trigger memories of past traumas, create spiritual crises, and affect hidden victims (people who are less obviously affected). Good coping advice includes being kind to yourself, keeping things in perspective, appreciating your mastery and resilience, and looking for opportunities for self-discovery.

Another important message, supported by my own research about the effect of disasters on relationship and intimacy, is that couples' relationships can be strained when they react differently to disaster (Kuriansky, 2002, 2003b; Richard, 2002). For example, one woman was ready to divorce her husband because he refused to talk about the horrors of 9/11, making her feel misunderstood and unsupported.

Psychology and Journalists' Trauma

Journalists themselves are affected by covering disasters and are part of the group of "hidden" or "unrecognized" victims whose suffering often goes unrecognized. Those in the field (especially freelancers) as well as in the studio are vulnerable to emotional reactions. The Dart Center for Journalism and Trauma was founded in 1999 to help journalists deal with covering stories about trauma. This global network of journalists, journalism educators, and health professionals is dedicated to improving media coverage of trauma and tragedy, providing a support system for journalists, and facilitating academic research, seminars, workshops, and training. "While it is not the Center's goal to get more quotes for psychologists," Dart's Executive Director Roger Simpson told me, "we do want to help journalists incorporate psychological science into reporting."

The center has worked closely with news teams and mental health professionals after bombings, school shootings, and multiple hurricanes. After 9/11, they dispatched a team to New York, headed by a psychologist and a school administrator. "Dart Center Ground Zero was a comprehensive approach to bring experts in trauma science together with media in the aftermath of a crisis. We focused on two goals: giving journalists information they needed to report knowledgeably and responsibly on mass trauma: and helping journalists and media organizations develop their own support systems," says Dart field director and Yale University journalism teacher Bruce Shapiro.

The center's inclusion and cooperation with psychologists, and its respect for the role of psychology in disasters, is impressive. Their Web site front page has a posting, "Need a source for your story? The Dart Center can direct you to mental health and trauma experts." Another place on the site posts, "As the facts of the tragedy sink in and stabilize—death toll, material damage and so on—remember there's also a powerful story to be told about both the immediate and longer-term psychological impact on the communities and individuals affected" (see http://www.dartcenter.org).

Another collaborative effort of psychologists working with media has been developed by trauma therapist and founder of the International Traumatic-Healing Institute, Gina Ross (Ross, 2003). Ross teaches techniques like somatic experiencing to help those who suffer from what she calls the "trauma vortex"—whirlpool of chaos with a magnetic pull that traps those who are traumatized. Describing the media as "the eyes, ears, and voice of our collective body," Ross facilitates the collaboration of media members and trauma specialists to create a "healing vortex" with messages of hope and healing.

Example of a Media Interview about Disaster

After America declared the start of military action in the war on Iraq in March 2003, I was asked to come on the local CBS television station for a series of weekly in-studio interviews with the anchor of the news show concerning how to cope. Each interview was about three minutes and ten seconds in length (long by news standards) and was preceded or followed by a commercial break, unrelated stories, or other terrorism news (something you can refer to in your story, to provide continuity). Each interview focused on a different age group: children, teens, adults, and grandparents. In each case, I was asked to describe the problems idiosyncratic to that age group, respond to common questions either from surveys or from e-mails sent to the station, and give specific advice.

Before the interview, there were e-mail and phone communications between myself and the producer and writer of the segment for me to give my ideas, statistics, studies, tips, and suggested questions. Then we would go over the topic, clarify the questions, and prepare lists of points (symptoms, advice, or survey results) that would be preproduced to appear on the screen during the interview, and that I would talk over. A script would be written for the anchor, with questions that he or she could follow or improvise.

Each story has an introduction. In the segment on teens, the anchor said, "We all know that many of the troops fighting in Iraq are still teens. Even rescued Jessica Lynch was only nineteen. So how do teens at home feel about the war and how can parents help them? Clinical psychologist Dr. Judy Kuriansky has talked to teens and is a columnist for *Cosmo Girl* magazine that has done a survey of young girls' feelings about the war." In the segment, I was asked about the survey results, and what parents can do to help teens. I explained that war can trigger direct conflicts for teens (like fears of going to war) and can also exacerbate problems in other areas of life (school performance, difficulties with boyfriends or girlfriends). The following sample script is from a segment about grandparents coping with the war:

ANCHOR LEAD: While some attention is given to how children are coping with this war, one age group is all-too-often neglected—older Americans. Yet, grandparents are also being affected by this war, and here to talk about that is clinical psychologist Dr. Judy Kuriansky, who has worked on a public awareness campaign about depression in mature America.

ANCHOR: Dr. Judy, how are older Americans coping with the stress of this war?

Dr. Judy answers (talks about disappointment over making a better life for their children and grandchildren; flashbacks triggered in vets and spouses from Vietnam, Korean War, and WWII, especially for Holocaust survivors).

ANCHOR: If older Americans are silently suffering, what can their children—who are adults—look for, as signs that there is a problem?

Dr. Judy answers: as the screen reveals these points:

SIGNS OF GRANDPARENTS SUFFERING:
INCREASED ACHES AND PAINS (including imaginary ones)
FEAR LEAVING HOME/HOUSEBOUND
CONSTANT REMINDING CHILDREN TO EAT, SLEEP, BE SAFE
PROBLEMS REMEMBERING
REPETITIVE STORIES ABOUT PAST LOSSES
DEPRESSION (can be misdiagnosed as cognitive disorder)

Back to Studio Shot:

ANCHOR: How can their adult children help?

Dr. Judy answers: (mentions calling, pointing out previous ability to cope, engage in cheerful family activities)

ANCHOR: How has this affected the relationship between grandparents and their grandchildren?

Dr. Judy answers

ANCHOR: What happens when grandparents have a different attitude toward the war than their grandchildren?

Dr. Judy answers

Throw to next story

The Role of Psychological Associations and Professional Media

In the aftermath of a disaster, local and national mental health associations should serve their members by giving guidelines about a proper response and about being available for media contacts. The Disaster Response Network of the American Psychological Association, which works in cooperation with the American Red Cross, provides an example of how psychological associations can create directories of members able to react to a disaster. Guidelines for effectively responding to mental health needs can be posted, and press releases and Web sites can be prepared and updated very rapidly, with fact sheets and recommendations that evolve as conditions change. Web sites should have places for posting experiences, relevant research, and articles; for example, my newspaper article, as well as reports on meetings at the United Nations about the tsunami, were submitted to the newsletters for International Association of Applied Psychology (http://www.iaapsy.org) and the American Psychological Association's International Division (Kuriansky, 2005a, 2005b).

Organizations may even have special media chapters or divisions, such as the Media Psychology Division of the American Psychological Association, which assists psychologists on how to use media effectively. The goals include "giving psychology away" to the public, informing the public about the science and profession of psychology, facilitating interaction between psychologists and media representatives, formulating ethical guidelines, and providing training for psychologists to interpret research to the lay public and communicate effectively. To ensure a psychological perspective, these professional organizations or individual members should also consider hosting and participating in events, workshops, and panels related to disasters and the media. For example, I recently chaired a symposium at the 2004 United Nations NGO conference on the topic, "Winning Ways: Media Approaches that Work."

Wearing Two Hats: The Psychologist as Media Professional

An excellent way to communicate psychology's message about trauma in the mass media is to have one's own mass media outlet. Some psychologists have the opportunity to do this by hosting radio or television shows or by writing columns. Such involvement can lead to further civic action, as my own experience in meeting with mayors to develop emergency preparedness manuals illustrates. Also, because of the control I have over the topics in my newspaper column on the Web, I have been able to post timely articles about coping after the tsunami (Kuriansky, 2005a) and to give voice to issues and experts that might not otherwise be covered.

Over decades of answering the questions of countless men and women, of all ages, dealing with crises on the radio, I developed a model of advice giving that is effective in such a public arena, with time constraints on contact with individuals. This Reassure Model is based on years of experience learning that people want reassurance that they are not the only one with their problem; that they are not "abnormal," as they may fear; and that there is help available. This model is proving useful in giving Internet advice (e-advice) as well, as I do through my newspaper column.

The psychologist as journalist can bring professional interviewing skills to public health communication during disasters, conducting sensitive interviews and eliciting revealing yet respectful interviews. There can, however, be dangers involved in these activities. Psychologist/journalists can put themselves in harm's way and need to exercise equally safe judgment as they advise others. A television interview I was doing in a dangerous foreign location was interrupted after a suspicious phone call, in order to get me into an armored car and driven away. On another occasion, at a bombing scene, officials herded reporters including myself away as the perpetrator was strapped to a stretcher, hands bound behind his back, and stripped naked to reveal hidden weapons. In such situations, this psychologist/journalist, for one, had to consider that pure intentions might not provide total protection in risky situations.

Cross-Cultural Issues

Culture plays a major role in how a country and its people, authorities, and media outlets react to a disaster. Therefore, the importance of taking cultural differences into account when working with the media regarding a disaster cannot be overstated. Even time zones matter (when being interviewed on live radio shows across the globe about the effect of SARS in China, I had to be aware of the time in that country, saying "yesterday afternoon" or "this evening" appropriately). Nevertheless, sharing information and techniques among countries is valuable and must continue, so that the combined knowledge, resources, and creativity of diverse people can be put to the best use possible. For example, three weeks after the 2004 Asian tsunami, the Sri Lanka Ministry of Health recognized their limited supply of mental health personnel and invited a mission from the Israeli Health Ministry to contribute expertise on psychological care, particularly for children and caregivers (Hadassah Medical Center, January 12, 2005). Apparently, a common ground was found, as the Israeli team leader said, "We explained how we lost families in the Holocaust, but that the survivors, their descendants, are living testimony of the ability to go on with life when so much is destroyed." This type of psychological rapport deserves to be another topic covered by the media in the interests of international cooperation.

Take Care of Yourself

Being a disaster relief worker inevitably leads to stress, possible "vicarious victimization," and "compassion fatigue," given exhaustion, frustration, time demands, extra workload, and exposure to trauma (Figley, 1995). Working with the media can increase stress as one struggles to keep up with breaking news and performance pressure. To prevent or handle such burnout, peer support and physical and emotional self-care are necessary. The FILL-UP model suggests that you focus inwardly on what is most important to you and your family today; look and listen to learn what you and your significant others are experiencing, so you will remember what is important and let go of what is not; and understand personally what these experiences mean to you, so that you will feel able to go on with your life and even grow personally (National Center for PSTD, 2003).

Future Possibilities and Directions for Psychologists and the Media in Disaster

Research has shown that public education and communication about the health facts and risks of a disaster can reduce the need for clinical mental health services (Reissman, 2004). There are several exciting avenues through which to mine the cooperation between psychology and the media for public mental health in the face of disasters:

- Further development of Internet use
- Researching the effect of psychologically oriented media messages in times of disaster
- "Partnering" among professional organizations, corporations, and media sources for purposes of communication and funding for disaster-related projects
- Highlighting the emerging role of community healing efforts and promoting comprehensive community education programs
- Focusing on prevention of panic as opposed to just disaster response
- Taking a long-term view (e.g., it is recognized that it will take at least 10 years for the Asian region to recover from the aftereffects of the tragic tsunami)
- Continuing to direct resources to affected areas other than those that are currently drawing the most attention

Where traditional media cannot be harnessed for psychological aid, community groups and schools can step in, as was the case in Sri Lanka after the 2004 tsunami, where the schools passed information to children to then bring home to their families.

A Personal Postscript

The hope of any mental health worker is to facilitate the health and happiness of others. That has certainly been my motivation, as my mother often reminds me that when asked as a child, "What do you want to do when you grow up?" my answer was, "To bring peace to the world." It continues to be an honor to strive to fulfill that dream, although it is sad that mass tragedies make such a goal necessary. As psychologists play a more public role in the healing process, the perception of psychology becomes more positive, the media more welcoming, and hope more possible for a future with efforts more focused on increasing joy than on healing pain.

Acknowledgments

Juan Rodriquez, graduate student at Long Island University, and Heather Butts, graduate student at Columbia University Teachers College, provided assistance in researching background journal articles.

References

Burroughs, C. (2002, May 11). Noted psychologist talks of emotions after Sept. 11. *Daily Mountain Eagle,* Jasper AL.

Diesch, C., & Caldwell, J. (1993). *Where are the experts? Psychologists in the media.* Paper presented at the annual convention of the American Psychological Association, Toronto, Canada.

Echterling, L. G., & Wylie, M. L. (1999). In the public arena: Disaster as a socially constructed problem. In R. Gist & B. Lubin (Eds.), *Response to disaster: Psychosocial, ecological, and community approaches* (pp. 327–346). Washington, DC: Taylor & Francis.

Edie Hand Foundation (2002). *ACCESS: Emergency Survival Handbook.* Retrieved October 9, 2005 from http://www.ediehandfoundation.org/access/

Figley, C. R. (Ed.). (1995). *Compassion fatigue: Coping with secondary traumatic stress disorder in those who treat the traumatized.* New York: Brunner/Mazel.

Hadassah Medical Center (2005, January 12). Hadassah child psychiatrist joins Israeli mission to Sri Lanka. Retrieved October 7, 2005, from http://www.hadassah.org/news/content/news-view.asp?pr_id=479

Hartog, K. (2002, August 23). Lessons from Ground Zero. *Jerusalem Post,* Jerusalem Section: Features, p. 4.

Heldring, M. (2004). Talking to the public about terrorism: Promoting health and resilience. *Families, Systems and Health, 22*(1) 67–71.

Kirschner, S., & Kirschner, D. (Eds.). (1997). *Perspectives of psychology and the media.* Washington, DC: American Psychological Association.

Kuriansky, J. (2002, September 8). Love in the time of terrorism. *South China Morning Post.*

———. (2003a). The 9/11 terrorist attack on the World Trade Center: A New York psychologist's personal experiences and professional perspective, *Psychotherapie Forum, 11,* pp. 37–47.

———. (2003b). *Peace and healing in troubled regions and times of terrorism: Impact on relationships, what East & West can learn from each other about treating trauma and a new integrated therapy model.* Paper presented at the Middle East/North Africa Regional Conference of Psychology, Dubai.

———. (2005a). Making sense of a senseless tragedy. Silver lining of this dark cloud lies in man's humanity to man. *The New York Daily News.* Retrieved from http://www.nydailynews.com/front/story/267597p-229217c.html

———. (2005b). Report on Meetings at the United Nations about the Tsunami Relief Effort, for IAAP newsletter, "Summary of the proceedings of two meetings held at the United Nations about the relief efforts concerning the tsunami disaster." Report on "Southeast Asia Tsunami: Response, Relief and Recovery" and Committee on Mental Health meeting, "Trauma and the Asian Tsunami Disorder." Meetings and notes from January 13, 2005.

Norris, F. H. (2005, January). "Psychosocial consequences of natural disasters in developing countries: What does past research tell us about the potential effects of the 2004 tsunami?" National Center for PTSD. Retrieved January 2, 2005, from http://www.ncptsd.org

NSW Institute of Psychiatry and Centre for Mental Health. (2000). *Disaster mental health response handbook*. North Sydney: NSW Health.

Reissman, D. B. (2004). New roles for mental and behavioral health experts to enhance emergency preparedness and response readiness. *Psychiatry: Interpersonal & Biological Processes, 67*(2), 118–122.

Richard, D. (2002). At Ground Zero, workers speak openly about sexuality. *Contemporary Sexuality, 36*, 6–7.

Ross, G. (2003). *Beyond the trauma vortex: The media's role in healing fear, terror and violence*. Berkeley, CA: North Atlantic Books.

Schwartz, L. L. (1999). *Psychology and the media: A second look*. Washington, DC: American Psychological Association.

Siegel, J. (2002, June 9). Los Angeles group donates $3.2 million for terror victims. *Jerusalem Post,* Daily Section, p. 4.

Stevens, M. J., & Wedding, D. (Eds.). (2004). *The handbook of international psychology*. New York: Brunner-Routledge.

Stout, C. (Ed.). (2002). *The psychology of terrorism* (Vols. 1–4). Westport, CT: Praeger.

Young, B. H., Ford, J. D., & Watson, P. J. (n.d.). *Disaster Rescue and Response Workers*. Retrieved October 7, 2005, from http://www.ncptsd.va.gov/facts/disasters/fs_rescue_workers.html

CHAPTER 9

NEGOTIATING THE SHRUNKEN HUMANITARIAN SPACE: CHALLENGES AND OPTIONS

Michael G. Wessells

Traditionally, the principles of independence, impartiality, and neutrality guided humanitarian agencies' emergency operations. These principles are enshrined in the Geneva Conventions of 1949 and in the "Code of Conduct of the International Federation of Red Cross and Red Crescent Societies and NGOs Engaged in Disaster Relief." Most nongovernmental organizations (NGOs) have viewed adherence to these principles as necessary for the creation of a space in which humanitarian work can be conducted apart from political and military agendas.

Departures from these principles frequently produce serious violations of the "do no harm" imperative and jeopardize the humanitarian enterprise (e.g., Anderson, 1999; Minear, 2002). For example, to provide food aid to only one party in an armed conflict while deliberately withholding it from the other party is to use aid as a weapon of war. This undermines the humanitarian imperative of assisting all people according to need, damages civilian populations, and reduces humanitarian assistance to the military's handmaiden. Traditionalists offer a well-defined formula for avoiding such problems. Humanitarian agencies should adhere strictly to a humanitarian agenda of providing assistance where it is needed, and the military should adhere to a separate, military agenda of providing security.

Most agencies that conduct psychosocial work in emergencies have accepted this division of labor and the commitment to adhere to humanitarian principles. By its nature, psychosocial intervention requires the establishment of a sense of security and trust between the interveners and the local population. Without security and trust, psychological processes of healing or reconciliation cannot occur. Security and trust become casualties, however, if local people view the psychosocial workers as spies or as arms of a government seen locally as wanting to dominate people. In addition, psychosocial workers are themselves at heightened risk if local people perceive them as part of a military force. According to traditional views, humanitarian psychosocial operations ought to be independent of and distinct from military operations and should adhere to humanitarian principles.

Although policies enacted during the Reagan administration forged tighter military–humanitarian connections, post-9/11 events constitute the greatest threat to the independence of military and humanitarian operations. As President Bush launched the "war on terror" and embarked on wars in Afghanistan and Iraq, U.S. policy makers built elaborate humanitarian–military connections, seeking to integrate into a seamless web the work of NGOs, for-profit contractors, and military forces. In addition, the U.S. government is both the primary combatant and the main donor for humanitarian operations in countries such as Afghanistan and Iraq. Colin Powell, the U.S. Secretary of State, declared that NGOs and humanitarian aid are "force multipliers" that boost the effect of U.S. political and military operations. The U.S. government views the politicization and militarization of aid as a natural response to the dangers posed by terrorism. Beyond the United States, international pressures exist for tightening the connections between peacekeeping and humanitarian operations in many postconflict situations. This unprecedented blurring of the boundaries separating military and humanitarian activities has already shrunken enormously the humanitarian space.

With respect to psychosocial interventions, this situation has raised profound concerns regarding ethics, security, operational feasibility, quality of humanitarian assistance, and peace building. At question is whether the humanitarian enterprise will survive as an independent set of collective activities or become an arm of the hyperpower's military operations and foreign policy. The magnitude of the changes that are under way is barely visible, and humanitarian agencies worldwide have only begun to think through how to position themselves in the new humanitarian context.

The purpose of this chapter is to outline the nature of the changes in humanitarian–military operations and to explore various options for humanitarian agencies in the new humanitarian environment. Using case studies of the humanitarian and rebuilding work in Afghanistan and Iraq, and drawing on my own field experience, critical aspects of the new humanitarian context are described. Although these cases are distinct and may not establish a new paradigm that governs humanitarian work in all countries, they merit attention because they illustrate most clearly the extensive blurring of the boundaries between military and humanitarian operations. Having sketched the dimensions of the problem, I also examine various options for psychosocial workers and NGOs in defining their role and the way forward. These options are offered not as solutions but as paths through which

NGOs may balance adherence to humanitarian principles with the practical realities of operating in the changed humanitarian context.

Afghanistan

In retaliation against the 9/11 attacks, the U.S. military and intelligence establishment collaborated with the Afghan Northern Alliance forces to overthrow the Taliban regime, which had spread religious extremism, severely oppressed women, and provided sanctuary to al Qaeda leader Osama bin Laden. The war, which lasted only from October to December 2001, was heralded as a success not only because the Taliban were routed so quickly but also because it entailed the use of a minimal number of U.S. ground troops, mostly special forces, and resulted in the death of only a small number of U.S. soldiers (Priest, 2004). The postwar environment, however, was far from secure. Southeastern areas such as Kandahar and Jalalabad remained hotspots where Taliban supporters fought, using guerrilla tactics. Over time, their attacks grew bolder and ultimately led to the withdrawal of many NGOs from the area. Speculation continued that Osama bin Laden himself was in the area, possibly hiding in the mountains along Pakistan's northwest frontier.

Other regions, although quieter on the surface, were controlled by commanders or warlords who retained strong militias or armies and who had a long history of fighting each other during the mujaheddin era. In these areas, local people reported that most of the Taliban troops had not been captured or killed but had shed their distinctive headgear, shaved their beards, and melted into the masses in the cities, where they could live free of suspicion and bide their time until the moment arose for renewed fighting. The fledgling Karzai administration had ample popular support but was unable to provide security. The war had devastated Afghanistan's infrastructure, and failures to meet people's basic needs could have undermined Karzai's popular support and plunged the country again into internecine conflict. Enormous needs existed for both international humanitarian assistance and military support to stabilize the situation and enable the reconstruction effort.

Provincial Reconstruction Teams

To address this situation, the U.S. government established in Afghanistan a new vehicle, the Provincial Reconstruction Team (PRT), for delivering aid and increasing security. Each PRT consisted of from 60 to 100 soldiers, aid personnel, and civil affairs officers (O'Brien, 2003). Although the PRTs are not mandated to intervene directly in fighting, they are intended to provide a stabilizing military and intelligence presence and to conduct a "hearts-and-minds" campaign of the kind that the United States invented in the Vietnam War and has used since in an increasing diversity of conflicts (Priest, 2004).

Because PRTs include psychological operations experts and civil affairs officers, they have the capacity to negotiate with local warlords and to keep the door open for humanitarian assistance by international NGOs (O'Brien, 2003). The PRTs also engage directly in humanitarian assistance by building structures such as schools or, more often, by contracting local workers or NGOs to conduct reconstruction projects. In all their activities, PRTs are expected to collect intelligence information that supports the "war on terror" that President Bush proclaimed.

On the surface, PRTs offer the advantages of small size, flexibility, and a joint civil–military platform for integrating humanitarian work, security, and the war on terrorism. Recognizing their potential advantages, the British and German governments also formed PRTs. The PRTs' military clout evoked respect from local power brokers, and many local people have said that they are happy to see U.S. and other troops in the region to help keep the peace. Despite their very limited powers of engagement, the presence of U.S. troops cautions potential troublemakers, who understand that killing a U.S. soldier could unleash a powerful U.S. reprisal. The PRTs have also helped to rebuild infrastructure such as schools, which are highly prized by Afghan parents and children. Many villages have never had a school, and girls frequently lack access to education because Afghan people view it as inappropriate for girls to walk unescorted outside their village. Although the intelligence information that PRTs have collected is not publicly available, it is likely that PRT staffs have obtained some useful intelligence information during visits to local communities and during regular interactions with local people, while conducting reconstruction projects.

Still, PRTs face powerful challenges and limits that outweigh their potential benefits. These challenges are intimately connected with the wider issues of the blurring of military and humanitarian operations in Afghanistan. During the war against the Taliban, U.S. bombers had carpeted areas where there were Taliban troops with cluster bombs, which kill by dispersing large numbers of explosive devices overhead, the detonation of which unleashes large amounts of shrapnel. The use of cluster bombs shatters humanitarian norms because they kill indiscriminately. In addition, approximately 5 percent of the cluster bomblets fall to the ground without exploding, creating large amounts of unexploded ordnance that randomly harms innocent civilians.

As U.S. planes dropped cluster bombs, they also dropped in the same areas humanitarian leaflets and food packages. This was unethical because hungry Afghan civilians were drawn into very dangerous areas. Whatever benefits such operations were expected to provide were undone by ineptitude and cultural insensitivity. The leaflets' messages, which were printed in English, French, and Spanish, were lost on Afghan villagers, who spoke Dari; in addition, many Afghans are illiterate. Also, the food packages lacked the nutritional value needed to enable a person to survive even a few days. This combination of bombs and inadequate food helped to galvanize Afghan people's perceptions that humanitarian aid is part of military operations by outside powers and that the humanitarian aid provided falls far short of the needs that exist in local villages. These themes resonated subsequently in the PRTs' activities.

The Trouble with PRTs

PRTs subvert the humanitarian enterprise by undermining humanitarian principles, delivering poorly designed assistance, and corroding security. Although the PRTs claim to conduct humanitarian work, their nonmilitary work is not genuinely humanitarian because it embodies the political agenda of winning a hearts-and-minds campaign and of collecting intelligence information. By definition, humanitarian work is conducted according to nonpolitical principles and seeks to meet humanitarian needs as defined through a careful situation analysis. In contrast, a hearts-and-minds campaign serves political agendas and seeks to win local people over to one's political point of view. If a PRT had conducted a presumably humanitarian project such as building a school, one may legitimately question whether the project were humanitarian because it may have been undertaken to collect intelligence and to sell a political agenda.

In addition, the military is poorly equipped to design and implement quality humanitarian work. It lacks the extensive humanitarian experience and technical expertise that enable assistance of high caliber. It also honors values such as hierarchy, order, and efficiency that support effective war fighting but conflict with the values of participation, capacity building, and partnership with local people that are the foundation of humanitarian assistance. In northeast Afghanistan, PRTs have supported school construction though nonparticipatory processes in which they contracted the school project to a local bidder. Little attention was given to consultation with local villages, collective design and planning of the school, or participation of local people in building it. As a result, local people felt no sense of ownership in the schools and no desire to maintain them. In some cases, people reported that the schools reflected poor quality of workmanship, had been built using the wrong materials, and had begun to deteriorate only six months following construction. In one case, Afghans said that the contractor had artificially inflated the price above fair local prices, knowing the United States had the money to pay. Local people reported that they could have helped to prevent the gouging and poor construction had they been consulted more thoroughly and engaged as participants who would watch over the quality of the project (A. Klaits, personal communication, March 10, 2003).

In addition, PRTs have sharply decreased security for humanitarian aid workers (ACBAR, 2003; Save the Children, 2004). Rural Afghan people have little familiarity with the relationship between NGOs and the governments of the countries in which the NGOs are based. They do not understand that U.S.-based NGOs are independent of the U.S. military, and most

NGOs devote considerable time and effort to explaining their independence. By blurring the military–humanitarian boundaries, PRTs strengthen the perceived linkage between NGO workers and the U.S. military.

In northeast Afghanistan, where I have helped to conduct psychosocial work, soldiers who are part of PRTs wear military uniforms, carry guns, and perform military missions 90 percent of the time. The other 10 percent of the time, they wear civilian clothes, carry no weapons, and conduct work such as overseeing the construction of schools. Dressed as civilians, they often take the same flights that NGO workers take. As a result, Afghan people see NGO workers and known military personnel dressed as civilians and taking the same flights and engaged in activities such as restarting education. It is only natural that they infer that all the outsiders are part of the U.S. military. The perceptions are strengthened by the fact that when the PRT members visit villages to conduct "humanitarian" work, they often collect intelligence information. This point is not lost on Afghan villagers, who have a long history of suspicion of outsiders related to their history of attempted domination by countries such as Russia and Britain. The monolithic categorization of the U.S. outsiders also gains strength from the fact that they seem to have similar values. Some of the values, notably those concerning women's equality, alcohol consumption, and sexual behavior, conflict sharply with those of Afghan society and raise fears of moral corruption by outside forces.

This situation sharply increases the target value of humanitarian workers. Taliban supporters who view the U.S. and European operations in Afghanistan as part of an occupation, as a pollution of Islamic society or another Crusade, or as an attempt to dominate the country, seek to strike back at the infidel outsiders. Direct strikes against U.S. military installations carry high costs because the U.S. military possesses overwhelming firepower and resources. In addition, armed U.S. troops are well protected and unlikely to suffer serious damage from small attacks. In contrast, humanitarian workers are "soft" targets because they are unarmed and unprotected, yet are seen as extensions of U.S. military operations. Attacks against humanitarian workers can be used to send a message that Afghans will resist domination or pollution by outsiders, as well as to undermine the humanitarian effort that would otherwise strengthen support for the Karzai administration. Taliban resisters understand well that the failure to deliver aid in a timely manner to Afghan villages will also blunt support for the presence of U.S. troops and strengthen the hands of warlords, whose internal fighting could scuttle national elections and undermine the national government.

It is not by chance, then, that humanitarian workers have become prime targets in Afghanistan. Before the end of 2003, most attacks on humanitarians had occurred in southeastern Afghanistan, where infamous incidents occurred such as the assassination of a UN High Commissioner for Refugees worker who was following direct orders that an extremist Muslim leader had issued via cell phone. In 2004, the situation deteriorated much further, culminating in the murder in June of five workers for Médicins Sans Frontières/Holland (MSF/Holland) in Northern Afghanistan. The murders prompted MSF, which has a long, respected history of neutrality and that had worked in Afghanistan throughout 24 years of the mujaheddin era and the Taliban rule, to withdraw from the country. Other NGOs struggle to maintain their operations in an increasingly dangerous situation. Since March 2003, over 30 humanitarians have been killed in Afghanistan. The risks to NGO workers have become so great that some NGOs have decided that it is impossible to conduct humanitarian work safely and have withdrawn from Afghanistan. Reductions in the international humanitarian presence in Afghanistan will probably strengthen the Taliban's hand and degrade the security situation even further.

Of course, many NGOs continue to operate in Afghanistan and face major questions about how to protect their workers while assisting local people. In response to the heightened insecurity, most NGOs have carefully limited their operations to areas that are relatively safe and have tightened protective measures, such as disallowing staff travel alone or at night. Some have also asked the U.S. government to increase its security support by adding International Security Assistance Force troops to help stabilize the situation. An omnipresent temptation for many NGOs is to increase the number of guards maintaining a 24-hour watch over nearly every NGO compound. There have also been discussions in Kabul of having U.S. military leaders notify NGO leaders in a general way that it might be a good idea to have staff avoid going to particular areas for the next few weeks.

These and other options present NGOs with profound ethical challenges. On one hand, NGOs have a powerful responsibility to protect their staff. If, however, they curtail their operations very significantly to protect their staff, will they still make a contribution to Afghans' well-being that justifies the NGO presence in the country? In desperate situations, the presence of NGOs that cannot deliver aid effectively creates among local people a sense of frustration, broken promises, and abandonment that only adds to the existing psychosocial burdens. Further, if terrorist activities influence NGO operations significantly, humanitarians risk becoming pawns in a political struggle that damages local people rather than supports them. Nor are the tactics of strengthening International Security Assistance Force forces or NGO security forces problem free. Arming one's compound guards, calling for additional International Security Assistance Force forces, or collaborating closely with the military all contribute to the militarization of the environment and also to the militarization of aid. Past experience in countries such as Somalia has shown that the militarization of aid often creates problems far outweighing the benefits of aid (Anderson, 1999; Prendergast, 1996; Shawcross, 2000). In many respects, NGOs are left to sort out the least bad among many problematic options.

These considerations underscore the dangers of intermixing military and humanitarian operations and of violating systematically the humanitarian principles of independence, impartiality, and neutrality. If aid workers had traditionally been protected by virtue of their mission, the PRTs have undermined this protection by making humanitarian aid an extension of a military and political effort. Afghan people's perceptions of NGOs as part of U.S. military operations gained strength as a result of the Iraq war and occupation. As explained below, these events confirmed what appeared to many Muslims as a pattern in which the United States and other powers combine aid with military means to dominate Muslim peoples.

Iraq

The humanitarian operations in Iraq can be understood only against the background of the strongly contested views of the legitimacy and causes of the war. President Bush, with the support of the U.K. Prime Minister Tony Blair, launched the war as a preemptive action, although the term "preemption" is generous because it implies the existence of an imminent threat, when most of the world believed that none existed (Chace, 2004). The ostensible purposes of the war were to remove the threatening regime of Saddam Hussein from power, to limit terrorism and the spread of weapons of mass destruction, and to enable democratic government to take root in Iraq, with hopes of strengthening democratic governance throughout the Middle East. The UN Security Council denounced the war as illegitimate because the evidence of imminent threat from Iraq was weak or nonexistent. French, Russian, and German leaders argued that the UN inspections of suspected Iraqi weapons of mass destruction activities should continue and that unilateral war set a dangerous precedent that encourages aggression. Bush's decision to launch the war in clear defiance of international norms created enormous difficulties for humanitarian operations even before the war had begun.

Before the War

In Washington, DC, and worldwide, as the prospects of war increased, humanitarian agencies debated hotly whether and how to prepare for relief operations in Iraq. One frequently heard argument was that humanitarian planning would only support an illicit war, and that humanitarian agencies should recognize that they will be used as pawns of the U.S. military and foreign policy machinery. Numerous organizations decided not to accept funding from the U.S. government because the acceptance of money from the attacker would tacitly support an illegitimate war. Practical concerns also thwarted NGOs' preparations. Some predicted that the war and the ensuing occupation would trigger widespread violence and instability, making it impossible to provide humanitarian assistance for months or even years.

Still others argued that the U.S. government had structured the humanitarian aid effort in a way that shattered humanitarian principles. In fact, the

Department of Defense had created an Office of Humanitarian Aid and Reconstruction to oversee the effort. Many NGOs felt marginalized by this arrangement and by the companion step wherein the U.S. government assigned large contracts for reconstruction and assistance to private, for-profit firms. Amid militarization and privatization of the aid planning, most NGOs questioned why the more traditional U.S. aid machinery such as that of the U.S. State Department and the NGO community were not guiding the effort or being engaged more fully. For many, the new arrangement placed humanitarian operations squarely under the wing of the military, thereby destroying most of the independent humanitarian space needed to operate in an ethical, effective manner.

Against these principled and pragmatic concerns, numerous agencies argued that the war, when it erupted, would create significant humanitarian needs and that humanitarian agencies have an obligation to prepare fully for humanitarian operations, as lack of preparation would lead to loss of lives. Expecting possible large flows of refugees to countries such as Jordan, some U.S.-based NGOs established offices in Jordan and prepared for humanitarian operations along the Iraqi border.

NGOs also struggled with the question of whether to help prepare U.S. troops to engage in humanitarian operations. Some argued that the U.S. military would be the only group that could provide necessary food and medical supplies during the fighting, and that NGOs should help train the military to provide aid in an effective, participatory manner. Other agencies argued that the provision of this type of training would blur the borders between military and humanitarian operations even further and legitimate the sidelining of NGOs. Most humanitarian agencies that had decided to engage had also taken deliberate steps to limit their support of the military and to work carefully to maintain what little independence was achievable. In this context, the humanitarian planning and preparations that preceded the war were limited, tenuous, and fraught with concerns about violating the "Do No Harm" principle. Numerous NGOs took a cautious, wait-and-see approach.

The Occupation

In most postconflict situations, the United Nations plays the lead role in the effort to keep the peace, alleviate suffering, establish a transitional administration, and rebuild the country for peace. The UN leadership is highly desirable because that organization answers to no particular government, and because it represents humanitarian interests, which are inherently transnational. Also, the United Nations is in the best position to coordinate the efforts of many different governments and to ensure that humanitarian principles are taken seriously. The United Nations has a long history of working with independent humanitarian partners such as NGOs that can maintain a healthy separation of military and humanitarian agendas.

In the case of Iraq, a strong UN role was impossible. First, U.S. military forces occupied Iraq following the war, and international law stipulates that the occupying power is responsible for providing security and meeting basic humanitarian needs. This meant that the United States had clear responsibility to take the lead role in the humanitarian effort. Second, the UN had strong conceptual and political grounds for limiting its engagement. To provide support for illegitimate wars and for military occupation is to increase the likelihood of the very acts of military aggression that the United Nations is designed to prevent. Also, the independence of the United Nations requires that it not become the servant of any particular country, particularly one that had disregarded international norms and the collective wisdom of the Security Council. Third, the UN typically fills its lead role by coordinating other actors, but the nature of the situation had shrunken the "coalition of the willing" to a small handful. Strong sentiments existed that peacekeeping and humanitarian assistance would tacitly support the war effort or reduce humanitarian operations to the level of mopping up the mess that many had warned against in advance.

Insecurity, however, provided the strongest limit on the UN role and the activities of humanitarian NGOs. A profound failure of the U.S. operation in Iraq was in not providing for civilian security. Immediately following the defeat of Saddam Hussein's regime, U.S. troops failed to stop or even to limit the looting of Saddam's palaces. With the constraints on crime having been removed, the looting and lawlessness spread into most neighborhoods. Even in July and early August 2003, NGOs reported from the field that insecurity had reached monumental proportions. In Baghdad, which had had relatively low levels of street crime under Saddam's regime, crime and looting became so widespread that many people feared leaving their homes and kept their children home from school (Wessells, 2003a). Girls were most often kept at home because of fears about the sudden upsurge in sexual violence, which had never been a problem before.

The way in which the U.S. government responded to the security situation posed enormous problems for humanitarian workers. To avoid the politically unpopular move of boosting the number of U.S. troops in Iraq, the U.S. government increasingly privatized and outsourced security (Singer, 2003). An estimated 20,000 people dressed as civilians provided so-called security services, and many private security firms masqueraded as humanitarian agencies in hopes of increasing their own security. This privatization of security strategy did not so much blur the military–humanitarian boundaries as obliterate them. The thorough military–humanitarian blending occurred also through the U.S. government's reliance on harsh military tactics such as storming homes in the middle of the night in neighborhoods where humanitarian assistance was administered. With no clear boundaries between military and humanitarian workers and anger growing over the occupation, the stage was set for increased attacks on humanitarian workers.

The threats to humanitarian workers had been strong since the beginning of the occupation, but no one anticipated how immense they would become in a period of several months. Headquartered in the Canal Hotel in Baghdad, the United Nations had deliberately avoided associating itself with U.S. troops and had sought protection by virtue of its mission. This hope was shattered by the car bomb that demolished the Canal Hotel on August 19, 2003. Among the dead were 18 UN staff, including Sergio De Mello, one of the United Nations' most accomplished leaders and the head of the UN operations in Iraq. As Kofi Annan said at an emotionally charged memorial held at UN headquarters in New York one month later, the United Nations could no longer assume that it would be protected by virtue of its humanitarian mission. Humanitarian operations had entered a new era rife with danger, uncertainty, and increased inability or unwillingness of local people to distinguish between combatants and humanitarians.

To understand why Iraq had become so dangerous for humanitarian workers, it is necessary to examine how Iraqi people viewed the occupation and to ask why the Iraqi insurgency was so strong, in sharp contrast to the Bush administration's rosy predictions that U.S. forces would be hailed as liberators and welcomed with open arms. In interviews conducted with over 400 Iraqis in Baghdad Governorate between July 1 and August 7, 2003, Shiite communities said they had supported the war, as had Kurdish peoples in Northern Iraq. Sunnis, who had been privileged in Saddam Husein's regime, said they had strongly opposed the war (Wessells, 2003b). However, all the participants said they opposed the occupation because it violated Iraqi independence and had made their lives much worse than they had been under Saddam's rule. They consistently pointed to the widespread breakdown in law and order, the rise in the use of drugs and in sexual violence, and the lack of electricity, which had increased poverty because shops could open only a few hours a day.

Many Iraqis viewed the occupation as yet another attempt of Western powers to dominate Muslims, as another Crusade or Holy War designed to seal the hegemony of Christianity, or as an attempt to control Arab countries and resources such as oil. Many Iraqi citizens in Baghdad said that the U.S. motivation in attacking Iraq was to dominate Muslim people and that this is obvious because the U.S. government has been the major patron of Israel during the decades of its oppression of Palestinians (Wessells, 2003b). Regardless of their veracity, these perceptions influenced people's behavior and contributed to negative attributions regarding failures of humanitarian assistance. Indeed, many participants said that the lack of electricity exemplified the U.S. desire to weaken and dominate Muslim people. After all, they reasoned, the United States, as the world's mightiest country, must surely have had the ability to supply electricity to a relatively small country such as Iraq if it had wanted to.

Preliminary evidence indicates that these perceptions strengthened the insurgency by encouraging youth radicalization. In most armed conflicts, teenagers are at risk of engaging in fighting because they frequently lack the supports and positive options that create hope for the future (Boyden & de Berry, 2004; Brett & Specht, 2004; Wessells & Jonah, in press). Being idealistic and easily frustrated, they often become disaffected and alienated from the current political and social system, making them susceptible to propaganda and political manipulation. At a developmental stage in which they are searching for meaning and identity, they are often lured into soldiering for a cause such as liberating one's people or fighting a religious war against the infidel. In Baghdad, some Iraqi teenagers said that they had never been involved in violence but that because of the occupation, they had become jihadis (Wessells, 2003b). To justify their decision, they frequently pointed out perceived transgressions of U.S. forces such as dishonoring Iraqi people, behaving in disrespectful ways toward women, and storming homes and arresting people without telling families what the charges were, where their sons were being held, and when they would be released. Even in its early days, the occupation had the effect of increasing terrorist motivation among youths (Wessells, 2003b). Extremist religious leaders such as Muqtada al Sadr knew well how to attract youth using a mixture of ideology, peer pressure, religious commitment, and appeals to avenge the transgressions committed daily by the occupiers.

In Iraq, it was inevitable that anti–United States sentiments would find expression in attacks on humanitarian agencies. For one thing, humanitarian workers were soft targets who were easy to harm in comparison to well-armed U.S. and British troops. There were also sentiments that all outsiders were polluting Iraqi culture and values. In this view, it made little difference whether the target of an attack was a soldier or a civilian. The visibility of U.S. workers and agencies was ensured when in June 2003, the USAID Administrator, Andrew Natsios, proclaimed at an annual meeting of U.S. NGOs that they are "an arm of the U.S. government" and should either use signs and other means to indicate that they are supported by U.S. funds or forfeit their contracts.

The biggest problem stemmed from the very structure of the humanitarian enterprise in Iraq. From its inception, the United States–led reconstruction effort was part of a political agenda of rebuilding Iraq in terms favorable to U.S. interests. This meant that humanitarian reconstruction workers were guilty by association with the larger United States–led effort and the forces that were most visible to Iraqi people.

The expansion and increasing organization of the fighting against U.S. forces, coupled with increased abductions, beheadings, and bombings of humanitarian workers, crippled the humanitarian effort in Iraq. Many NGOs, particularly those based in the United States and the United Kingdom, and outraged by atrocities such as the murder of Margaret Hassan, a longtime aid worker with CARE in Iraq, decided that the dangers to their workers vastly outweighed the limited good they might be able to accomplish. The humanitarian space had not just shrunk but in cities that were mired in fighting had disappeared completely. Many NGOs either curtailed their operations severely or withdrew entirely. Christian Children's Fund, the NGO with which I work, had lost one of its most gifted child protection workers, Jill Clark, in the bombing of the Canal Hotel and decided to withdraw. The withdrawal of independent NGOs and the severe cutback in UN operations in Iraq meant that privately employed firms, many of whom had little commitment to traditional humanitarian principles, conducted an increasing share of the humanitarian and reconstruction effort in Iraq. This situation only increases the blurring of the boundaries between military and humanitarian operations that contributes to the targeting of humanitarian workers.

Options

In considering options for humanitarian agencies, it is vital to recognize that the problems outlined above extend beyond Iraq and Afghanistan. If the problems were limited to situations in which the United States were both cobelligerent and a major humanitarian donor, one could perhaps deal with the problems by constructing a contingency plan for handling special cases. In fact, some NGO workers have argued that two cases do not make a new paradigm and that the situations of Iraq and Afghanistan are special because they involved humanitarian assistance by co-belligerents, and in the case of Iraq, the war was not sanctioned by the UN.

This view, however, overlooks the facts that the war on terror is global in scope and that the U.S. operations in Afghanistan and Iraq, coupled with the rhetoric about the "axis of evil," have sparked powerful resentments against the United States. Many nations, including European allies, see current U.S. behavior internationally as arrogant and dangerous to world security. It is likely that any U.S. humanitarian response, particularly in a Muslim country, will arouse the suspicions of some people that the goal of humanitarian operations is U.S. political, economic, or military domination. In the Darfur crisis, numerous murders of USAID workers have occurred, most likely by people who perceived the U.S. humanitarian intervention as threatening. Also, enemies of the United States who flee Iraq or Afghanistan will probably work in other countries to harm the United States. Although they are ill equipped to attack the U.S. military or government directly, they may seek to use violence against humanitarian workers to advance their political agendas. As insecurity increases, the international community tends to respond by increasing military forces and forging ever tighter connections between military and humanitarian operations. This trend is embodied most clearly in attempts to construct a "military humanitarianism" in which deadly force is used without the consent of nation states to enforce human values and meet basic needs (Weiss & Collins, 1996).

The rapid evolution and complexity of this situation defy the quest for simple answers and challenge the success of business-as-usual approaches. Although many options are conceivable, the main options fall into three broad categories: principled resistance, pragmatic accommodation, and strategic engagement.

Principled Resistance

Principled resistance is a strategy of adhering closely to the traditional humanitarian principles of independence, impartiality, and neutrality and of actively resisting attempts to blur the military–humanitarian boundaries. By refusing to compromise core values, this option provides a means of keeping clear boundaries between military and humanitarian operations and taking decisive action when encroachments on humanitarian principles occur. Agencies that exercise this option may take steps such as refusing to engage in humanitarian work in contexts in which blurring is inevitable or even pre-planned, avoiding training military forces in how to conduct humanitarian operations, refusing to accept funding from donor governments that are belligerents in the conflict, and advocating with other NGOs to resist activities that contribute to the militarization and politicization of aid. For example, in regard to Iraq, Oxfam announced that it would not accept funding from the United Kingdom since it was a cobelligerent.

Although laudable, this option faces significant conceptual challenges such as whether it is ethical to sit on the sidelines in a situation in which unmet humanitarian needs exist on a mass scale and one has the capacity to respond. Also, practical issues arise such as how to protect humanitarian workers in a context in which opponents of humanitarian aid are well armed and cannot be stopped by forming positive relations with local communities. In an age of increased coupling of military and humanitarian operations, purists' rigid adherence to principle may be tantamount to being sidelined or marginalized permanently.

Pragmatic Accommodation

A second option, pragmatic accommodation, accepts the reality that humanitarian agencies work in a changed environment and adapts by working in whatever humanitarian space remains. Although this realists' approach is grounded in the belief that humanitarians should be pragmatic, its conceptual underpinning is that in an age of unprecedented threats to civilians, the humanitarian imperative to save lives trumps traditional humanitarian principles. Critics of this approach have contended that this option amounts to an "anything goes" strategy. Proponents, however, claim that the presence of international humanitarians in war zones helps to prevent the worst abuses of civilians and that the self-sidelining that the principled resistance approach often engenders contributes to an anything-goes situation on the ground. Too often, the pieties of humanitarian resistance frequently fall on deaf ears, creating an enabling environment for massive human rights abuses and suffering among war-affected people.

Supporters of this option point out that traditional humanitarian principles such as neutrality are outdated in an era of mostly internal wars. For example, the entry of a humanitarian agency into Angola during its 40-year civil war required government approval, and security concerns often made it impossible to work in areas controlled by UNITA, the opposition group. How, many agencies asked, could neutrality be maintained amid these circumstances? Further, many humanitarian agencies have challenged the neutrality principle in situations in which one side is clearly responsible for the murder and rights abuses of civilians. In the Darfur crisis of 2004, many agencies saw it as their duty to oppose the Sudanese government's support of Janjaweid militias or the government's plans to force displaced people to return home when killings, rapes, and abductions continue in the areas of return. Critics of the neutrality principle question whether neutrality would save lives in such contexts.

Proponents also point out that military–humanitarian integration can be advantageous in dangerous situations and that the advantages of military engagement in humanitarian activities have been underestimated. In Bosnia, for example, the U.K. military helped to deliver vitally needed aid to areas in which NGOs were unable to operate because of high security risks (Wieloch, 2003). In the Goma refugee camps following the 1994 Rwandan genocide, French and U.S. troops contributed significantly to the humanitarian effort by digging latrines, burying bodies, and purifying water (Minear, 2002). Having significant logistics and transport capacities, many militaries are in a strong position to help in desperate circumstances. Supporters of this option frequently provide training for military troops on humanitarian assistance, collaborate in transport by having humanitarian vehicles travel with military escort, and cooperate on humanitarian service delivery by, for example, having the military transport materials while the humanitarian agency works with local people on the design, construction, and use of the school.

This option, like the first, is fraught with difficulties. If practicality rules over traditional humanitarian principles, the door is opened ever more widely to the problems of militarization and politicization of aid. In addition, military humanitarianism strikes many as an oxymoron because guidance by humanitarian principle is at the heart of the humanitarian enterprise (Minear, 2002). To abandon or compromise excessively on humanitarian principles is to risk falling prey to a slippery slope problem in which a slow accretion of accommodations to military–humanitarian mixing undermines the boundaries between military and humanitarian operations. This approach may also open the door to for-profit contractors appropriating the term "humanitarian assistance" and using it in ways that have more to do with hearts-and-minds campaigns than humanitarianism. Although civil–military relations are important in protecting staff security, the case of the PRTs in Afghanistan shows clearly that one cannot assume that the presence of military forces or their engagement in humanitarian activities will increase security. These problems have stimulated interest in a third option that lies between the extremes of the first two.

Strategic Engagement

The third option, strategic engagement, is a form of principled pragmatism in which humanitarian agencies adapt their operations to the particular situation but with a careful eye toward maintaining humanitarian principles. This approach entails considerable flexibility and continuous monitoring of the situation. If in a particular situation the humanitarian space had shrunken too far, some humanitarian agencies might decide not to engage or to engage in a minimal way that enables preparation but premature commitment. In Iraq, for example, some agencies collaborated with UNICEF in the conduct of a national psychosocial and child protection assessment shortly following the war. The deterioration of the security situation, coupled with the extensive military–humanitarian blurring, led a number of the partner agencies to withdraw following the completion of the assessment. In other situations, agencies might decide that the urgent need to save lives argues in favor of continued humanitarian intervention. The difference from the second option, however, is that strategic engagement implies continuous interrogation of one's actions in light of humanitarian principles.

Strategic engagement disallows abandonment of principles but opens the door to negotiating a position between the first two options. Relative to principled resistance, this option provides increased latitude with regard to civil–military relations. Some NGOs may decide to engage in joint planning with both civilian and military government officials. Many will decide to share information on issues such as security. And many will seek to educate the military about genuinely humanitarian operations and the role of NGOs. However, this option avoids the anything-goes problem because it challenges humanitarians to review their work and options vis-à-vis the humanitarian principles. In a highly insecure situation, NGOs might be faced with the choice of delivering aid by means of a military escort or not delivering it at all. Following the strategic engagement approach, many agencies would decide that the use of military escort departs too far from humanitarian principles and ought to be avoided. Whereas the first two options offer black-and-white alternatives, this option recognizes the shades of gray in between and invites principled adaptation to complexity and situationally grounded ethics. In contrast to the all-or-none approaches, it leaves room for compromise, for applications of principles in context, and for negotiation of the complex web of ethical, political, military, cultural, and humanitarian issues that arise in complex emergencies.

In implementing strategic engagement, NGOs typically pay careful attention to security issues. Most recognize that the foundation of security for NGOs is gaining local acceptance (Von Brabant, 2000), which in most situations entails maintaining independence of military operations. A key part of gaining local acceptance is to work through national staff members who are respected in the local community and who can help tailor NGO activities to the local cultural, historical, and political context. Many NGOs also seek to improve security through the use of protective measures such as not marking agency vehicles and prohibiting travel to particularly dangerous areas. However, most NGOs would not travel with a military escort as a means of increasing security because this constitutes too great a departure from humanitarian principles and blurs excessively the military–humanitarian boundaries.

Critics of this approach argue that it starts the humanitarian community down a path of compromising the very principles on which it stands. Pragmatists object that it leans too heavily in the direction of adherence to principles, when the reality is that the humanitarian context has changed. For psychosocial workers and agencies, however, the strategic engagement option offers the best means of assisting war-affected people while protecting the security and trust with local people who provide the foundation for efforts at healing, reconciliation, and peace building. If psychosocial work abandons humanitarian principles, the good that it yields will be eclipsed by harm that it causes.

References

ACBAR. (2003). *NGO position paper concerning the Provisional Reconstruction Teams.* Kabul: Author.

Anderson, M. (1999). *Do no harm: How aid can support peace—or war.* Boulder, CO: Lynne Rienner.

Boyden, J., & de Berry, J. (Eds.). (2004). *Children and youth on the front line. Studies in forced migration* (Vol. 14). New York: Berghahn.

Brett, R., & Specht, I. (2004). *Young soldiers: Why they choose to fight.* Boulder, CO: Lynne Rienner.

Chace, J. (2004). Empire, anyone? *The New York Review of Books, 51*(15), 15–18.

Minear, L. (2002). *The humanitarian enterprise.* Bloomfield, CT: Kumarian.

O'Brien, P. (2003). PRTs–guaranteeing or undermining a secure future in Afghanistan? *Forced Migration Review, 18,* 38–39.

Prendergast, J. (1996). *Frontline diplomacy: Humanitarian aid and conflict in Africa.* Boulder, CO: Lynne Rienner.

Priest, D. (2004). *The mission: Waging war and keeping peace with America's military.* New York: Norton.

Save the Children. (2004). *Provincial reconstruction teams and humanitarian-military relations in Afghanistan.* London: Author.

Shawcross, W. (2000). *Deliver us from evil: Peacekeepers, warlords and a world of endless conflict.* New York: Simon & Schuster.

Singer, P. (2003). *Corporate Warriors: The rise of the privatized military industry.* Ithaca, NY: Cornell University Press.

Von Brabant, K. (2000). *Operational security management in violent environments.* London: Overseas Development Institute.

Weiss, T., & Collins, C. (1996). *Humanitarian challenges and intervention: World politics and the dilemmas.* Boulder, CO: Westview.

Wessells, M. (2003a). *Children on dangerous streets: A child-focused assessment of Baghdad Governorate.* Richmond: CCF International.

————. (2003b). *The impact of U.S. anti-terrorist interventions on terrorist motivation: A preliminary study in Afghanistan and Iraq.* Research report prepared for the APA Task Force on the Psychological Effects of Efforts to Prevent Terrorism.

————, & Jonah, D. (in press). Reintegration of former youth soldiers in Sierra Leone: Challenges of reconciliation and post-accord peacebuilding. In S. McEvoy-Levy (Ed.), *Troublemakers or peacemakers? Youth and post-accord peacebuilding.* South Bend, IN: University of Notre Dame Press.

Wieloch, R. (2003). The humanitarian use of the military. *Forced Migration Review, 18,* 32–33.

Conclusions and Recommendations for Further Progress

Gilbert Reyes

A frequently expressed concern in humanitarian circles is that we are chronically engaged in the inefficient process of "reinventing the wheel." Frustrations regarding this issue seem justified, given the tendency of humanitarian organizations to operate in a more territorial and insular manner than is either necessary or wise. Counterarguments point to frequent conferences among these NGOs, but such meetings seldom result in substantive changes in policies or operations, and cooperative agreements are the exception rather than the rule. A reasonable inference can be drawn that some humanitarian organizations would rather take a proprietary stance toward "wheel development," preferring the autonomy and distinctiveness of creating their own "wheel" to the efficiency and communality involved in working cooperatively with others of their kind. Similar observations can be made regarding mental health professionals, who are sometimes better rewarded for relabeling borrowed "wheels" than they would be for adopting existing wheels with minimal adaptations to suit the particular conditions of their situation. One might say that, rather than reinventing the wheel (i.e., the general model of psychological support), a more efficient procedure is to adapt elements of wheels successfully used by others to fit the characteristics of one's own particular terrain. The responsibility for ensuring that a modified "wheel" (i.e., a situation-specific model) will be culturally congruent rests with the people in the affected areas, who are free to select what to keep or discard and choose the placement and timing of its use. Thus, what gets adopted in any given situation will be generally useful principles, but the operational details and practices will vary in accordance with needs, cultures, and conditions.

A major intention of the *Handbook of International Disaster Psychology* has been to establish a sufficiently diversified base of information on when, where, why, and how disaster psychosocial services are implemented, as well as what is done and by whom. Accordingly, the contributing authors have articulated many of the most important ideas that have influenced the development of psychosocial humanitarian operations over the past decade. They have also shared their own activities and experiences in a transparent manner so that others might learn from their successes and failures. Their descriptions of the practices and principles that have been employed to help heal the psychological and social wounds among populations affected by potentially traumatic events offer a rich resource from which others with similar goals may borrow to formulate their own programs and practices.

Volume 1 provided an overview of the field and addressed the fundamentals issues and principles of concern to those who design and implement psychosocial programs for disaster survivors. Volume 2 described a variety of programs conducted around the world and the recommended practices for promoting effect healing at both individual and collective levels. Volume 3 focused specifically on mental health issues of refugees and the favored approaches to needs assessment and psychosocial care under a complex set of conditions and stages of migration. Volume 4 identified several populations whose special needs and circumstances tend to be overlooked and thus require conscientious consideration to ensure adequate care. The authors, all of whom are experienced members of the international humanitarian community, represent a broad spectrum of nationalities, cultures, and viewpoints. The stories told in these pages should prove instructive and inspiring to anyone concerned with promoting the psychosocial welfare of people who have endured the fear and loss that accompany widespread violence and social upheaval. Readers are encouraged to glean from these works the most useful and inspiring ideas from which they can develop their own skills, practices, and programs.

Politics, Cultures, and Controversies Cannot Be Ignored

International psychosocial support activities have not unfolded without controversy. Some have argued that the humanitarian psychosocial movement reflects Western ideology with a vision of life and its norms that is at odds with native cultures indigenous to those places where catastrophic events are most likely to occur. Critics invoke images of cultural imperialism perpetrated by the former colonial aggressors against the relatively innocent and primitive captives of their misguided ministrations. There is certainly some truth in these accusations, given the asymmetry of a humanitarian community dominated by lighter-skinned people of the Northern Hemisphere "serving" the darker-skinned peoples of the Southern Hemisphere in a present version of *White Man's Burden* (Kipling, 1899). But the comparisons employed by these critics are commonly as dramatic, overwrought, and anecdotal as the claims their adversaries use to compel the forces of "compassionate" action. In the absence of reliable evidence, what poses for truth may be unfounded but persuasive claims which better serve the political or religious agendas of their purveyors than they do the psychosocial needs of their targets.

Cultural differences are often invoked as obstacles to effective helping. Cultures do have expectations and values that set boundaries around actions and influence the effectiveness of our means and the appropriateness of our goals. But that does not mean that intercultural collaboration is all about obstacles (Marsella & Christopher, 2004; Szegedy-Maszak, 2005). Cultures are also resilient and malleable to conditions, and can be understood as resources rather than obstacles. Moreover, because the most prominent voices against disseminating "Western models" of psychological support are often Western intellectuals (Pupavac, 2001; Summerfield, 1999, 2005), the discourse is suspiciously devoid of non-Western voices. That is, it would appear to be an argument among "Western" factions, rather than between Western and non-Western voices. This invites a comparison with the colonial era, during which factions within the dominant powers argued over what was in the best interest of the cultures and people whom they held in subordination. The time for Western speakers to serve as proxies for non-Westerners should be passing, and the fact that non-Western speakers often call for more collaboration casts suspicion on the claims of the anti-Western Westerners.

This state of affairs is not specific to the debates over models or intervention strategies, but instead cuts across almost every issue and area of concern in humanitarian intervention. Representatives of developing nations are shamefully underrepresented in the discourse of assertions, arguments, and deliberations that converge to influence the development of humanitarian psychosocial policies affecting their regions. Moreover, even when governments and ministries from the developing world are somewhat represented, the same cannot be said for less affluent groups with little access to state power. This means that women, religious and ethnic minorities, indigenous tribes, and underclasses may have little say in the planning, implementation, and distribution of psychosocial services. Thus, a strong recommendation is presently expressed for greater inclusion of non-Western voices and perspectives in the discourse over which psychosocial beliefs and practices are appropriate, welcome, or desirable for use among disaster survivors in developing countries. Beyond this, it is also important to seek the insight and wisdom of groups at the margins of national and international power circles. Of particular concern is the muted influence of women from the least developed nations, whose lives (and those of their children) are among those most frequently and severely affected by war and other disasters.

Concerted International Efforts Are Needed

Humanitarian stakeholders share values and interests that should improve their prospects for collaborating toward commonly held aspirations.

Nevertheless, it is a widely held perception that they often function with a greater emphasis on autonomy than on cooperation. While it is understandable and predictable that the social psychology of these organizations would mirror those of governments and corporations, it is unfortunate that humanitarian organizations would rather tolerate waste and duplication than pursue cooperative partnerships that might allow a more efficient division of efforts and responsibilities. For example, psychosocial support for expatriate delegates has received considerable attention, and some, but not all, organizations have the requisite resources to provide mental health care for their field personnel. Cooperative agreements would allow psychosocial delegates from one NGO partner to share their services with personnel from another, resulting in better distribution of preventive care without the need for each NGO to develop its own psychosocial services.

As recently as 2001, the World Health Organization issued a declaration requesting that the international community agree to consensual guidelines for improving cooperation in the best interest of serving the psychosocial needs of refugees and other displaced populations (WHO, 2001). Such cooperation and collaboration would require division of roles and activities, a consequence of which would be to limit the autonomy of any given signatory organization. Unfortunately, the sovereignty of governments and NGOs alike tends to supersede such noble ideals as cooperative action or the placing of a beneficiary's interests above organizational politics. Nevertheless, leaders in the humanitarian community, faced with inadequate funding and an escalating spiral of mission objectives, should take a progressive route toward the forging of collaborative agreements that would improve efficiency and decrease unnecessary duplication of services.

International Standards of Care Are Needed

Psychosocial services have become a staple part of humanitarian relief operations around the world. Much of this progression has been driven by an increasing emphasis on the psychologically "traumatic" impact of war, disasters, and other tragic events. The fundamental propositions of international disaster psychology begin with the belief that extreme psychological distress and trauma predictably follow from events in which death, injury, and massive loss are involved. Specific claims are seldom made regarding the magnitude of the psychosocial consequences, but the impact is expected to include profound distress and substantial impairment of adaptive behavior among a large proportion of the population. A sense of extreme urgency is also evident in the alarming tone of news reports quoting claims by international mental health experts that major portions of populations affected by the 2004 Indian Ocean tsunami will develop trauma or other mental disorders (e.g., WHO, 2005). The responses to these alarms vary, with some ad hoc psychosocial emergency teams responding within the first few weeks (e.g., Kuriansky, 2005), while larger organizations take a more cautious, measured, and deliberative stance (Anderson, 2005).

Given the generally predictable occurrence of disasters, wars, and other catastrophic events, there would seem to be a third alternative in which planned action strategies are prepared well in advance. Once an activating event occurs, the strategy can quickly be reviewed and revised to fit any unanticipated conditions and the action plan can then be implemented without unnecessary delay. In fact, many governmental and nongovernmental organizations do exactly that with regard to material supplies such as food, water, medicines, munitions, and plastic sheeting. Indeed, this policy of preparedness for the unexpected is quite common for most goods that are considered essential to survival or social stability. Countless institutions, from police and fire departments to hospitals and insurance companies, exist to respond quickly when chronic problems arise, and many communities now have emergency mental health response capacities as well. Yet the global community, after more than a decade of experience with international disasters, remains relatively unprepared to respond to the psychosocial aspects of a major disaster in any systematic and concerted manner.

After nearly a decade of discussion regarding "best practices," no widely accepted standards of care have emerged. Contributing to this problem is the paucity of real research in this area. The present author recommends that humanitarian psychosocial organizations and experts (e.g., Psychosocial Working Group, 2004), convene not only to establish consensual endorsement of interventions, but also to develop action strategies for responding with all deliberate speed and coordination to address the psychosocial needs of disaster survivors. Organizations with an historical head start in developing psychosocial programs can help to inform others, and the sharing of lessons learned and approaches to delivering services can be exchanged in the service of all concerned. A more provocative suggestion would include establishing an international NGO dedicated specifically to providing psychosocial support in a manner analogous to that of Médecines Sans Frontières (Doctors Without Borders) in the arena of medical care.

Rapid Assessment of Psychosocial Needs Should Be a Standard Practice

Recent efforts directed toward the rapid assessment of psychosocial needs in disaster-affected populations have been helpful and instructive (e.g., Dodge, 2006; Jacobs et al., 2006), but episodic and limited in scope. The history of medical and psychosocial interventions demonstrates the importance of accurately assessing problems and resources before devising a plan to provide services. In the rush to relieve human suffering after catastrophic events, there is a danger in assuming the nature and magnitude of psychosocial needs while ignoring existing resource capacities in favor of imported experts. Although it is true that some presuppositions based on past experience are likely to prove true, important information may be missed or delayed unless needs assessment is granted a formal role in the overall service plan. To ease the succession from needs assessment to intervention, it is possible to begin assessing very early and in tandem with the deploying and tailoring of services (i.e., listening to the beneficiaries and tailoring the service model). It is also crucial to build an evaluation component into the service model so that the lessons learned are less subject to global appraisals that suit political rather than developmental aims.

Psychological Trauma versus Disaster Psychology

The international humanitarian community must operate on assumptions that are either self-evident or adapted from analogous circumstances. Thus, it is self-evident that supplies of clean water will be critically needed in remote regions where refugees often assemble, and it stands to reason that the emotional needs of people displaced by a wildfire will be analogous to those of people displaced by an earthquake. Historical trends in the mental health fields have elevated the concept of psychological trauma to a position from which it eclipses any other explanatory framework or descriptive terminology. This has led to a condition where psychological trauma is treated as though its existence and importance are self-evident across every type of human catastrophe, from war to flood and famine to disease. In turn, the proper response to these events must center foremost on preventing or alleviating the formation of a traumatic disorder. Evidence to support the proposition that refugees (Fazel, Wheeler, & Danesh, 2005), torture survivors (Silove, 1999), and others who have suffered terribly in disasters often develop trauma-related symptoms and clinical disorders is abundant and convincing. But there are many psychosocial consequences other than trauma that carry great importance and that are often more amenable to change without intrusive interventions that may not be welcomed or valued by disaster survivors. Thus, the emphasis on trauma may inadvertently obscure the importance of less dramatic issues that are not as "sexy," compelling, and provocative in tone. Nevertheless, what is actually provided in many instances is not "trauma-focused treatment," but instead consists of more mundane-sounding approaches such as education, stress management, and crisis intervention, which are often what is most useful for prevention activities and immediate relief of acute stress.

Disaster psychology, while closely connected to traumatology, is also distinct in several ways, including a decidedly normalizing stance toward short-term responses to acute stress and a pronounced emphasis on community-based interventions. In contrast to the clinical therapies typically applied in cases of post-traumatic stress disorder, the techniques preferred by disaster psychologists are more akin to crisis intervention and stress management and emphasize reduction of emotional arousal with brief support for problem solving and other effective coping strategies. Disaster survivors are not referred to as either clients or patients, and no "case" is ever formulated or assigned to a particular provider. Privacy is almost impossible, confidentiality is very limited, and no formal therapeutic relationship is either acknowledged or terminated. Rather, if the disaster psychologist detects the need for "clinical" services, a referral is made to an appropriately skilled provider who need not be experienced in disaster mental health. More often, the approach taken could best be described as a "public health" approach, with the purpose of taking steps to prevent the need for more targeted interventions by reducing the impact of known risk factors. This proactive model is superior in many ways to reactive models, but it requires very different skills and objectives from those needed for working with a more select group of survivors who display symptoms of clinical disorders. Thus, the qualifications for disaster psychologists are substantially different from those of traumatologists, and these areas of expertise are not interchangeable. Therefore, while skilled trauma-clinicians have much to offer in response to disaster survivors, they should also acknowledge the need to develop the pertinent skills for disaster field assignments.

Humanitarian Assistance and Military Aggression Are Incompatible

Interventions can take countless forms, and it is debatable whether the aims are indeed wholly altruistic and compassionate (i.e., humanitarian), or if there is another, more selfish agenda being disguised. The secular humanitarian movement has long been encumbered by the historical example of religious charities that blended compassionate deeds with missionary indoctrination. Selective governmental humanitarian efforts in the late twentieth century were often suspected of being part of a global propaganda struggle between the opposing powers of communism and capitalism during the Cold War. These examples illustrate the fragile credibility of altruistic acts across national and cultural boundaries and should inform true humanitarians of the dangers of blended agendas. In a spate of publications over the past decade, contributors have called the humanitarian community to task over its questionable behavior or suspect motives (Holzgrefe & Keohane, 2003; Moore, 1999; Smillie & Minear, 2004). Concurrently, the rates of intentional violence against humanitarian personnel have reached historically high levels (Sheik, Gutierrez, Bolton, Spiegel, Thieren, & Burnham, 2000), as illustrated by the 2003 bombings of the United Nations and Red Cross offices in Iraq during the American occupation. In such a climate of scrutiny, criticism, and profound security concerns, it is more important than ever that humanitarian motives be kept wholly distinct from partisan politics and military adventures.

Since its inception, the Red Cross/Red Crescent movement has wisely promoted and subscribed to principles of neutrality and impartiality in the pursuit of humanitarian goals. Only the strictest adherence to such principles can possibly serve to shield humanitarian workers and the people they seek to serve from becoming targets of terror, torture, and death. This is not to say that military means cannot be employed in the service of humanitarian ends. Indeed, the ostensible rationale behind many if not most wars is to serve the greater good of humanity while defeating some evil force. But in violence the ends are often believed to justify any means of achieving them, and this includes the resort to instrumental aggression in the service of geopolitical goals of domination, pacification, and exploitation. Conversely, in humanitarianism the means must conform to principles of compassion, dignity, and human rights if the ends are to maintain legitimacy. Anything less threatens to destroy the very foundation upon which the international humanitarian enterprise has been erected.

Psychosocial Issues Need Better Advocacy

In the competition for disaster relief resources, psychosocial concerns are given more lip service than action. Basic survival needs are so clear and compelling that humanitarian mental health advocates find themselves relegated to the margins while central planning concerns are pursued with fervor. This is to some extent a necessary and reasonable situation, since mental health is a relative luxury in the face of mass destruction and death. Nevertheless, if psychosocial interventions are ever to be both timely and effective, they must move from being marginal concerns toward being integral and influential in the overall scheme of disaster response planning.

At present the priorities are such that mental health and psychosocial support activities have more propaganda value than actual influence. This helps to keep the mental health sector in a reactive role, rather than supporting systematic, strategic development of responsive operational abilities and the undertaking of initiatives for building more resilient local capacity . Instead, the current state of affairs allows for a public voicing of compassion and vague claims of action for the anguish and trauma of the affected people, while the pace of response is more timid and tentative. This is to some extent due to legitimate doubts regarding the need for psychosocial interventions and an absence of evidence supporting the effectiveness of what is presently being offered. Thus, disaster mental health advocates will need to consider their steps carefully if they are to advance their cause while avoiding the temptation to overstate their importance at the risk of further undermining their precarious progress.

References

Anderson, N. B. (2005). The APA tsunami relief effort, part 2. *APA Monitor, 36*(4), 9.

Dodge, G. R. (2006). Assessing the psychosocial needs of communities affected by disaster. In G. Reyes & G. A. Jacobs (Eds.), *Handbook of international disaster psychology, Vol. 1. Fundamentals and overview.* Westport, CT: Praeger Publishers.

Fazel, M., Wheeler, J., & Danesh, J. (2005). Prevalence of serious mental disorder in 7000 refugees resettled in Western countries: A systematic review. *Lancet, 365,* 1309–1314.

Holzgrefe, J. L., & Keohane, R. O. (2003). *Humanitarian intervention: Ethical, legal, and political dilemmas.* New York: Cambridge University Press.

Jacobs, G. A., Revel, J. P., Reyes, G., & Quevillon, R. P. (2006). A tool for rapidly assessing the mental health needs of refugees and internally displaced populations. In G. Reyes & G. A. Jacobs (Eds.), *Handbook of international disaster psychology, Vol. 3. Refugee mental health.* Westport, CT: Praeger Publishers.

Kipling, R. (1899, February). The white man's burden: The United States and the Philippine Islands. *McClure's Magazine*, p. 12.

Kuriansky, J. (2005, February 21). Finding life in a living hell. Retrieved March 31, 2005, from http://www.nydailynews.com/front/story/283039p-242333c.html

Marsella, A. J., & Christopher, M. A. (2004). Ethnocultural considerations in disasters: An overview of research, issues, and directions. *Psychiatric Clinics of North America, 27*, 521–539.

Moore, J. (1999). *Hard choices: Moral dilemmas in humanitarian intervention.* New York: Rowman & Littlefield.

Psychosocial Working Group (2004). *Considerations in planning psychosocial programs.* Retrieved February 15, 2005, from http://www.forcedmigration.org/psychosocial/papers/PWGpapers.htm

Pupavac, V. (2001). Therapeutic governance: Psycho-social intervention and trauma risk management. *Disasters, 25*, 358–372.

Sheik, M., Gutierrez, M. I., Bolton, P., Spiegel, P., Thieren, M., & Burnham, G. (2000). Deaths among humanitarian workers. *British Medical Journal, 321*, 166–168.

Silove, D. (1999). The psychosocial effects of torture, mass human rights violations, and refugee trauma: Towards an integrated conceptual framework. *Journal of Nervous and Mental Disease, 187*, 200–207.

Smillie, I., & Minear, L. (2004). *The charity of nations: Humanitarian action in a calculating world.* Bloomfield, CT: Kumarian Press.

Summerfield, D. (1999). A critique of seven assumptions behind psychological trauma programmes in war-affected areas. *Social Science & Medicine, 48*, 1449–1462.

———. (2005). What exactly is emergency or disaster "mental health"? *Bulletin of the World Health Organization, 83*, 76.

Szegedy-Maszak, M. (2005, January 17). The borders of healing. *U.S. News & World Report, 138*(2), 36–37.

World Health Organization (WHO). (2001). Declaration of cooperation: Mental health of refugees, displaced and other populations affected by conflict and post-conflict situations. Author: Geneva.

———. (2005, January 19). Press release (SEA/PR/1384): WHO warns of widespread psychological trauma among Tsunami victims. Retrieved April 25, 2005, from http://w3.whosea.org/en/Section316/Section503/Section1861_8571.htm

EPILOGUE

Yael Danieli

This impressive, thoughtful *Handbook of International Disaster Psychology* succeeds in conveying and mapping many of the key issues and complex challenges that have confronted the field and influenced the development of psychosocial humanitarian operations over the past decade. The scope and depth of this superb compilation would not have been possible even a decade ago, demonstrating how far we have come as a field. But much of it is also a reminder of how far we have yet to go in a world that has unremittingly produced disasters that, despite growing awareness, are met at best by episodic and inconsistent response and a rather limited commitment to preventing them and their long-term—possibly multigenerational—effects.

Created on the ruins of the World War II, the United Nations (UN) was formed in a spirit of optimism. Never again would the world community permit such a devastating war to take place. The world organization was joined by numerous nongovernmental organizations (NGOs) in its efforts to create a new, intensified impetus to alleviate poverty, eradicate illness, and provide education to shape a better world. But despite 60 years of energetic action, problems abound, and are even increasing. Disasters and their consequences continue to torment individuals and societies, leaving trails of illness, suffering, poverty, and death. Life expectancy has increased in most countries, and the proportion of children in the world has risen dramatically as well, with a corresponding growth in the need for food, health care, and education.

Tragically, trauma is clearly as ubiquitous today as it was during and immediately following World War II, when the UN was created, in the words of the Charter, "to save succeeding generations from the scourge of war, which twice in our lifetime has brought untold sorrow to mankind, and to reaffirm faith in fundamental human rights, in the dignity and worth of the human person, in the equal rights of men and women and of nations large and small, and to establish conditions under which justice and respect for the obligations arising from treaties and other sources of international law can be maintained, and to promote social progress and better standards of life in larger freedom."

The end of the Cold War, and the vanishing of its ideological barriers, has given rise, not to a more peaceful world, but to a world in which nationalist and ethnic tensions have frequently exploded into conflict. International standards of human rights, although largely accepted by states, are discarded in the face of fanaticism and stored-up hatred. In addition, issues between states North and South—developed and underdeveloped—are growing more acute, and call for attention at the highest levels. The most recent recognition of this in the context of the UN is the Secretary-General's report, *In Larger Freedom: Towards Development, Security and Human Rights for All* (United Nations, 2005).

People today know more about what goes on in the world than ever before. Cameras transmit their revelations within minutes to living rooms around the globe. Modern mass communication has erased geographical distance and informs us of suffering immediately as it occurs. But increasing and intense coverage may lead to desensitization and apathy as efforts to cope with ever present, overwhelming news of disturbing events result in a psychological distancing from the suffering (Figley, 1995). With the parallel exposure to fictional film and video, the distinction between reality and fantasy becomes blurred. War and disasters may even become entertainment (note the proliferation of reality shows on television). The worst-case scenario occurs when the world is a helpless eye witness and its efforts merely symbolic, with the sole intention of giving the appearance that something is being done (among Sarajevo's 85,000 children, a symbolic group of 32 injured were evacuated). A contrasting scenario is the unprecedented, overwhelming generosity of pledges and outpouring of philanthropy, likely inspired by its proximity to gift-giving holidays, to the victims of the December 26, 2004, Asian tsunami. However, even if we accept that this response was due to the seemingly inherent political neutrality of natural disasters, how do we explain international neglect in the case of other natural disasters, as in El Salvador? The constant threat of terrorism and the aching persistence of war crimes, crimes against humanity, and genocide—previous, ongoing, and current—with the continued suffering of their victims, keep the international community ashamed.

Because the scars of traumatic stress can be both deep and long-lasting, their treatment is imperative. Such treatment, all too often neglected, is crucial in conflict resolution and in the building of peace—possibly the best preventer of further war and violence—among individuals and groups. Unless treated, the germ of hatred and holding on to the image of the enemy—both consequences of traumatic stress—may give rise to new conflicts and bloody clashes between ethnic or religious groups in an endless cycle of violence. Victims may become perpetrators as individuals, as members of families and communities, or as nations. Genuine peace cannot exist without the resolution of trauma. If traumatic stress constitutes one element in this terrible cycle, its interception could be one way to break the cycle. The cessation of wanton violence and abuse of power without full multidimensional integration of trauma (e.g., political, psychological, social, legal) will impair a nation's ability to maintain peace, to rebuild so that sustainable development is possible.

International Response

In addition to documenting the ubiquity of exposure to extreme events, history has recorded a wide variety of sociopolitical efforts to intervene in ways that address the needs of those who have been exposed and to prevent or minimize the impact of future exposures. Since the creation of the United Nations in 1945, the response by the organized international community and in particular by the UN system has been largely political. The main political imperatives have been from two opposite poles of conflict in finding political solutions: on the one hand, the continued existence of international concern about human suffering, stimulated by the modern media, and on the other hand, conceptions of state sovereignty that lead states to resist international interference in matters that they consider to be under their control and within their jurisdiction. By and large, the joint arrival of intergovernmental and nongovernmental organizations has been able to bring much relief to many victims of disasters, even though such relief tends to be temporary, may not alleviate all the hardships suffered by the victims, and will frequently not address the psychosocial damage. This book should help in keeping attention focused on remedying this unacceptable situation.

Trauma and the Continuity of Self: A Multidimensional, Multidisciplinary Integrative (TCMI) Framework

In my own attempt to describe the diverse and complex destruction caused by massive trauma such as is examined in this volume, I concluded that only a multidimensional, multidisciplinary integrative framework (Danieli, 1998) would be adequate. An individual's identity involves a complex interplay of multiple spheres or systems. Among these are (1) the physical and intrapsychic; (2) the interpersonal—familial, social, communal; (3) the ethnic, cultural, religious, spiritual, natural; (4) the educational/professional/occupational; and (5) the material/economic, legal, environmental, political, national, and international. These systems dynamically coexist along the time dimension to create a continuous conception of life from past through present to the future. Ideally, the individual should simultaneously have free psychological access to and movement within all these identity dimensions.

Trauma Exposure and "Fixity"

Trauma exposure can cause a rupture, a possible regression, and a state of being "stuck" in this free flow, which I (Danieli, 1998) have called *fixity*. The intent, place, time, frequency, duration, intensity, extent, and meaning of the trauma for the individual, and the survival strategies used to adapt to it (see, for example, Danieli, 1985) as well as post-victimization traumas, will determine the degree of rupture and the severity of the fixity. Fixity can be intensified in particular by the *conspiracy of silence* (Danieli, 1982, 1998), the survivors' reaction to the societal indifference (including that of health care and other professionals), avoidance, repression, and denial of the survivors' trauma experiences (see also Symonds, 1980). Society's initial emotional outburst, along with its simultaneous yet unspoken demand for rapid return to apparent normality, is an important example. This *conspiracy of silence* is detrimental to the survivors' familial and sociocultural (re)integration because it intensifies their already profound sense of isolation from and mistrust of society. It further impedes the possibility of the survivors' intrapsychic integration and healing, and makes the task of mourning their losses impossible. Fixity may increase vulnerability to further trauma. It also may render *chronic* the immediate reactions to trauma (e.g., acute stress disorder), and, in the extreme, become lifelong *post-trauma/victimization adaptational styles* (Danieli, 1985, 1997). This occurs when survival strategies generalize to a way of life and become an integral part of one's personality, repertoire of defense, or character armor.

Viewed from a family systems perspective, what happened in one generation will affect what happens in the next, though the actual behavior may take a variety of forms. Within an intergenerational context, the trauma and its impact may be passed down as the family legacy even to children born *after* the trauma. The awareness of the possibility of pathogenic intergenerational processes and the understanding of the mechanisms of transmission should contribute to finding effective means for preventing their transmission to succeeding generations (Danieli, 1985, 1993, 1998).

The possible long-term impact of trauma on one's personality and adaptation and the *intergenerational* transmission of victimization-related pathology still await explicit recognition and inclusion in future editions of the diagnostic nomenclature. Until they are included, the behavior of some survivors, and some children of survivors, may be misdiagnosed, its etiology misunderstood, and its treatment, at best, incomplete.

This framework allows evaluation of each system's degree of rupture or resilience, and thus informs the choice and development of optimal multilevel interventions. Repairing the rupture and thereby freeing the flow rarely means going back to "normal." Clinging to the possibility of "returning to normal" may indicate denial of the survivors' experiences and thereby fixity.

Exposure to trauma may also prompt review and reevaluation of one's self-perception, beliefs about the world, and values. Although changes in self-perception, beliefs, and values can be negative, varying percentages of trauma-exposed people report positive changes as a result of coping with the aftermath of trauma (called "post-traumatic growth," by Tedeschi & Calhoun, 1996). Survivors have described an increased appreciation for life, a reorganization of their priorities, and a realization that they are stronger than they thought. This is related to Danieli's (1994) recognition of competence vs. helplessness in coping with the aftermath of trauma. Competence (through one's own strength and/or the support of others), coupled with an awareness of options, can provide the basis of hope in recovery from traumatization.

Integration of the trauma must take place in *all* of life's relevant dimensions or systems and cannot be accomplished by the individual alone. Routes to integration may include reestablishing, relieving, and repairing the ruptured systems of the survivor and his or her community and nation, and restoring the surviving community's or nation's place in the international community. For example, in the context of examining the "Right to restitution, compensation and rehabilitation for victims of gross violations of human rights and fundamental freedoms" for the United Nations Centre for Human Rights (1992), some necessary components for integration and healing in the wake of massive trauma emerged from my interviews with victims/survivors of the Nazi Holocaust, interned Japanese-Americans, victims of political violence in Argentina and Chile, and professionals working with them, both in and outside their countries. Presented as goals and recommendations, these components are organized from the following perspectives: (A) individual, (B) societal, (C) national, and (D) international.

A. **Reestablishment of the victim's equality, power, and dignity—the basis of reparation.** This is accomplished by (a) compensation, both real and symbolic; (b) restitution; (c) rehabilitation; and (d) commemoration.

B. **Relieving the victim's stigmatization and separation from society**. This is accomplished by (a) commemoration; (b) memorials to heroism; (c) empowerment; (d) education.

C. **Repairing the nation's ability to provide and maintain equal value under law and the provisions of justice**. This is accomplished by (a) prosecution; (b) apology; (c) securing public records; (d) education; (e) creating national mechanisms for monitoring, conflict resolution, and preventive interventions.

D. **Asserting the commitment of the international community to combat impunity and provide and maintain equal value under law and the provisions of justice and redress**. This is accomplished by (a) creating ad hoc and permanent mechanisms for prosecution (e.g., ad hoc tribunals and ultimately an International Criminal Court); (b) securing public records; (c) education; (d) creating international mechanisms for monitoring, conflict resolution, and preventive interventions.

It is important to emphasize that this comprehensive framework, rather than presenting *alternative* means of reparation, sets out necessary *complementary* elements, to be applied in different weights, in different situations and cultures, and at different points in time. It is also crucial that victims/survivors participate in the choice of the reparation measures adopted for them.

To fulfill the reparative and preventive goals of psychological recovery from trauma, perspective and integration through awareness and containment must be established so that one's sense of continuity, belongingness, and rootedness are restored. To be healing and even potentially self-actualizing, the integration of traumatic experiences must be examined from the perspective of the *totality* of the trauma survivors' and family members' lives.

With survivors it is especially hard to draw conclusions based on outward appearances. Survivors often display external markers of success (e.g., occupational achievement or established families) that in truth represent survival strategies. Clearly, such accomplishments may facilitate adaptation and produce feelings of fulfillment in many survivors. Thus, the external attainments do represent significant adaptive achievement in their lives. Nevertheless, even survivors in the "those who made it" category (Danieli, 1985) still experience difficulties related to their traumatic past, suggesting that overly optimistic views of adaptation may describe defense rather than effective coping. In fact, it is within this category that we observe the highest rates of suicide among survivors as well as their children. Furthermore, these optimistic views and accounts may cause survivors, who may have already felt isolated and alienated from those who did not undergo similar traumatic experiences, to see themselves as deficient, especially when compared to their "supercoper" counterparts, and deter them from seeking help.

The finding that survivors have areas of both vulnerability and resilience is not paradoxical when viewed within a multidimensional framework for multiple levels of post-traumatic adaptation. And tracing a history of multiple traumas along the time dimension at different stages of development reveals that, while time heals ills for many, for *traumatized* people time may not heal but may magnify their response to further trauma and may carry intergenerational implications.

Future Directions

In the context of prevention, an absolutely necessary precondition is the creation of a network of early warning systems, which necessitates thorough familiarity with, understanding of, and genuine respect for the local, national and regional culture(s) and history (Danieli, 1998). The United Nations and its related organizations have developed such systems concerning environmental threats, the risk of nuclear accident, natural disasters, mass movements of populations, the threat of famine, and the spread of disease. It is now time to include the potential effects of traumatic stress in preparing to confront these and other events.

Comparing this book's conclusions with our conclusions of "International Responses to Traumatic Stress: Humanitarian, Human Rights, Justice, Peace and Development Contributions, Collaborative Actions and Future Initiatives" (Danieli, Rodley, & Weisaeth, 1996), I felt delighted with the editor's assertion that psychosocial services have become "a staple part of humanitarian relief operations around the world" (Reyes, 2006, p. XX). But I must agree with him that, despite this progress, psychosocial issues still need further and greater advocacy. We have a long way to go toward ensuring that mental health concerns become integral and influential in the overall architecture of disaster response planning, in order to support systematic, strategic development of operational capabilities and initiatives to build more resilient local capacity.

I am saddened by the inefficient process of "reinventing the wheel" that persists among both national and international humanitarian organizations. It might be helpful for humanitarian psychosocial organizations and experts, without sacrificing their diversity and richness, to endorse core, evidence-based standards of care and interventions. It would also be useful to develop coordinated action strategies for flexibly available psychosocial preparedness to enable speedy, systematic responses that address the psychosocial needs of disaster survivors.

Although mostly Western, the authors are experienced members of the international humanitarian community, representing a broad spectrum of nationalities, cultures, and viewpoints. I agree with the editors that the time for Western speakers to serve as proxies for non-Westerners should be passing and that *all* voices and perspectives—not only those of the imported experts—must be included in the discourse over which psychosocial frameworks and practices are appropriate for use among disaster survivors in developing countries. The resources, insight, and wisdom of groups at the margins of national and international power circles must be included as well.

Concurring with the guidelines generated by the Task Force on International Trauma Training of the International Society for Traumatic Stress Studies (Weine, Danieli, Silove, van Ommeren, Fairbank, & Saul, 2002), the editor argues for rapid assessment of psychosocial needs to become standard practice, and for building an evaluation component into the service to assess its effectiveness. Such assessment and evaluation practices will guarantee that lessons learned are less subject to appraisals that suit political rather than developmental aims. The concern over the incompatibility of humanitarian assistance, partisan politics, and military aggression is repeated in this book as well, and reinforced by the recognition of the cost paid by humanitarian aid workers and others on the front line (Danieli, 2002).

The five Cs of disaster work—Communication, Cooperation, Collaboration, Coordination, and Complementarity—apply here, too. So does the need for leadership strategies, such as compassionate articulation (Spratt, 2002), that can reduce chaos and terror and thereby diminish the effectiveness of terrorism.

Nongovernmental organizations must improve their efforts at coordination. The greatest obstacle still seems to be competition for visibility and credit, which is essential if they are to compete effectively for increasingly scarce resources. At both the organizational level and in the field, the desire to have highly visible, quantitatively impressive programs can lead to competitiveness and jealousies that work against unified efforts.

There is a risk that the uncritical use of concepts such as coordination, which creates the impression of easy, quick solutions irrespective of the complexities of traumatic stress, may result in the loss of an operational meaning for these concepts. For example, the result may be too many coordinators and too few doing the work, or the actual work may be being reserved to nonprofessional and insufficiently trained volunteers. Such volunteers may serve for short periods of time, with traumatic detriment to themselves, and without contributing to the pool of accumulated knowledge that ought to move the field forward.

It is essential for UN agencies and programs, and for NGOs, to further define and develop complementary roles in their responses to traumatic stress. Complementarity involves the tolerance of, respect for, and capitalizing on the differing strengths of the various partners—UN bodies, governments, NGOs, and the communities they serve.

Some of the programs described in this work are inspiring in their excellence. But what comes through most of all is that, however superb some programs are, they are too few, and the challenges they must face are overwhelming. Each of the noble examples of programs is dwarfed by the needs with which our world is faced. In fact, the most striking theme that keeps emerging in the field is the enormous gulf between what needs to be done and the resources available to do it with. Although difficult in the short term, providing the international community with this needed expertise will lessen long-term costs, and possibly prevent intergenerational effects and the resulting much larger costs—both human and financial.

Another resource-related issue is that available funds tend to be used for emergency shipments of food, medicine, housing, and the like in reaction to situations that have been widely publicized by the media. Once the emergency is no longer new, and the dramatic pictures are no longer on the nightly news, funds usually dry up and are not available for sustaining the short-term gains or for long-term care.

The work in this area radiates good will, idealism, and commitment, despite cynicism and despair, and despite the realization—emerging from situations such as those in the former Yugoslavia, Rwanda, Kosovo, East Timor, Democratic Republic of Congo, and Darfur/Sudan—that humanity has failed to learn the lessons and honor the commitments made after World War II.

The same world that created the circumstances for the crime, the victimization, has also created the circumstances for good and kind and compassionate people to be there for each other, for the victims in time of need. Viewing our work through the prism of traumatic stress, within the multidimensional, multidisciplinary integrative (TCMI) framework, should thus have not only a healing, but also a humanizing, effect on the victims and on society as a whole.

We must pursue primary, secondary, and tertiary prevention. We must continue efforts to reduce the stigma that still exists against the field of mental health while broadening its reach to join hands with other disciplines. We must partner with others in fields at and beyond the boundaries of mental health and extend our investigations and preventive suggestions also to the root causes of disasters.

The danger of bioterrorism, with medically unexplained physical symptoms challenging patients, clinicians, scientists and policy makers, necessitates special training for all public health professionals. Its psychological casualties far outweigh the physical ones (Flynn, 2004), and its long-term social and psychological effects are likely to be as damaging as the acute ones, if not more so (Wessely, Hyams, & Bartholomew, 2001). The threat of bioterrorism also calls for revamping the health/mental health systems on all levels/dimensions—before, during, and after such attacks.

Despite growing awareness and the accumulated body of knowledge, there are still policy makers who either deny the existence of the invisible, psychological wounds, or feel that they have a lesser priority in an era of dwindling resources. At every level, government policy has yet to fully comprehend and embrace the centrality of psychosocial issues in understanding and responding to disasters, particularly to terrorism. For any nation to become optimally prepared to cope, homeland security must include, integrate, and adequately fund psychosocial security (Danieli, Brom, & Sills, 2005) and the full participation of the social sciences in all aspects of preparedness. This book should certainly advance this undertaking.

References

Danieli, Y. (1982). *Therapists' difficulties in treating survivors of the Nazi Holocaust and their children.* Dissertation Abstracts International, 42(12-B, Pt 1), 4927. (UMI No. 949-904).

———. (1985). The treatment and prevention of long-term effects and intergenerational transmission of victimization: A lesson from Holocaust survivors and their children. In C. R. Figley (Ed.), *Trauma and its Wake* (pp. 295–313). New York: Brunner/Mazel.

———. (1992). Preliminary reflections from a psychological perspective. In T.C. van Boven, C. Flinterman, F. Grunfeld & I. Westendorp (Eds.), *The Right to Restitution, Compensation and Rehabilitation for Victims of Gross Violations of Human Rights and Fundamental Freedoms.* Netherlands Institute of Human Rights [Studie-en Informatiecentrum Mensenrechten], Special issue No. 12.

————. (1993). The diagnostic and therapeutic use of the multi-generational family tree in working with survivors and children of survivors of the Nazi Holocaust. In J. P. Wilson & B. Raphael (Eds.) *International handbook of traumatic stress syndromes* [Stress and Coping Series, Donald Meichenbaum, Series Editor]. (pp. 889–898). New York: Plenum Publishing.

————. (1994). Resilience and hope. In G. Lejeune (Ed.), *Children Worldwide* (pp. 47–49). Geneva: International Catholic Child Bureau.

————. (1997). As survivors age: An overview. *Journal of Geriatric Psychiatry, 30* (1), 9–26.

————, Rodley, N.S., & Weisaeth, L. (Eds.) (1996). *International responses to traumatic stress: Humanitarian, human rights, justice, peace and development contributions, collaborative actions and future initiatives.* Amityville, NY: Baywood Publishing.

————. (Ed.). (1998). *International handbook of multigenerational legacies of trauma.* New York: Kluwer Academic/Plenum Publishing.

————. (Ed.). (2002). *Sharing the front line and the back hills: International protectors and providers, peacekeepers, humanitarian aid workers and the media in the midst of crisis.* Amityville, NY: Baywood Publishing.

————, Brom, D., & Sills, J. (Eds.). (2005). *The trauma of terrorism: Sharing knowledge and shared care. An international handbook.* Binghamton, NY: The Haworth Press.

Figley, C. R. (Ed.). (1995). *Compassion fatigue: Coping with secondary traumatic stress disorder in those who treat the traumatized.* New York: Brunner/Mazel.

Flynn, B. W., (2004) Letters to the Editor: Behavioral Health Aspects of Bioterrorism. *Biosecurity and Bioterrorism: Biodefense Strategy, Practice, and Science, 2,* 232.

Green, B. L., Friedman, M. J., de Jong, J., Solomon, S. D., Keane, T. M., Fairbank, J. A., Donelan, B., & Frey-Wouters, E. (Eds.) (2003). *Trauma interventions in war and peace: Prevention, practice, and policy.* New York: Kluwer Academic/Plenum Publishers.

Reyes, G. (2006). Conclusions and recommendations for further progress. In G. Reyes & G. A. Jacobs (Eds.), *Handbook of International Disaster Psychology.* Westport, CT: Praeger Publishers.

Spratt, M. (2002, August 28). 9/11 media may comfort, terrify. Retrieved on August 29, 2002, from http://www.dartcenter.org/articles/headlines/2002/2002_08_28.html

Symonds, M. (1980). The "second injury" to victims. *Evaluation and Change* [Special issue], 36–38.

Tedeschi, R. G., & Calhoun, L. G. (1996). The posttraumatic growth inventory: Measuring the positive legacy of trauma. *Journal of Traumatic Stress, 9,* 455–471.

United Nations (2005). *In larger freedom: Towards development, security and human rights for all. Report of the Secretary-General.* Retrieved May 31, 2005, from http://www.un.org/largerfreedom/contents.htm

Weine, S., Danieli, Y., Silove, D., Van Ommeren, M., Fairbank, J. A., & Saul, J. (2002). Guidelines for international training in mental health and psychosocial interventions for trauma exposed populations in clinical and community settings. *Psychiatry, 65*(2), 156–164.

Wessely, S., Hyams, K., & Bartholomew, R. (2001). Psychological implications of chemical and biological weapons. *British Medical Journal, 323,* 878–879.

INDEX

About the Volume Editors

GILBERT REYES, PhD, is a licensed clinical psychologist and the Associate Dean for Clinical Training at Fielding Graduate University in Santa Barbara, California. He has responded to several major disasters in the United States, including the September 11, 2001, attack on the World Trade Center. Reyes has also consulted with the International Federation of Red Cross and Red Crescent Societies on various projects and in 2002 co-authored that organization's training manual for community-based psychological support. He recently co-authored a training course for the American Red Cross on children's disaster mental health needs and is now collaborating with the Terrorism and Disaster Center of the National Child Traumatic Stress Network on the development of interventions for children in disasters.

GERARD A. (JERRY) JACOBS, PhD, is Director of the Disaster Mental Health Institute (DMHI) and a Professor at the University of South Dakota. He is active in field work, training, program development, and consultation nationally and internationally for the Red Cross movement and the American Psychological Association. He is a co-author of the WHO *Tool for the Rapid Assessment of Mental Health* and served on the Institute of Medicine Committee on Responding to the Psychological Consequences of Terrorism. He also works with the Asian Disaster Preparedness Center in psychological support training and program development.

ABOUT THE CONTRIBUTORS

ALISTAIR AGER is Professor of Applied Psychology and Director of the Institute for International Health & Development at Queen Margaret University College, Edinburgh. He has field experience across Malawi, Nigeria, Sri Lanka, Bangladesh, India, Romania, Palestine, and Montserrat, having worked with a wide range of international agencies, including UNHCR, UNICEF, WHO, and a number of nongovernmental agencies, both local and international. He has authored over 50 published works, including the edited volume *Refugees: Perspectives on the Experience of Forced Migration* (1999). He is co-convenor of the Psychosocial Working Group, a consortium of five universities (Columbia, Harvard, Oxford, Queen Margaret, and University of Pennsylvania) and five humanitarian agencies (CCF, IRC, MSF-Holland, Mercy Corps, and Save US) involved in the development of best practice in the field of psychosocial intervention in complex emergencies. He is a member of the Board of the Antares Foundation, committed to the development of national and international NGO capacity in the care and deployment of humanitarian workers.

DEANNA R. BEECH is Chair of the Psychologists for Social Responsibility Action Committee for Trauma, Resiliency and Social Reintegration, and is the Co-chair of their conference series on Working with Communities Affected by Ethnopolitical Conflict. She is also a founding member of the Alliance for Resilient Communities, a for-profit organization whose mission is to design, train, and implement programs that weave psychological knowledge with the resilient aspects of cultures affected by ethnopolitical conflict to benefit the well-being of the people. Her field experiences in the Balkans include evaluations of psychosocial programs for children and supervision of the psychologists at the hospital in Sarajevo. During the war in Kosovo she worked in Montenegro, designing and implementing psychosocial programs for displaced Albanians. When the war ended, she did the same for displaced Serbians who fled in the wake of retaliations.

YAEL DANIELI, PhD, is a clinical psychologist in private practice in New York City, a traumatologist, and victimologist. She is also Co-founder and Director, Group Project for Holocaust Survivors and Their Children; Founding President, International Network for Holocaust and Genocide Survivors and their Friends; and Co-founder, past-President, Senior United Nations Representative, International Society for Traumatic Stress Studies (ISTSS). Dr. Danieli integrates treatment, worldwide study, teaching/training, publishing, expert advocacy, and consulting to numerous governments, news, international and national organizations, and institutions on victims rights and optimal care, including for their protectors and providers. Most recently she received the ISTSS Lifetime Achievement Award.

GORDON R. DODGE is the clinical director for Lakes Area Human Services, Inc., Forest Lake, Minnesota. He has over 35 years of experience as a psychologist in clinical, consultative, and educational services. He also heads the Trauma Division of his agency, addressing workplace and community crises and trauma. As a disaster psychologist he has extensive experience working with private industry, emergency services personnel, and other local, national, and international public agencies. He has had international assignments, including in the former Yugoslavia, Kosovo, Albania, the Burmese-Thai refugee camps, India, Guam, and two consultation and training assignments to Nairobi. Domestic assignments have included an Oklahoma City bombing hotline and natural disaster responses for the American Red Cross. He was assigned a leadership position in New York following the World Trade Center attack.

AMY C. HUDNALL was educated in History (MA) and History and German Studies (BA) at Appalachian State University. She studied at the Goethe Institute and the Bayerische Julius-Maximilians-Universität, Germany. She is a lecturer in the History and Women's Studies Departments, Appalachian State University, and a Research Assistant Professor at the Institute of Rural Health, Idaho State University. Her work focuses on cross-cultural trauma and genocide from psychological and historical references, and she teaches courses on peace and conflict. She has presented and published on captivity trauma, human rights, secondary trauma, cultural relativism, and cross-cultural conflict.

JUDY KURIANSKY is a journalist and a clinical psychologist at Columbia University Teachers College as well as the Department of Psychiatry at Columbia Medical School. Trained by the Red Cross and honored with the first "International Outreach Award" from the American Women in Radio and TV, she has been involved with disaster relief after 9/11, after SARS hit in China, bombings in Jerusalem, and the Asian tsunami. A United Nations representative for the International Association of Applied Psychology and the World Council for Psychotherapy, and Fellow of the American Psychological Association Media Psychology division, she is a radio call-in host, television commentator, and columnist for the *New York Daily News* and *Singapore Straits Times*, and has been featured in the *International Herald Tribune*, on CBS News, CNN, and China's CCTV.

NANCY PEDDLE, PhD, educated in early childhood development at Bank Street College (MS) and human organization and development at Fielding Graduate Institute (MA, PhD), is Executive Director of LemonAid Fund, Chicago, working with individuals who have experienced violence changing their lives and those of their families and communities. Peddle's expertise has taken her to more than 20 countries worldwide focusing on community-based programs, participatory research, and psychosocial needs of children. She was a Research Fellow at Prevent Child Abuse America and was the first Executive Director for the International Society for the Prevention of Child Abuse and Neglect. She has lived the experiences and published and presented on community-based approach to addressing violence.

VANESSA PUPAVAC is a lecturer in the School of Politics, University of Nottingham, and has previously worked as a consultant to the United Nations and other organizations. She has published widely on human rights and international aid policies. She was awarded the Otto Klineberg Intercultural and International Relations Award in 2003.

BENEDETTO SARACENO, MD, an internationally admired psychiatrist, is the Director of the Department of Mental Health in the World Health Organization (WHO). He has been a committed mental health reformer for over three decades, both in Italy and in the global arena. As a progressive voice for patients' rights and de-institutionalization, he has contributed to the reduction of the stigma associated with mental illnesses. Dr. Saraceno works closely with nongovernmental humanitarian organizations to promote greater awareness of the growing burden of mental illness around the world. He has recently worked tirelessly to ensure adequate and appropriate psychosocial support for victims of the Indian Ocean tsunamis.

CHARLES D. SPIELBERGER is Distinguished Research Professor of Psychology and Director of the Center for Research in Behavioral Medicine and Health Psychology at the University of South Florida. He previously directed the USF Doctoral Program in Clinical Psychology. An ABPP Diplomate in Clinical Psychology and Distinguished Practitioner of the National Academies of Practice, Spielberger focuses his current research on anxiety, curiosity, and the experience, expression, and control of anger; job stress and stress management; and the effects of stress, emotions, and lifestyle factors on hypertension, cardiovascular disorders, and cancer. During 1991–92, Spielberger served as the 100th president of the American Psychological Association.

B. HUDNALL STAMM, PhD, educated in psychology and statistics at Appalachian State University (BS, MA) and University of Wyoming (PhD), is a Research Professor, the Director of Telehealth, and Director of the Institute of Rural Health at Idaho State University. She is also the Director of the National Child Traumatic Stress Network Center for Rural, Frontier, and Tribal Traumatic Stress. Working primarily with rural underserved peoples, Stamm has focused on health policy, cultural trauma, and work-related traumatic stress where telehealth figures prominently. The author of over 100 professional papers, her work is used in diverse fields in over 30 countries. See www.isu.edu/~bhstamm and www.isu.edu/irh for more information.

HENRY E. STAMM IV holds a PhD in history from the University of Wyoming, with an MA from Appalachian State University and a BA from Rice University. Currently an independent historian living in Pocatello, Idaho, Stamm was a research scholar at Dartmouth College and taught history at the University of Alaska Anchorage and SUNY-Oswego. He is the author of *People of the Wind River: The Eastern Shoshones, 1825–1900* (1999) and has appeared in a documentary film about Chief Washakie and the Shoshones. His work emphasizes the historical context for understanding cultural trauma among indigenous peoples. His current project examines the cultural transformation of the Eastern Shoshones.

MICHAEL G. WESSELLS, PhD, is Senior Child Protection Specialist for Christian Children's Fund and Professor of Psychology at Randolph-Macon College. He has served as President of the Division of Peace Psychology of the American Psychological Association and of Psychologists for Social Responsibility and as Co-Chair of the InterAction Protection Working Group. His research on children and armed conflict examines child soldiers, psychosocial assistance in emergencies, and postconflict reconstruction for peace. He regularly advises UN agencies, donors, and governments on the situation of children in armed conflict and issues regarding child protection and well-being. In countries such as Afghanistan, Angola, Sierra Leone, Uganda, East Timor, Kosovo, and South Africa, he helps to develop community-based, culturally grounded programs that assist children, families, and communities affected by armed conflict.

ABOUT THE SERIES

As this new millennium dawns, humankind has evolved—some would argue has developed—exhibiting new and old behaviors that fascinate, infuriate, delight or fully perplex those of us seeking answers to the question, "Why?" In this series, experts from various disciplines peer through the lens of psychology telling us answers they see for questions of human behavior. Their topics may range from humanity's psychological ills—addictions, abuse, suicide, murder, and terrorism among them—to works focused on positive subjects including intelligence, creativity, athleticism, and resilience. Regardless of the topic, the goal of this series remains constant—to offer innovative ideas, provocative considerations, and useful beginnings to better understand human behavior.

Chris E. Stout
Series Editor

ABOUT THE SERIES EDITOR AND ADVISORY BOARD

CHRIS E. STOUT, PsyD, MBA, is a licensed clinical psychologist and is a Clinical Full Professor at the University of Illinois College of Medicine's Department of Psychiatry. He served as an NGO Special Representative to the United Nations, was appointed to the World Economic Forum's Global Leaders of Tomorrow, and has served as an Invited Faculty at the Annual Meeting in Davos. He is the Founding Director of the Center for Global Initiatives. Dr. Stout is a Fellow of the American Psychological Association, past-President of the Illinois Psychological Association, and a Distinguished Practitioner in the National Academies of Practice. Dr. Stout has published or presented over 300 papers and 30 books/manuals on various topics in psychology, and his works have been translated into six languages. He has lectured across the nation and internationally in 19 countries, visited 6 continents, and almost 70 countries. He was noted as being "one of the most frequently cited psychologists in the scientific literature" in a study by Hartwick College. He is the recipient of the American Psychological Association's International Humanitarian Award.

BRUCE BONECUTTER, PhD, is Director of Behavioral Services at the Elgin Community Mental Health Center, the Illinois Department of Human Services state hospital serving adults in greater Chicago. He is also a Clinical Assistant Professor of Psychology at the University of Illinois at Chicago. A clinical psychologist specializing in health, consulting, and forensic psychology, Mr. Bonecutter is also a longtime member of the American Psychological Association Taskforce on Children & the Family. He is a member of organizations including the Association for the Treatment of Sexual Abusers, International; the Alliance for the Mentally Ill; and the Mental Health Association of Illinois.

JOSEPH FLAHERTY, MD, is Chief of Psychiatry at the University of Illinois Hospital, a Professor of Psychiatry at the University of Illinois College of Medicine, and a Professor of Community Health Science at the UIC College of Public Health. He is a Founding Member of the Society for the Study of Culture and Psychiatry. Dr. Flaherty has been a consultant to the World Health Organization, the National Institutes of Mental Health, and also the Falk Institute in Jerusalem. He has been Director of Undergraduate Education and Graduate Education in the Department of Psychiatry at the University of Illinois. Dr. Flaherty has also been Staff Psychiatrist and Chief of Psychiatry at Veterans Administration West Side Hospital in Chicago.

MICHAEL HOROWITZ, PhD, is President and Professor of Clinical Psychology at the Chicago School of Professional Psychology, one of the nation's leading not-for-profit graduate schools of psychology. Earlier, he served as Dean and Professor of the Arizona School of Professional Psychology. A clinical psychologist practicing independently since 1987, he has focused his work on psychoanalysis, intensive individual therapy, and couples therapy. He has provided Disaster Mental Health Services to the American Red Cross. Mr. Horowitz's special interests include the study of fatherhood.

SHELDON I. MILLER, MD, is a Professor of Psychiatry at Northwestern University, and Director of the Stone Institute of Psychiatry at Northwestern Memorial Hospital. He is also Director of the American Board of Psychiatry and Neurology, Director of the American Board of Emergency Medicine, and Director of the Accreditation Council for Graduate Medical Education. Dr. Miller is also an Examiner for the American Board of Psychiatry and Neurology. He is Founding Editor of the American Journal of Addictions, and Founding Chairman of the American Psychiatric Association's Committee on Alcoholism. Dr. Miller has also been a Lieutenant Commander in the U.S. Public Health Service, serving as psychiatric consultant to the Navajo Area Indian Health Service at Window Rock, Arizona. He is a member and Past President of the Executive Committee for the American Academy of Psychiatrists in Alcoholism and Addictions.

DENNIS P. MORRISON, PhD, is Chief Executive Officer at the Center for Behavioral Health in Indiana, the first behavioral health company ever to win the JCAHO Codman Award for excellence in the use of outcomes management to achieve health care quality improvement. He is President of the Board of Directors for the Community Healthcare Foundation in Bloomington, and has been a member of the Board of Directors for the American College of Sports Psychology. He has served as a consultant to agencies including the Ohio Department of Mental Health, Tennessee Association of Mental Health Organizations, Oklahoma Psychological Association, the North Carolina Council of Community Mental Health Centers, and the National Center for Health Promotion in Michigan. Dr. Morrison served across 10 years as a Medical Service Corp Officer in the U.S. Navy.

WILLIAM H. REID, MD, is a clinical and forensic psychiatrist, and consultant to attorneys and courts throughout the United States. He is Clinical Professor of Psychiatry at the University of Texas Health Science Center. Dr. Miller is also an Adjunct Professor of Psychiatry at Texas A&M College of Medicine and Texas Tech University School of Medicine, as well as a Clinical Faculty member at the Austin Psychiatry Residency Program. He is Chairman of the Scientific Advisory Board and Medical Advisor to the Texas Depressive & Manic-Depressive Association, as well as an Examiner for the American Board of Psychiatry & Neurology. He has served as President of the American Academy of Psychiatry and the Law, as Chairman of the Research Section for an International Conference on the Psychiatric Aspects of Terrorism, and as Medical Director for the Texas Department of Mental Health and Mental Retardation. Dr. Reid earned an Exemplary Psychiatrist Award from the National Alliance for the Mentally Ill. He has been cited on the Best Doctors in America listing since 1998.